AIR WAR AND EMOTIONAL STRESS
Psychological Studies of Bombing and Civilian Defense

The RAND Series

The RAND Series

This is one of a series of publications which will present results of research undertaken by The RAND Corporation, a nonprofit organization, chartered "to further and promote scientific, educational, and charitable purposes, all for the public welfare and security of the United States of America."

AIR WAR AND EMOTIONAL STRESS

Psychological Studies
of
Bombing and Civilian Defense

Irving L. Janis

The RAND Corporation

First Edition

NEW YORK • TORONTO • LONDON
McGRAW-HILL BOOK COMPANY, INC.
1951

1.1
J

AIR WAR AND EMOTIONAL STRESS

Psychological Studies
of
Bombing and Civilian Defense

Copyright, 1951
The RAND Corporation
Printed in the United States of America

Foreword

THIS book is one of a series of monographs in which the results
of research by members of the staff of The RAND Corporation
will be made available to the public.

The author of this volume, Dr. Irving L. Janis of the Department
of Psychology, Yale University, prepared the present study under
the sponsorship of The RAND Corporation as a part of its program
of research for the U.S. Air Force.

The study was undertaken in order to evaluate the psychological
effects of air warfare and to indicate the nature of problems in this
field which may arise in planning the defense of the United States
against air attack.

Author's Note

DURING the past three years, as a research consultant to The RAND Corporation, I have prepared a series of special reports on the psychological effects of air war. The reports were intended primarily to survey the relevant observations on reactions to conventional and atomic bombing that had been accumulated during World War II and to delineate major problems for further research in the human sciences. After having been circulated among specialists in national defense research, the reports were consolidated and rewritten, forming the substance of the present volume.

It is a pleasure to express my appreciation to the following social scientists on the staff of The RAND Corporation: to Hans Speier, Joseph M. Goldsen, and Herbert Goldhamer for their guidance, suggestions, and encouragement throughout every phase of the preparation of this book; to Nathan Leites, Paul Kecskemeti, Victor Hunt, and Leo Rosten (formerly a member of the RAND staff) for many important criticisms and recommendations; to Harry Hall for assistance in carrying out the content analysis of interviews from Hiroshima and Nagasaki.

Many valuable suggestions pertinent to this work were derived from informal discussions with colleagues at Yale University: Carl I. Hovland, Neal E. Miller, and John Dollard of the Department of Psychology; Frederick C. Redlich of the Department of Psychiatry; George Dession and Harold D. Lasswell of the Yale Law School. I am indebted to Burton R. Fisher of the University of Michigan for his highly informative comments in conversations about the implications of the U.S. Strategic Bombing Survey findings, particularly with respect to the phases of the research he directed in connection with the morale survey in Japan.

I also wish to thank Irma Janoff for her assistance in preparing bibliographic notations. Special thanks are due to Elizabeth Kellers for preparing and correcting typescript copies of the manuscript. Finally, I wish to acknowledge my gratitude to Marjorie Graham Janis for the important contributions she has made to the content of the book and for the aid she has given in editing the final manuscript.

Irving L. Janis.

Yale University,
New Haven, Connecticut,
    April, 1951.

Contents

Contents

PART I
REACTIONS AT HIROSHIMA AND NAGASAKI

CHAPTER 1
INTRODUCTION

The study of reactions to disaster may prove to have important implications for general behavior theory by illuminating basic processes of human adjustment that occur under conditions of severe environmental stress. Moreover, sound information about the psychological impact of wartime catastrophes is a fundamental requirement for developing effective civil defense policies, for planning over-all military strategy, and for appraising the political, social, and moral consequences of atomic warfare.

Although a considerable amount of information is available on "conventional" air warfare, there is a dearth of relevant material on atomic warfare. Very little psychological research has been carried out among the tens of thousands of Japanese survivors who lived through the disasters at Hiroshima and Nagasaki.

In the chapters comprising Part I, all the available observations on reactions of survivors are brought together in an attempt to arrive at a comprehensive description of the psychological impact resulting from the atomic-bombing disasters. Whenever possible, an effort is made to discern similarities and differences between atomic and other types of bombing, with a view to exploring the question of whether atomic weapons might have unique psychological effects.

The more extensive material on effects of "conventional" air warfare will be described in Part II. Unless one knows how people reacted at Hiroshima and Nagasaki, one cannot be certain that the conclusions derived from the extensive studies of other kinds of

1

bombing apply equally to atomic disasters. Both types of situations will be taken into account in later chapters, where an attempt will be made to specify, at least tentatively, the general conditions under which various reactions—fear, aggression, neurosis, disorganized action, demoralization, etc.—are evoked in large-scale catastrophes.

The only published case studies of atomic disaster experiences are those in John Hersey's popular book, *Hiroshima.*[1] There has been only one systematic study of a cross section of A-bombed survivors: a small sample survey by the Morale Division of the United States Strategic Bombing Survey,[2] conducted about three months after the A-bombs were dropped.[3]

In the USSBS survey, the standard interview was focused mainly on questions of morale. Consequently, there is a fair amount of empirical data on postdisaster attitudes. Only a small part of the interview, however, was devoted to personal experience of the bombing; among the standard set of questions there were none which dealt directly with overt behavior, subjective feelings, or emotional tension during the crisis phases of the disaster. Nevertheless, many of the interviews contain spontaneous comments that tell us something about the emotional impact resulting from the A-bombing.

In order to make as full use as possible of this unique source of information, the original protocols of the interviews (which are now available for the use of research scholars in the National Archives at Washington, D.C.) were examined and analyzed. The reanalysis of the interviews provides new information which supplements the findings published in the USSBS report on Japanese morale.[4] In addition to the USSBS interviews and the case studies published by Hersey, there are a few eyewitness reports which are also used as source materials.

---

[1] John Hersey, *Hiroshima,* Alfred A. Knopf, New York, 1946.

[2] Throughout this book, the United States Strategic Bombing Survey will be referred to by the initials USSBS.

[3] USSBS Report, *The Effects of Strategic Bombing on Japanese Morale,* U.S. Government Printing Office, Washington, D.C., 1947.

[4] *Ibid.*

Unfortunately, the small amount of relevant data, often based on observations of questionable reliability, is insufficient to meet adequately either the scientific need for empirical evidence concerning the dynamics of emotional stress or the practical need for sound predictions and guidance in current planning on atomic disaster control. Nevertheless, it is essential to examine carefully all the available evidence, despite its limitations, if we are to extract tentative conclusions and suggestive leads concerning the psychological effects of atomic warfare.

CHAPTER 2
EMOTIONAL IMPACT OF THE A-BOMB

UNPREPAREDNESS OF THE POPULATION

At both Hiroshima and Nagasaki, disaster struck without warning. Whether intended so or not, an extraordinarily high degree of surprise was achieved by both A-bomb attacks. At the two target cities, prior to the bombing, there had been relatively little anxiety about the threat of heavy B-29 raids. When the planes carrying the A-bomb arrived over their targets, the population was almost completely unprepared. At the time, not even a light air raid was expected. People were caught at home, at work, out on the city streets, calmly going about their usual daily affairs.

When the first A-bomb was dropped, on August 6, 1945, very few residents of Hiroshima were inside air-raid shelters. An all-clear signal from a previous alert had sounded less than half an hour earlier and the normal routine of community life had resumed. Shortly after eight in the morning, when the explosion occurred, the working-class population was arriving at the factories and shops. Many workers were still out-of-doors en route to their jobs. The majority of school children, along with some adults from the suburbs, were also outside, hard at work building firebreaks as a defense against possible incendiary raids. Housewives, especially in middle-class families, were at home, preparing breakfast. Only a few minutes later, their flaming charcoal stoves were to create hundreds of local fires, adding to a general conflagration of such intensity that even if the assiduous labor of Hiroshima's school children had been completed, the fire storm still would have been beyond control.

At Nagasaki, three days later, the populace had heard only vague reports about the Hiroshima disaster. Here again, people were at work in factories and offices, tending their homes, engaging in their normal daily activities. A few hours earlier a raid alert had been canceled; before the raid signal could be repeated, the bomb had already exploded. Only 400 people out of a population of close to a quarter of a million were inside the excellent tunnel shelters that could have protected some 75,000 people from severe injury or death.

It is generally recognized that the element of surprise was an important factor contributing to the unprecedented casualty rates at Hiroshima and Nagasaki. Many of those who were exposed to lethal gamma radiation, struck down by flying debris, or trapped in collapsed buildings would not have been killed if they had been warned in time to flee to the outskirts of the city or if they had been in adequate shelters. Thousands of people who were out-of-doors or standing in front of windows would have been protected from incapacitating flash burns if they had been under any sort of cover.[1]

Whether or not they suffered severe injury, those who survived the explosion were also affected by the element of surprise in quite another way. The absence of warning and the generally unprepared state of the population undoubtedly augmented the emotional effects of the disaster. "I was just utterly surprised and amazed and awed." This brief remark, by a newspaper reporter who was living in Nagasaki at the time of the disaster, epitomizes the way in which survivors described the terrifying events to which they were so suddenly exposed.

Of great importance in the predispositional set of the population is the fact that there was not a state of readiness to face danger or to cope with the harsh exigencies of a major catastrophe. The stage was well set for extreme emotional responses to dominate the action. It is against this background of psychological unpreparedness that the emotional impact resulting from the atomic disasters should be viewed.

---

[1] USSBS Report, *The Effects of Atomic Bombs on Hiroshima and Nagasaki,* U.S. Government Printing Office, Washington, D.C., 1946.

TYPICAL DISASTER EXPERIENCES

The total pattern of emotional stress created by the surprise attack emerges most clearly from a qualitative examination of individual eyewitness accounts of the disaster. A single illustrative case (based on the original interview data recorded by a member of the USSBS Morale Survey Team) will be described in order to give a preliminary over-all view of the characteristic sequence of disaster experiences. This will be followed by a detailed discussion of the generalizations which emerge from the available qualitative and quantitative evidence.

The account given by a fifty-year-old woman, who was a part-time worker in a flower shop at Hiroshima, is fairly typical. On the morning of the attack, while alone at breakfast, this woman heard the sound of planes flying overhead. She thought nothing of it and merely continued her meal. Suddenly there was a terrific flash outside, to which she reacted automatically by ducking down. A split second later her body was hurled against the table and, at the same moment, she realized that the entire house was crashing down. Her instantaneous thought was that she was going to be killed.

For a short time, this woman remained in a stunned, semiconscious condition, buried beneath the debris of her household. Gradually she became aware of faint, unrecognizable voices calling out to her, as from far away: "Are you all right?" At first she was unable to reply, but after a few minutes she recovered full consciousness and found that she could extricate herself from the wreckage without requesting aid.

While working her way out of the destroyed dwelling, she realized that an explosion had occurred, but she was convinced that it was only her own house that had been bombed—by a direct hit. When she emerged into the street she was amazed and deeply shocked by the sight of mutilated human beings and by the sound of "the faint and loud groans of the victims." Perceiving so many people in agony, lying about in the midst of so much wreckage and destruction, she felt terrified.

Like the other survivors who were capable of using their legs, the woman fled from the destroyed area toward the outskirts of the city. As she ran past more and more dead and dying people while escaping from the burning city, her terror persisted. In a state of acute emotional excitement, she remained totally unaware of a large and severe burn on her forehead until a fellow refugee called it to her attention.

Having reached the countryside outside the city, she "hid" in a country field, fearfully expecting more bombs to be dropped. Here she remained for many hours before her emotional excitement subsided.

The above case illustrates many of the important features of the powerful emotional stress engendered in those who survived the atomic disasters. We catch a glimpse of the sudden, startling way in which the presence of danger flashes into the focus of awareness. There are indications of a feeling of utter helplessness evoked by the traumatizing impact of the violent physical concussion. And then, after emotional recovery is beginning to occur, there comes a second emotional shock, produced by the inescapable sight of mutilated human beings. Moreover, it becomes apparent to the survivor that the magnitude of the destruction far exceeds that of any understandable source of danger. Nowhere in view is there an intact sanctuary where aid, emotional relief, and normal contact with people can be secured. On the contrary, with a flaming conflagration rapidly menacing the entire area, the urgent sense of danger cannot be dispelled. Prolonged, effortful escape becomes essential.

From the total pattern of disaster behavior, as exemplified by the initial case material, it is possible to discern a number of component factors. In the sections which follow, each of the components will be considered more or less independently in order to specify the types of reaction which occurred fairly frequently, if not ubiquitously, among the A-bombed population.

AWARENESS OF PERSONAL DANGER

Sudden awareness of immediate danger appears to have been the initial experience of almost all survivors in Hiroshima and Nagasaki.

A considerable period of time elapsed before people realized that their entire community had been stricken. Initially, each individual was totally preoccupied with the immediate danger that confronted him personally. It was only after they had already carried out various emergency actions that the survivors began to realize the magnitude of the disaster. In the accounts given by those who lived through it, the A-bomb attack is described primarily as a personal catastrophe, a horrible event in the individual's life experience, during which his personal survival was at stake.

People who have been in other wartime disasters, i.e., exposed to high-explosive attacks or to incendiary raids, do not uniformly describe their experiences in terms of direct personal involvement. A fairly sizeable proportion express a "remote-miss" attitude.[2] They discuss their bombing experience as though they had been relatively detached bystanders who merely observed what was happening to their community. However, practically all the people interviewed at Hiroshima and Nagasaki talked about the disaster in highly personal terms. For them, it was a severe "near-miss" or "direct-hit" experience accompanied by sharp awareness of the threat of personal annihilation. Evidently, there were very few remote-miss cases in the A-bombed cities. Even when viewing their experiences retrospectively three months later, most of the survivors displayed little evidence of having developed a detached or impersonal attitude toward it.

Typical examples of the narrow escapes reported by survivors will be found in the interview excerpts quoted later in this chapter. But some indication of the nature of near-miss experiences has already been provided by the initial case study in the preceding section. Many people were exposed to even more severe conditions of danger. Some described being painfully lacerated by missiles of flying glass. Others vaguely remembered having been knocked unconscious after being hurled through the air and then, in a semi-dazed and helpless condition, facing the harrowing dangers of raging fires. A few alluded to themselves as being the

---

[2] See Chap. 6.

sole survivors of a shattering blast that killed everyone else in the same room.

Not all of the survivors reported such extreme experiences. But in almost every case there was some mention of personal exposure to actual physical danger. This is borne out by some of the quantitative findings from the content analysis of the USSBS interviews of survivors who were in Hiroshima or Nagasaki at the time the A-bomb exploded. Approximately 98 per cent of the cases mentioned that they had personally experienced some form of danger. More than 60 per cent spoke about being physically affected by the powerful blast, i.e., knocked down, severely shaken, trapped inside a falling building, buried beneath debris, etc.[3]

Along with the vivid awareness of danger, there was often the belief that it was "my house" or "my neighborhood" that had been directly bombed, as was true of the Hiroshima woman whose experiences were described earlier. According to the Nagasaki Prefectural Report on the bombing:

> . . . The people of Nagasaki, even those who lived on the outer edge of the blast, all felt as though they had sustained a direct hit. . . . People who were in comparatively damaged areas reported their condition under the impression that they had received a direct hit.[4]

In the USSBS interviews from Hiroshima and Nagasaki, one finds fairly frequent reference to this initial, egocentric conception of the disaster. Although not questioned about any specific aspect of their experiences, approximately one-fourth of the respondents volunteered the information that they thought, at first, that a bomb had hit their own buildings or had exploded very close by. Typical of such responses are the following:

> ". . . I was working in the shop rationing out wheat. Then came a flash—the wall caved in. I threw myself next to the lot of rice piled up and I was saved by it. My son in the room was only cut by the glass. I first thought our home was bombed. But as I

[3] See the table on p. 11.
[4] USSBS, *op. cit.*

looked out I saw all the buildings were down." [Ration clerk in Hiroshima]

"All of a sudden a sort of flash and then my home caved in. I really thought this was the end. I thought the bomb had fallen in our immediate neighborhood. . . ." [Housewife in Nagasaki]

"I saw the strong flash which blinded me so I ducked. Then I heard a big explosion at the same time. I thought I was a near miss bomb hit. Everything was falling down on me and hitting my body." [Transportation supervisor in Nagasaki]

"Then a big noise came and dust clouds rose up. At that time I thought it an ordinary bomb. I felt it fall close to me—but there was no sign of it." [Mechanic in Nagasaki]

"When the atomic bomb fell, I and my wife and my six year old girl stayed in the house. I thought the bomb hit very near . . . the ceilings, walls, windows, and doors fell down and only the frame of my house remained." [Office worker in Nagasaki][5]

As is apparent from these excerpts, the awareness of immediate danger was touched off by a complex pattern of unusual and intense stimuli. The blast effects, by arousing violent kinesthetic and disequilibrium sensations, often accompanied by acute pain, probably played a primary role as the danger stimuli evoking an excited state of emergency in the human organism. In this respect, the traumatic impact resulting from the atomic explosion would not have been different from that of other types of bombing. Perhaps this is reflected by the fact that so many of the people in the A-bombed area—in the absence of any prior knowledge about the nature of the attack—initially interpreted the situation in terms of the conventional air attacks about which they had heard so much; i.e., they thought it was a small-scale disaster in which they happened to be close to the focal point of the explosion.

There were also some fairly unique sights and sounds which may have strongly influenced disaster responses: the flash, heat, and noise of the explosion probably contributed to the initial awareness of immediate danger. Other stimuli present during subsequent

---

[5] These quotations and similar ones are taken from the original protocols of the USSBS interviews in Hiroshima, Nagasaki, and the towns surrounding those two cities.

phases of the disaster became important determinants of mass behavior. In the next section some of the outstanding sources of
emotional stress will be examined.

SPECIFIC DISASTER EVENTS

In examining the original USSBS interviews, a systematic content-
analysis technique was applied to determine the frequency with
which various disaster events were mentioned. The results shown
in the following table form the basis for inferences concerning the
relative importance of various aspects of the atomic disasters.

**DISASTER EVENTS MENTIONED IN PERSONAL ACCOUNTS OF
ATOMIC-BOMBING EXPERIENCES**

(Based on the entire USSBS sample of Hiroshima and Nagasaki survivors)

Disaster Events	Hiroshima Survivors (No. = 55) (%)	Nagasaki Survivors (No. = 46) (%)
Flash of the explosion	62	76
Knocked down by blast	13	4
Personal exposure to indirect blast effects:		
building destruction or falling debris	60	61
Noise of the explosion	29	28
Presence of large numbers of casualties	69	64
Presence of widespread devastation	31	17
Fires in the immediate vicinity	14	20

When interpreting these findings, it is necessary to bear in mind
that the respondents had not been asked any direct questions about
disaster events. The percentages probably underestimate the true
incidence of exposure and should be regarded as indicating only
the *minimal* incidence. For instance, some of the respondents who
actually did perceive the flash of the explosion may not have mentioned it in their disaster accounts, since they were not asked about

it; nevertheless, the results in the table show that *at least* 62 per cent of the Hiroshima respondents and 76 per cent of the Nagasaki respondents perceived this preliminary disaster stimulus. This way of interpreting the findings is based on the assumption that those respondents who spontaneously mentioned each stimulus were reporting accurately. Such an assumption would appear to be fairly safe, especially since there are no observations which suggest that the respondents were withholding the truth or remembering incorrectly on matters of this sort.

The particular values of the percentages listed in the table apply only to the sample of survivors interviewed. Since the Hiroshima and Nagasaki samples are referred to in the USSBS morale report[6] as representative cross-sections, it would seem safe to assume that the true percentages for the total population of survivors would be roughly of the same order of magnitude. Even if sampling difficulties were encountered which made the sampling error slightly larger than usual for peacetime community surveys, the results would nevertheless serve to indicate the approximate rank order of the stimuli. Consequently, the results are useful as a rough answer to the question: Which events were experienced most frequently?

In general, the results indicate that there were three major disaster events which were reported by the majority of the survivors: (1) the flash of the atomic explosion; (2) the blast effects; and (3) the presence of large numbers of casualties. Presumably these were the three aspects of the disaster most likely to be prominent in the survivors' subjective experiences and to leave a deep impression in their memories.

The Flash of the Explosion

When the A-bomb exploded, the brilliant flash was the first thing that was observed. For those who were not close to ground zero, there was a discernible time interval between the visual per-

---

[6] USSBS Report, *The Effects of Strategic Bombing on Japanese Morale,* U.S. Government Printing Office, Washington, D.C., 1947.

ception of the flash and the subsequent waves of heat and blast.[7]
Although exceedingly brief, this time interval was apparently sufficient for executing some forms of protective action.

A substantial proportion of the respondents in Hiroshima and
Nagasaki reported having reacted immediately to the intense flash
alone, as though it were a well-known danger signal, despite the
fact that they were unaware of its significance at the time. A number of them said that they voluntarily ducked down or "hit the
ground" as soon as the flash occurred and had already reached the
prone position before the blast swept over them. A Nagasaki housewife told about being suddenly frightened by "something shining in
the sky" as she was entering her home; she managed to run into her
bedroom "to hide" before the blast wave reached the house and
shattered all the windows. A worker in Nagasaki reported that he
was out in the street waiting for a streetcar when the big "flash-
like electric spark" occurred; he promptly dashed into a nearby
public shelter and was inside by the time the blast wave struck.
These examples indicate that the atomic flash was not merely an
impressive visual stimulus but also, in some cases at least, a danger
signal evoking semi-automatic overt responses. The examples culled
from the interviews serve to amplify one of the incidental observations mentioned in the USSBS medical report: "Japanese claim
that in some instances persons were able to shield their faces with
their hands between the time the flash was seen and the time the
heat wave reached them."[8]

In the instances cited so far, the prompt action proved to be of a
highly adaptive character in that it minimized exposure to the secondary heat and blast waves, preventing burns and concussive blows.
The interviews also indicate that this was not always the case. The
opportunity to minimize the danger was sometimes missed because
the individual remained fixed, staring at the place where he saw
the flash, or because the prompt action proved to be wholly in-

---

[7] Los Alamos Scientific Laboratory, *The Effects of Atomic Weapons,* U.S. Government Printing Office, Washington, D.C., 1950.

[8] USSBS Report, *The Effects of Atomic Bombs on Health and Medical Services in
Hiroshima and Nagasaki,* U.S. Government Printing Office, Washington, D.C., 1947.

appropriate. The following is an example of the latter type of nonadaptive behavior: A young woman in Nagasaki stated that "when I saw the flash of light in the sky I thought it was an incendiary so I started running around looking for water to put it out." It was in the midst of this futile activity that the concussion wave arrived and bombarded her with flying debris.

From the above discussion, it is apparent that some of the survivors immediately perceived the flash as a danger signal. It also appears that for those who were not located near the center there was an opportunity to take protective action that could reduce injuries from the secondary heat wave and from flying glass, falling debris, and other blast effects. It is noteworthy that some survivors evidently failed to make use of this opportunity, as is to be expected when there has been no prior preparation for it.

In a later chapter on the problems of civil defense, we shall have occasion to take account of these findings, since they suggest that casualties in an A-bomb attack might be reduced if the population has been well prepared in advance to react appropriately to the flash of the explosion.

Blast Effects and Noise of the Explosion

The high incidence of personal exposure to blast effects has already been mentioned in connection with the survivors' awareness of immediate danger. It was this aspect of the disaster which apparently was most responsible for bringing people face-to-face with the threat of injury or annihilation. As is indicated by the results in the preceding table, only a small percentage reported having been knocked down by the blast, but a high percentage spoke about personal experiences in connection with indirect blast effects, e.g., building destruction and falling debris.

In some cases the terrifying impact of the crushing blast wave was augmented by a tremendous roaring sound. The results in the table, however, indicate that only slightly more than one-fourth of the respondents mentioned having heard the noise of the explosion. This relatively low proportion probably reflects the fact that the noise of the explosion was a highly variable stimulus. One of the USSBS reports states: "Curiously enough, this sound was not distinctly noted by those who survived near the center of the explosion, although it was heard as far as fifteen miles away."[9] From the interviews, it was found that inside the target cities some people heard an extremely intense roar, whereas others explicitly denied having heard a loud sound.

In some cases the absence of a perceptible loud noise may have contributed to bewilderment. For example, a woman who lived on the periphery of Hiroshima said that when the walls of her house shook and a sensation of heat suddenly occurred on one side of her face, she felt surprised and puzzled; she did not realize that there had been an explosion because "I heard no blast of any kind."

Perception of Casualties

In the case of most uninjured survivors, the initial blast phase of the disaster was followed by a period of high activity—extricating oneself from collapsed buildings, searching for and rescuing relatives, fleeing from fires. It was during this second phase that people became increasingly aware of the magnitude of the catastrophe. Signs of destruction were to be seen everywhere throughout the stricken area. The following are typical of the experiences reported by survivors:

"... When I came to my senses, a worker was trying to help me up. We got out [of the destroyed factory] through a high window. It was unusually bright outside. I noticed that chimneys in the distance were shattered and here and there a fire had started. ... We ran toward the hills in front of the plant, with my friends. ... Houses we passed by were all crumbled down ... rains came like a shower. When it stopped a strong wind began to blow and lasted until four. About that time houses in the neighborhood began to burn." [Female student in Nagasaki]

"Fires started from the direction of the railway station. Fires started from everywhere. They grew bigger and bigger as time

---

[9] USSBS, *The Effects of Atomic Bombs on Hiroshima and Nagasaki.*

went on. The whole city was aflame. Fire fighting was power-less." [Horsecart driver in Nagasaki]

"I saw a lightning-bright flash ray and all I knew was that every-thing collapsed around us. I was knocked unconscious and when I came to I saw all my surroundings [fallen] to the ground and flames raging here and there. My home is nearby the factory. Since the factory was on fire, I ran home for my family without bothering or knowing I was burned around my head. When I arrived home, our house was devastated and destroyed in flames. . . . I saw people here and there burned and dead, heard groans, and cries that could not be forgotten, persons here and there yell-ing, *'Tasukete kure'* ["Help, if you please"] who were pinned beneath walls. . . ." [Factory worker in Hiroshima]

The presence of large numbers of dead, dying, and injured, the uniform obliteration of buildings, and the outbreak of local fires gradually developing into a general conflagration—these were the salient stimuli in the disaster situation that came as the immediate aftermath of the atomic explosion.

In the preceding table it will be noted that approximately two-thirds of the A-bombed survivors mentioned having perceived the dead and injured. From the nature of their comments about the casualties, it is apparent that such perceptions gave rise to intense emotional reactions.

In order to obtain some systematic evidence on the relative amount of emotional disturbance evoked by the various disaster events, an analysis was made of all interview statements describing the respondents' affective responses to each of the events listed in the table. Many respondents spoke about the fear or terror evoked by their disaster experiences in general (as will be seen in the next section), but very few attributed these reactions to specific danger events. Only 5 per cent or less asserted that they experienced fear or some other form of emotional disturbance in connection with each of the following: the flash of the explosion, the noise, the blast and concussion effects, the widespread devastation, and the fires. In marked contrast, almost one-third of the respondents spoke about having been emotionally upset because of the casualties witnessed. The following illustrate the sort of comments that were made:

> "I don't know how I escaped from death. People around my neighborhood were burned or killed. The bodies of those who were killed were all puffed up. It was a terrible and horrible sight." [Female domestic worker in Hiroshima]

> "Then [after the explosion] I escaped into the shelter with my child where many people were lying down injured. Their faces and hands looked so terrible. Their clothes were torn into many pieces. I have no words to explain this atmosphere—just like hell." [Housewife in Nagasaki]

> "On the way back, the bodies of half the dead people lay on the roadside, on the bridge, in the water, in the garden, and everywhere. . . . Practically all these people were burned. It was a sight no one wants to see. . . . The color of these people was brownish and blackish and some of the bodies were dripping." [Male shop worker in Hiroshima]

> "It was really fearful and I thought I was going to die—seeing people all burnt when I went to look for my daughter." [Housewife in Hiroshima]

The fact that emotionalized references to casualties occurred fairly frequently, whereas such references to other types of disaster events were of rare occurrence, suggests that a differential effect may have occurred at the time of the disaster; the sight of dead, mutilated, and maimed people may have had a more powerful emotional impact than the other aspects of the disaster.

There is always the possibility, however, that because of purely extraneous factors emotional responses evoked by the casualties tended to be played up in the retrospective accounts given by the survivors. For instance, it may have been a socially approved act to express sympathy in this way toward less fortunate fellow citizens. Although such potential sources of distortion cannot be fully excluded, there is no particular evidence that would lead one to discount the value of the interview statements. On the basis of a qualitative examination of the original protocols, it appears that there are no indications of insincerity, exaggeration, or stereotyped conventional expressions in the comments about casualties. On the contrary, the variation from one respondent to another with respect to circumstantial details and the personal ways that the affective disturbances are expressed strongly suggest that the verbalizations reflect genuine emotional experiences. It seems fairly probable, therefore, that the perception of casualties at the time of the disaster evoked extremely intense emotional reactions.

There is one important feature of the postdisaster period which should be mentioned at this point because it may have played some role in reviving and strengthening disturbing memories of the disaster. During the weeks following the atomic explosion, many survivors witnessed the outbreaks of radiation sickness and were also exposed to the sight of severely injured people suffering from intractable burns, unhealed lacerations, etc. Repeated exposures of this kind may have strongly reinforced the psychological effects of the original disaster experience.

Even without any subsequent reinforcement, however, it is likely that the original experience of perceiving large numbers of burned, cut, and maimed bodies was a major source of emotional trauma. Many people located only a short distance from the center of the explosion appear to have undergone a double emotional shock—the first, from the physical impact of the explosion and, the second, after they ran out into the streets and saw human devastation everywhere about them. The latter seems to have been the primary emotional stimulus among those who were at the periphery of the target cities and who escaped the full physical violence of the explosion. For such cases, the moment of the bomb burst was relatively nontraumatic and the initial emotional impact seems to have occurred when they saw the endless streams of maimed victims pouring out of the destroyed areas. The same sort of reaction was noted in the interviews of people in Kabe and Hera, small towns close to Hiroshima; and also in Isahaya, a city near Nagasaki.

Slightly more than one hundred residents in the three nearby towns were interviewed by the USSBS Morale Division. These respondents were physically unaffected by the atomic disasters but were located at close enough range to be eyewitness spectators; their disaster accounts were analyzed by the same procedures that were applied to the interviews from Hiroshima and Nagasaki.

From the results, it appears that perception of the casualties was the most outstanding feature which created strong emotional reactions among those located in nearby areas. Although the flash of the explosion, the noise, and the widespread devastation were mentioned by 20 to 50 per cent of those respondents, only a very small proportion reported experiencing any emotion in response to such stimuli. The casualties, however, were mentioned by 35 to 50 per cent of the respondents, and in most cases their statements indicate that some degree of affective disturbance was experienced. A very strong degree of emotional upset was reported by over one-fourth of the residents in the nearby towns. It was by no means rare to find interview comments suggesting emotional shock, as in the following excerpt from the interview of a local official in Hera village:

". . . The burns on the faces were horrible. . . . The eyes appeared as a mass of melted flesh. The lips were all split up and they looked like a mass of molten flesh. Only the nose appeared the same as before. Their clothes were all badly burned and all the open portions of the body were badly burned. The wounded were suffering awful pains. It was to me a sickening scene. We assembled the people in the public schools and in the old village-office. We had about eleven wounded persons in the mayor's office. Everyone in the group died except for one person. The death scene was awful. The color of the patient would turn to blue, and when we touched the body, the skin seemed to stick to our hands. We felt that if America had such a weapon, it was no use for us to go on."

Evidently, many people located in towns several miles away from the target cities, like those within the bombed areas, were acutely disturbed by the magnitude and the character of the casualties inflicted by the atomic weapon. It is relevant to note in this connection that systematic comparisons between the A-bomb and other weapons have highlighted the exceptionally high casualty rate produced by the combination of heat, blast, and gamma rays emitted by the

atomic explosion.[10] The mortality rate per square mile and the
total casualty rate per square mile were from 15 to 20 times greater
at Hiroshima and Nagasaki than the average result of the Twen-
tieth Air Force's intensive campaign against 93 Japanese cities.
There were approximately 245,000 people in Hiroshima at the time
the A-bomb was dropped; 30 per cent of the population lost their
lives and an additional 30 per cent were seriously injured. Out of a
population of 220,000 in the built-up areas of Nagasaki, about
35,000 were killed (16 per cent) and a somewhat larger number
were seriously injured. According to USSBS statistics, only a small
fraction of the total number of A-bomb casualties at Hiroshima
and Nagasaki would have been produced by a striking force employing the amount of high explosive and incendiary bombs necessary
to achieve the equivalent physical damage to buildings and installations.[11] In other words, to produce a given amount of physical
destruction in a metropolitan area, the use of the A-bomb (under
the Hiroshima-Nagasaki type of conditions) results in an excessive
number of killed and injured people, as compared with the use of
"conventional" bombs. This antipersonnel feature of the atomic
weapon seems to have definite psychological implications.

From the interview evidence, we have seen that the inordinate
numbers of casualties were highly visible to survivors within the
target area, evoking strong emotional reactions. People located on
the periphery and at a safe distance away from the explosion were
also likely to witness the disturbing sight of injured victims as they
came streaming out of the bombed area. Apparently, it was not
simply the large numbers of casualties but also the specific character
of the injuries, particularly the grossly altered physical appearance
of persons who suffered severe burns, that had a powerful effect
upon those who witnessed them. Hence, it appears to be highly
probable that, as a correlate of the exceptional casualty-inflicting
properties of the atomic weapon, there was an unusually intense
emotional impact among the uninjured evoked by the perception

---

[10] Los Alamos Scientific Laboratory, *The Effects of Atomic Weapons;* USSBS, *The
Effects of Atomic Bombs on Hiroshima and Nagasaki.*

[11] USSBS, *ibid.*

of those who were casualties. From the material presented so far, we cannot specify whether perception of the casualties produced affective disturbances that were inconsequential, momentary feelings of unpleasantness, or more persistent states of emotional tension with pronounced behavioral effects. We shall return to the question of whether or not the A-bomb produced severe disturbances of a unique sort after examining other relevant observations on emotional reactions.

FEAR AND TERROR REACTIONS

From the material in the preceding sections, it is clear that the A-bomb produces an extraordinarily high incidence of exposure to immediate danger and to a variety of severely disturbing disaster stimuli. One of the consequences of experiences of this kind is acute anxiety and temporarily impaired ego functioning, the symptoms of which are likely to last for days, weeks, and even months after the traumatic event.[12] Discussion of incapacitating neurotic breakdown and persistent emotional shock following the atomic bombings will be postponed until the next chapter, which describes the psychological effects that carried over into the postdisaster period. In the present section, attention will be focused mainly upon the immediate emotional responses evoked during the crisis phases of the Hiroshima and Nagasaki disasters, when objective conditions of danger required swift and effective emergency action.

All available sources of information consistently indicate that a dominant reaction to the bombing was acute anxiety. From statements made by survivors, one gains some inkling of the intensity of the overwhelming emotional excitement evoked during the disasters. It will be recalled that the formal USSBS interviews, conducted several months after the A-bombs were dropped, dealt primarily with questions of morale. Only a few general questions about bombing experiences were included and there were no direct questions about fear or other emotional reactions to the disaster. Never-

---

[12] See Part II, Chap. 5.

theless, one finds spontaneous comments such as the following, which allude to fairly severe terror states:

"I became hysterical seeing my grandmother bleeding and we just ran around without knowing what to do." [Domestic worker in Nagasaki]

"[After recovering from the blast] I got up and ran to the mountains where the good shelter was. I just ran like the crazy. I stayed in the shelter for three days. . . ." [Office worker in Nagasaki]

"My children were injured and I was in such emotional upset that I couldn't think straight." [Factory worker in Hiroshima]

Only a few respondents volunteered information of this kind. Nevertheless, in at least a small percentage of cases, the emotional excitement reached such a high level that there was temporary loss of inhibitory control over primitive, automatic manifestations of acute anxiety, as is implied in the interviews just cited.

In other cases, the acute emotional disturbance took the form of profound apathy and depression. John Hersey refers to several such cases in his report on Hiroshima.[13] He describes one extreme case in detail: A fifty-year-old man, uninjured by the explosion, stood weeping at the window of a burning building. When an attempt was made to rescue him, his only response was "Leave me here to die." After being forcibly carried to safety, he managed to break away and then ran back into the fire.

Instances of less severe depressive reactions are to be found among the respondents in the USSBS survey. A Nagasaki housewife, for example, spoke about manifestly suicidal feelings: "I carried my son on my back and we rushed toward the hills. It was very cold and the rain started to fall. At that time I wished we had died in the explosion of the bomb." A few other respondents verbalized similar depressive tendencies which, from the context, do not seem to be mere expressions of conventional Japanese attitudes concerning the appropriateness of suicide.

Feelings of profound hopelessness and pessimism were sometimes evoked, as is illustrated by the following statement which describes

[13] John Hersey, *Hiroshima*, Alfred A. Knopf, New York, 1946.

the thoughts of a Nagasaki workman at the moment when he looked down from the top of a hill and saw the entire city devastated and aflame: "I thought at that time I would not mind leaving all my tools to their fate; I thought Japan could not win."

In general, the acute symptoms of anxiety and depression among the A-bombed survivors do not appear to differ in any unique way from those observed among the British and Germans who were subjected to exceptionally severe air attacks. Psychodynamic hypotheses concerning such symptoms will be elucidated in a later chapter. The same hypotheses probably apply equally to the intense emotional reactions evoked in the A-bomb disasters. From clinical observations in the European war, it appears that experiencing a narrow escape from danger often has the effect of temporarily shattering the individual's psychological defenses—defenses which had formerly prevented the outbreak of anxiety in the face of environmental threats by maintaining feelings of personal invulnerability.[14] That the same psychodynamic processes may have been evoked in the overwhelming terror experiences at Hiroshima and Nagasaki is suggested by certain of the interview comments, which link intense emotional reactions with subjective awareness of personal vulnerability.

A number of respondents explicitly referred to vivid expectations of personal annihilation:

"I thought I was killed when the atomic bomb fell." [Housewife in Nagasaki]

". . . we almost suffocated from the dust which was caused by the explosion. I thought it was the end of my life." [Clerk in Nagasaki]

. . . we all yelled and ran into the forest and then a loud explosion was heard. The trees began to sway. I thought we were done for." [Personnel officer in Nagasaki]

"It was really fearful and I thought I was going to die." [Housewife in Hiroshima]

Although there was only a small percentage of respondents who made such direct references to the imminence of death, a fairly

14 See Chap. 8.

sizeable proportion made indirect allusions to the same type of expectation. In some cases, awareness of personal vulnerability seems to have been expressed when the respondent talked about his close proximity to death in connection with narrow-escape experiences. For example, the Nagasaki newspaper reporter, who asserted that he was "utterly surprised, and amazed and awed" when the violent explosion hurled him to the ground, went on to say: "If I had been sleeping inside the house [instead of lying awake on the front porch], I would have been killed." In other cases, there were references to expectations of violent death that had been projected into the immediate future. A Nagasaki transportation supervisor, who was badly injured by falling debris, described his state of mind in these terms: "I thought we would be killed by the next one." As is indicated by some of the quotations cited earlier, experiences of traumatic helplessness apparently gave rise to marked anxiety and to an intense, preoccupying concern about the possibility of new exposures to the traumatic situation.

The material presented so far has dealt only with qualitative aspects of the intense emotional stress evoked by A-bomb experiences. We turn now to the quantitative analyses of the morale survey interviews, which provide some rough indication of the incidence with which strong affective responses occurred.

According to the USSBS report on Japanese morale,[15] approximately 47 per cent of the people interviewed in the A-bombed areas mentioned that they had experienced "fear or terror." An additional experience, "fear for own life," is reported as the reaction of 16 per cent. The total sample of 248 cases on which these percentages are based included people from nearby towns as well as residents of the target cities.

The supplementary content analysis included various categories of affective responses. This analysis was systematically applied to the total sample of 101 respondents who were actually in Hiroshima or Nagasaki at the time of the bombing. (Twenty-seven respondents from Hiroshima and Nagasaki were eliminated from

---

[15] USSBS, *The Effects of Strategic Bombing on Japanese Morale.*

the sample, as were all the residents of nearby towns, because they were not located inside the target city at the time of the atomic explosion.) The following supplementary findings were obtained:

1. Approximately two-thirds of the respondents described some form of affective disturbance that they had experienced during the atomic disaster. In most cases, the disturbance took the form of either (*a*) intense fear in the face of danger, (*b*) emotional upset from witnessing casualties, or (*c*) depressive feelings.

2. The most frequently mentioned emotion was fear or "objective" anxiety. Approximately one-third of the respondents explicitly stated that they experienced intense terror, fright, or apprehensiveness—generally in the context of describing exposure to actual danger. An additional 15 per cent made implicit or indirect references to anxiety reactions, such as "felt I was done for" or "felt very worried about my family."

3. In one-fifth of the cases, the *only* affective reaction mentioned was some form of upset or unpleasant feeling evoked by witnessing the dead and injured ("shocked," "couldn't stand the sight," "felt strong pity," etc.).

4. In about 5 per cent of the cases, feelings of depression were expressed ("felt hopeless," "wanted to die," etc.).

It is probable that the percentage of cases who experienced each of the various forms of affective disturbance was actually much higher than in the above results inasmuch as these findings are based on spontaneous comments given in response to general questions about bombing experiences. In the standard USSBS interview questionnaire there were only three questions that elicited answers containing some information about emotional responses:

No. 34. What did you think about the atomic bomb?
No. 35. What bombing experiences have you personally had?
No. 36. Can you tell me more about your experiences?

With the exception of a probing question that was occasionally asked by some of the interviewers after No. 36 ("How did you feel?"), none of the standard questions in the USSBS interviews dealt specifically with emotional reactions. Consequently, the fact that a respondent made no mention of a given type of reaction cannot be taken as an indication that he or she did not experience the reaction—or that a negative answer would have been given if a direct question had been asked. Hence, the above results provide *minimal* estimates of the incidence of affective disturbances among a cross section of disaster survivors. As such, they tend to be consistent with the general picture that has emerged from the qualitative study of intense affective reactions produced by the A-bombs.

PANIC AND DISORGANIZED BEHAVIOR

The material in the preceding sections has dealt almost exclusively with subjective aspects of emotional reactions, i.e., feelings, perceptions, anticipations, and thoughts that are indicative of a person's emotional state. But information about overt action is of even greater importance for an adequate comprehension of the problems of atomic-disaster control. To what extent was overt behavior irrational, disorganized, or maladaptive? Was there widespread panic? How many people engaged in frantic escape attempts without regard for the antisocial consequences of their behavior?

From the fact that many survivors *felt* emotionally upset, it is not safe to assume that they actually displayed panic behavior or that they engaged in actions which were inappropriate or antisocial. Studies of people in comparable stress situations repeatedly have shown that, in the face of extreme danger, a person may suffer from acute anxiety but nevertheless perform actions that are highly adaptive and efficient, if not impressively "heroic." Spiegel has emphasized this point in describing his observations of American soldiers in the Tunisian Campaign:

> . . . A state of tension and anxiety is so prevalent in the front lines that it must be regarded as a normal reaction in this grossly abnormal situation. Where ordinary physiological signs of fear end, and where signs and symptoms of a clinical syndrome begin, is often difficult to decide. This is an important consideration because not only was some of the gallant and heroic work done by men and officers in acute anxiety states, but a considerable

amount of the ordinary combat accomplishment was performed by ordinary men experiencing rather severe anxiety.[16]

Clinical observers, such as Glover, have called attention to similar phenomena among the bombed civilian population of Britain:

> Such signs of panic as have been manifested after the heaviest attacks never assumed a serious form. The pathological reactions noted have been due less to fear than to lack of adequate social organization.[17]

It is true that in very extreme states of emotional excitement, overt panic behavior and other pathological manifestations are likely to occur. But in the absence of precise behavioral observations, the occurrence of disorganized overt behavior cannot be inferred from the mere fact that intense affect was subjectively experienced. Hence, even though we know that those who survived the atomic explosions had strong feelings of fear, a separate inquiry is required in order to determine whether or not they manifested overt panic or disorganized behavior.

Unfortunately, there is a dearth of reliable, empirical observations on overt behavior at Hiroshima and Nagasaki. If there were adequate data we could expect to obtain a more complete picture of the psychological impact of atomic weapons and to gain some additional insights into the dynamics of danger reactions under conditions of total community breakdown. So little information is available, however, that our inquiry hardly yields any substantial facts which could settle differences in speculative opinion about the way A-bombed populations are likely to behave. At most, reviewing the scanty observations will serve only to insert qualifications and reservations into the blanket generalizations that have been put forth on the basis of a priori, stereotyped conceptions of "mass panic."

One of the most widely quoted eyewitness accounts of the Hiroshima disaster is that of Father Siemes, who was at the Jesuit

---

[16] H. X. Spiegel, "Psychiatric Observations in the Tunisian Campaign," *Am. J. Orthopsychiat.*, Vol. 14, 1943, pp. 381–385.

[17] E. Glover, "Notes on the Psychological Effects of War Conditions on the Civilian Population," Part III, "The Blitz," *International J. Psychoanal.*, Vol. 23, 1942, pp. 17–37.

Novitiate in Nagatsuke (about three miles away from Hiroshima) on the day the bomb was dropped. According to this German priest, the behavior of the Japanese survivors was impulsive, disorganized, and socially irresponsible:

> . . . Among the passersby, there are many who are uninjured. In a purposeless, insensate manner, distraught by the magnitude of the disaster most of them rush by and none conceives the thought of organizing help on his own initiative. They are concerned only with the welfare of their own families. It became clear to us during those days that the Japanese displayed little initiative, preparedness, and organizational .skill in preparation for catastrophes. They failed to carry out any rescue work when something could have been saved by a cooperative effort, and fatalistically let the catastrophe take its course. When we urged them to take part in rescue work, they did everything willingly, but on their own initiative they did very little.[18]

The implicit criticism of the Japanese people contained in this passage (lack of initiative, etc.) is noteworthy because, in the last sentence of the preceding paragraph, the author had said that ". . . we did not want to go into town, except under pressure of dire necessity, because we thought that the population was greatly perturbed and that it might take revenge on any foreigners which they might consider spiteful onlookers of their misfortune, or even spies." Whether or not this belief was justified, it may have exerted a predisposing influence upon the author's perceptions of the people he was observing. Nevertheless, his testimony warrants careful consideration as that of a participant observer who was in a position to perceive relevant aspects of disaster reactions.

Father Siemes' testimony contains two main assertions about overt behavior. The first is that many survivors from Hiroshima and its environs behaved in a distraught and purposeless manner. Presumably, this is a summary statement of the author's impressions from seeing hundreds of people who, during the hours immediately after the explosion, came into or passed close to the Novitiate building in Nagatsuke where he was participating in first-aid activity. The sec-

---

[18] Father Siemes, "Hiroshima—August 6, 1945," *Bull. Atomic Scientists*, Vol. 1, May, 1946, pp. 2–6.

ond assertion is that the survivors failed to engage in essential rescue work on their own initiative and were generally deficient in co-operating with each other to mitigate the effects of the disaster—a failure which is attributed, in part, to their distraught state. In making this claim, Father Siemes may have been drawing upon additional experiences he had while carrying out rescuing sorties into the destroyed city, the first of which began about eight hours after the explosion.

In order to evaluate the accuracy and generality of the two descriptive generalizations, it is necessary to examine them carefully in the light of all available sources of information. Father Siemes is not the only one who has put forth such generalizations. Similar summary statements are to be found in certain of the USSBS monographs. The Medical Division's report on the effects of atomic bombs, devoted largely to a careful examination of data on casualties, medical facilities, environmental sanitation, and problems of public health, contains the following introductory remarks about the Hiroshima disaster:

> . . . There was no organized activity. The people seemed stunned by the catastrophe and rushed about as jungle animals suddenly released from a cage. Some few apparently attempted to help others from the wreckage, particularly members of their family or friends. Others assisted those who were unable to walk alone. However, many injured were left trapped beneath collapsed buildings as people fled by them in the streets. Pandemonium reigned as the uninjured and slightly injured fled the city in fearful panic. . . . there were physically intact teams on the outskirts of the city which did not function. Panic drove these people from the city just as it did the injured who could walk or be helped along.[19]

With respect to the second atomic disaster, the report asserts:

> In Nagasaki a similar, but slightly less catastrophic picture occurred. . . . Nagasaki was less completely destroyed than Hiroshima and the panic was apparently less.

In the final section of the report, which presents the summary and conclusions, the evacuation of the target areas is again characterized

---

[19] USSBS, *The Effects of Atomic Bombs on Health and Medical Services in Hiroshima and Nagasaki.*

in extreme terms: "All thoughts except that of self-preservation seem to have been forgotten."

The above assertions about the alleged panic sound like authoritative, well-established propositions, as though the panic were in the same category as the fact that there was a mass exodus from the burning cities. But the report presents no evidence to support the assertions about panic behavior and there is not a single reference to any source from which relevant evidence was obtained. Perhaps the original source for some of the assertions was the report by the British Mission to Japan, published a year earlier, which contains the following sentence: "Witnesses report a panic flight of population, in which officials and civil defense personnel joined, abandoning even the rescue services."[20] Unfortunately, there is no description of the witnesses to indicate who they were, how reliable their testimony was, or what they actually observed, other than the hasty evacuation of survivors from the area where fires were raging.

In the over-all report on the effects of atomic bombs, issued by the USSBS Chairman's Office, there is some material which tends to refute any claim that there was a complete failure on the part of civil defense personnel in Hiroshima to engage in disaster-relief activities:

> Surviving civilians assisted; although casualties in both groups had been heavy, 190 policemen and over 2,000 members of the Civilian Defense Corps reported for duty on 7 August.[21]

In addition, there is a description of the enormous loss of skilled personnel and facilities, followed by the conclusion that "With such elimination of facilities and personnel, the lack of care and rescue activities at the time of the disaster is understandable." But in the very same report there are unsubstantiated generalizations about disorganized overt behavior of the survivors:

> The behavior of the living immediately after the bombings, as described earlier, clearly shows the state of shock that hindered rescue efforts.

---

[20] Report of British Mission to Japan, *The Effects of the Atomic Bombs at Hiroshima and Nagasaki*, His Majesty's Stationery Office, London, 1946.

[21] USSBS, *The Effects of Atomic Bombs on Hiroshima and Nagasaki*.

The two typical impulses were these: Aimless, even hysterical activity or flight from the city to shelter and food.

The phrase "as described earlier" apparently refers only to the passage by Father Siemes, quoted earlier in that same report. There is only one relevant piece of evidence cited to support the generalization that "Aimless, even hysterical activity" was "typical" of the behavior of the population. This was a quotation from a morale-survey interview which refers to a temporary state of acute emotional excitement in one individual ("I became hysterical seeing my grandmother bleeding . . ."). Although it is introduced with the statement that it "illustrates succinctly the mood of survivors" and is referred to as "typical," this particular quotation was found by the present author to be one of very few instances—and probably the most extreme example—of severe emotional breakdown mentioned in the entire set of interviews from Hiroshima and Nagasaki.

The report by the Morale Division, which presents the findings from a systematic analysis of all the interviews, makes no mention whatsoever of aimless or disorganized behavior. As will be described shortly, the morale interviews do not, in fact, provide substantial support for the claim that a sizeable proportion of the population *behaved* in an ineffective or distraught way, even though they do indicate that many people *felt* momentarily terrified or fearful. In only a few cases could one surmise from the individual's statements that he or she might have exhibited uncontrolled emotional behavior; in most cases, such an inference could not be drawn without resorting to extremely tenuous, speculative assumptions.

Before looking into the detailed findings from the USSBS interviews, most of which contain very little information relevant to our present inquiry, it will be useful to consider the case studies presented by John Hersey.[22] The latter material, presumably based on intensive interviews of a few individuals, contains more detailed information about the overt actions of survivors than any other available source.

---

[22] *Op. cit.*

In one of the case studies, Hersey gives the following description of the refugees as they fled from the burning city immediately after the explosion:

> Many, although injured themselves, supported relatives who were worse off. Almost all had their heads bowed, looked straight ahead, were silent, and showed no expression whatever.

In another passage, the large numbers of people who sought refuge in a park on the day of the bombing are described in similar terms:

> To Father Kleinsorge, an Occidental, the silence in the grove by the river, where hundreds of gruesomely wounded suffered together, was one of the most dreadful and awesome phenomena of his whole experience. The hurt ones were quiet; no one wept, much less screamed in pain; no one complained; none of the many who died did so noisily; not even the children cried; very few people even spoke. And when Father Kleinsorge gave water to some whose faces had been almost blotted out by flash burns, they took their share and then raised themselves a little and bowed to him, in thanks.

The inexpressiveness and impassivity of both the injured and uninjured, as emphasized by Hersey, does not preclude the possibility of severe emotional shock, which may have been manifested in symptoms of affectlessness and apathy. Nevertheless, his description is not consonant with the image of survivors rushing excitedly about, engaging in distraught, purposeless actions—as conveyed by Father Siemes and by the more extreme characterization ("like jungle beasts . . ," etc.) presented in the USSBS medical report.

One of Hersey's general statements does appear to be in accord with Father Siemes' comments about the absence of rescue work:

> Under many houses, people screamed for help, but no one helped; in general, survivors that day assisted only their relatives or immediate neighbors, for they could not comprehend or tolerate a wider circle of misery.[23]

It is highly questionable, however, whether Hersey intended this statement to imply that there was a general tendency among the

---

[23] *Ibid.*

survivors to withhold aid to other people or to fail to engage in rescue work at times when it would have been possible to do so. He cites only a few instances where survivors failed to rescue trapped victims and in all such instances it was under conditions of dire emergency, when the fire hazard was so great that the would-be rescuers as well as the rescued would probably have been trapped by the flames. None of his examples provide clear-cut support for the conclusion that the survivors behaved in a socially irresponsible or negligent way. Moreover, in the six case studies to which Hersey's book is devoted there are so many examples of rescue work, spontaneous cooperative effort of mutual aid, and care of the wounded that it is very difficult to believe that these were the exceptions rather than the general rule.

Since this very small group of case studies contains the most detailed information available on overt actions, it is worth while to review briefly the material relevant to mutual aid:

Case 1. Father Kleinsorge, who was affiliated with the same Jesuit Novitiate as Father Siemes, was inside the city of Hiroshima at the time of the disaster. Not only was he extremely active in aiding others, but his experiences brought him into contact with numerous Japanese survivors who were likewise engaging in rescue and relief work. Among them was Mrs. Murato, the mission housekeeper who helped to dig the kindergarten teacher out from under a collapsed dwelling. At Asano park, where hundreds of survivors had congregated, Father Kleinsorge was enlisted into various relief activities by a Japanese man who had organized teams of volunteer crews to fight fires, feed the wounded, etc.[24] Evidently this German priest was deeply impressed by some of his personal experiences of cooperative behavior among the Japanese survivors:

> Father Kleinsorge began to be thirsty in the dreadful heat, and he did not feel strong enough to go for water again. A little before noon, he saw a Japanese woman handing something out. Soon she came to him and said in a kindly voice, "These are tea leaves. Chew them, young man and you won't feel thirsty." The woman's gentleness made Father Kleinsorge suddenly want to cry. For

---

[24] See Case 6.

weeks, he had been feeling oppressed by the hatred of foreigners that the Japanese seemed increasingly to show, and he had been uneasy even with his Japanese friends. This stranger's gesture made him a little hysterical.

Case 2. After rescuing her children from her destroyed home, one of the very first acts of Mrs. Nakamura, a widowed housewife, was to engage in a laborious enterprise in order to respond to a neighbor's request for bandages: ". . . she crawled into the remains of her house again and pulled out some white cloth that she had been using in her work as a seamstress, ripped it into strips, and gave it to Mrs. Nakamoto." While packing up to leave for the designated evacuation area, she suggested to another neighbor that they postpone their flight in order to fight a nearby fire, but decided against doing so when it was pointed out to her that it was too risky. At the evacuation area, she and her children received food and various forms of aid from fellow survivors.

Case 3. Miss Sasaki, a file clerk, sustained an incapacitating leg injury and was buried under wreckage in the factory where she worked. Within a relatively short time she was dug out, along with several others who had been in the same room, by men who were total strangers. One of the members of a rescuing party constructed a crude shelter for her and for two other incapacitated people. After being rescued, however, she received no further aid until two days later, when some strangers transported her to a hospital.

Case 4. Dr. Fujii, despite being injured, extricated himself from the ruins of his hospital and promptly took refuge from the surrounding fires. But he caught sight of two nurses trapped in the wreckage and thereupon left his refuge in order to save them: "He enlisted the help of some of the others under the bridge and freed both of them." Later on, he escaped from the fires, and, with his shoulder in an extremely painful condition, gave some limited medical aid to others and received some aid himself.

Case 5. Dr. Sasaki, the only uninjured physician on the staff of Hiroshima's largest hospital, began administering first aid within a few seconds after the A-bomb explosion. To hundreds of patients requiring prompt attention, he administered whatever medical aid he could give them. "At the Red Cross Hospital, Dr. Sasaki worked for three straight days with only one hour's sleep."

Case 6. Mr. Tanimoto, a Japanese Methodist minister, devoted himself as unceasingly to helping others as did Dr. Sasaki. In Hersey's lengthy chronicle of Mr. Tanimoto's "five days of ministering to the wounded," one finds several instances of spontaneously organized rescue and relief activities that occurred among the refugees in an evacuation area:

> . . . When he saw the fire, he shouted, "All the young men who are not badly hurt come with me!" . . . The team [of volunteers] fought the fire for more than two hours, and gradually defeated the flames.

> In the park, Mr. Tanimoto organized the lightly wounded women of his neighborhood to cook. . . . Altogether, the rice was enough to feed nearly a hundred people.

It is interesting to note that on one occasion, when this man was giving aid to a small group of German priests, he came into contact with Father Siemes, who describes him in the following terms:

> Our rescuing angel in this difficult situation is a Japanese Protestant Pastor. He has brought up a boat and offers to take our wounded up stream to a place where progress is easier. First, we lower the litter containing Father Schiffer into the boat. . . . The boat returns about one-half hour later and the pastor requests that several of us help in the rescue of two children whom he had seen in the river.[25]

The case-study material does not seem to bear out Father Siemes' generalization about the lack of cooperation and the absence of initiative among the Japanese survivors, nor does it tend to substantiate the more limited assertion that there was a tendency to give assistance only to relatives and friends, without regard for others. The glimpses we get of the overt behavior of the few survivors described by Hersey give the impression that by and large they behaved in a socially responsible way and that their activities generally consisted of fairly sensible attempts at coping with an unusually severe disaster situation. As was already mentioned, a few instances

---

[25] Siemes, *loc. cit.*

are noted of survivors neglecting to rescue others who were trapped inside burning houses, but these occurred during the period when rapid escape from the conflagration was essential. For example, Hersey tells us:

> From every second or third house came the voices of people buried and abandoned, who invariably screamed with formal politeness, *"Tasukete kure!"* ["Help, if you please!"] The [German] priests recognized several ruins from which these cries came as the homes of friends, but because of the fire it was too late to help.[26]

Father Siemes describes the very same situation and asserts: "They must be left to their fate."[27]

Among the nine eyewitness accounts from Nagasaki published by Dr. Nagai, there are numerous references to spontaneous relief activities and mutual aid. Only one clear-cut instance of failure to give aid is cited—a confession made to a seven-year-old boy:

> Mr. Tanaka, who lived near us in Urakami, said to me a few days after the bomb, "Satoru, I saw your brother Masaru sitting along the side of the road near Mori. I heard somebody calling for help but I couldn't stop for him—you understand, don't you sonny? I had to get home to my own family!" [Satoru Fukabori's story in *We of Nagasaki*][28]

Dr. Nagai claims that many survivors felt guilty about having failed to risk their lives to save others; but he asserts that generally such action would have been suicidal—people in the bombed area met quick death if they stopped to help someone instead of running from the enveloping flames. According to a U.S. Army Medical Bulletin:

> . . . It took some time, perhaps one hour as stated above, for the fires that were started following the blast to spread within the city. Consequently, those who did not escape were burned to death.[29]

---

[26] Hersey, *op. cit.*

[27] Siemes, *loc. cit.*

[28] T. Nagai, *We of Nagasaki: The Story of Survivors in an Atomic Wasteland,* Duell, Sloan and Pearce, Inc., New York, 1951.

[29] U.S. Army Medical Department, "What Every Medical Officer Should Know about the Atomic Bomb," *Bull. U.S. Army Med. Dept.,* Vol. 8, April, 1948, pp. 247–326.

Under such conditions, rapid, uninterrupted flight would generally be the most adaptive response. In the absence of precise, detailed observations of escape behavior, one cannot make an adequate evaluation of the degree of emotional control exhibited by the survivors. To stop and to attempt to extricate others in the face of a rapidly spreading conflagration would sometimes be tantamount to futile sacrifice of one's own life. We cannot be sure, therefore, that those who fled without stopping to help others were behaving impulsively, since we cannot exclude the possibility that they may have been acting on the basis of a realistic appraisal of the danger situation. Our information is too incomplete to permit any fine judgments to be made; from what little is available, it would be unwarranted to conclude that there was a sizeable frequency of inappropriate, negligent, or asocial behavior merely because some instances of abandonment have been reported.

Although Hersey's case material offers little support for the notion that overt panic states were widely prevalent at Hiroshima, it does suggest that under certain local hazardous circumstances, when a large number of people were crowded together, there may have been outbreaks of excited, disorganized group behavior with antisocial consequences. One clear-cut instance of this kind is mentioned by Hersey:

> As Mr. Tanimoto's men worked, the frightened people in the park pressed closer and closer to the river, and finally the mob began to force some of the unfortunates who were on the very bank into the water. Among those driven into the river and drowned were Mrs. Matsumoto of the Methodist school, and her daughter.[30]

A single reference to disorganized group behavior also occurs in one of the eyewitness accounts from Nagasaki: A child who was seven years old at the time of the disaster reports that there was "almost a panic" among the adults in a neighborhood shelter when planes flew over on the night after the bombing.

> The ones near the entrance started pushing to get inside more. They shouted, "Get inside! Move back farther! Let us in, there'll

---

[30] Hersey, *op. cit.*

be another flash!" They were so scared! And the ones inside yelled when they got squeezed, because their burns hurt. [Satoru Fukabori's story in *We of Nagasaki*][31]

It should be mentioned that these two incidents are the only examples of group panic or near-panic that were found after a thorough search of all published accounts of the atomic disasters. All the original USSBS interviews from Hiroshima and Nagasaki were also examined. No indications that would suggest the occurrence of mass panic behavior were found in those interviews. A sizeable proportion of the A-bombed survivors do mention that they ran away from the burning city after the explosion, but, in the sparse accounts of themselves and of the people whom they saw, there are no references to excited, uncontrolled behavior that could be characterized as overt "panic."

In only a handful of cases, out of more than a hundred interviewed, is there any allusion to distraught or impulsive behavior that had occurred at least momentarily. The four most extreme examples have already been quoted under "Fear and Terror Reactions," page 21. To these, only a few more could be added, all of which involve only momentary impulsive actions that were immediately brought under control. For example, one woman said that she had been so frightened by the blast that she had already run out of her destroyed house before realizing that her children were left behind, whereupon she immediately returned to the ruins and rescued them.

In contrast to the high percentage of respondents who reported having experienced feelings of fear, less than 10 per cent referred to any action carried out "without knowing what I was doing" or to any other kind of behavior that might remotely imply temporarily disorganized activity.

Obviously, the above negative evidence with respect to panic behavior cannot be taken at face value. There is no way of knowing to what extent the respondents were distorting, suppressing, or repressing their memories of the actual events of the disaster. Since no direct questions were asked about overt actions, some of the

---

[31] Nagai, *op. cit.*

respondents may have simply avoided volunteering any information about the unfavorable aspects of their own and others' behavior. Nevertheless, insofar as the interviews constitute relevant evidence, they provide no substantiation for the assertion by Father Siemes and others that the survivors generally acted in a distraught or purposeless manner.

The interviews also provide no support for the claim that when fellow disaster victims were in urgent need of assistance the more fortunate survivors tended to be inordinately lacking in initiative or in social responsibility. Even the more limited assertion—that rescue activity tended to be confined to close relatives and immediate neighbors—is not borne out. The examination of the total sample of Hiroshima interviews yields the following results: 17 per cent mentioned having received aid from strangers and 4 per cent mentioned aid from family members or close friends. Furthermore, 17 per cent mentioned giving help to strangers and 11 per cent, to members of their own families or to close friends. In general, a fairly sizeable proportion of the Hiroshima interviewees (over one-third) referred to rational, practical actions carried out in order to assist other people, whereas no one spoke about any form of neglect.

There were fewer references to mutual aid in the Nagasaki interviews: 7 per cent mentioned giving aid to strangers and 4 per cent mentioned aid to family or friends; none mentioned receiving aid from strangers and 2 per cent, from family or friends. Here again, the interview evidence is ambiguous and does not settle the issue one way or the other. On the one hand, the very low frequency of references to mutual aid among the Nagasaki respondents could be construed as indirect evidence supporting the assertion that the survivors failed to help each other. Furthermore, a sizeable proportion of the respondents in Hiroshima as well as Nagasaki spoke about seeing injured people, but only a small proportion mentioned having given them assistance. Taking account of the findings on intense subjective feelings of fear and terror, it would be by no means unreasonable to speculate that in many such cases the individual might have been so dominated by emotional excitement as to ignore others who were in need of help. On the other hand, the interviews contain no direct, clear-cut evidence of such occurrences: none of the respondents complained about *not* receiving aid when in need of it, and none admitted that they failed to render aid. Moreover, it was on the basis of the Hiroshima disaster that Father Siemes and the USSBS writers originally made their claims and, as we have seen, the manifest content of the interview statements made by survivors of that disaster tend to contradict such claims.

Thus, although we cannot exclude the possibility that the respondents may have intentionally or unintentionally distorted the truth, the fact remains that the findings from the USSBS interviews, like the intensive case studies recorded by Hersey, provide no substantial support for generalizations about disorganized overt behavior.

Let us now return to a central question about which our inquiry has been centered: Was there "mass panic" during the atomic disasters? Only a very tentative and highly qualified answer can be given. If "panic" is defined in terms of inappropriate or socially negligent behavior, we can point to only one clear-cut instance where a sizeable group of Hiroshima survivors behaved in such a way: the pushing-crowd incident reported by Hersey. We also know that there were at least a few individuals who, in a state of acute terror, behaved impulsively, and perhaps irrationally, for a brief period of time. These few instances, when viewed in the context of a high incidence of intense anxiety feelings, create the presumption that there may have been a tendency for many people to lose the normal restraints that ordinarily govern their behavior. Under the catastrophic conditions of an atomic disaster, when so many people are in a state of acute excitement, it is to be expected that the threshold for uncontrolled, disorganized action would generally be much lower than normal. When obvious escape routes are not apparent, many individuals, temporarily dominated by powerful emotional impulses, might engage in frantic efforts to attain safety without regard for the negative consequences of their behavior. Excited stampedes and other typical manifestations of mass panic could easily be touched off by a multiplicity of threatening circumstances that ordinarily, when encountered singly, would not evoke such behavior.

The available evidence suggests that there probably was a latent disposition of this kind among the survivors at Hiroshima and Nagasaki. But how often did it break through into actual behavior? Was the excited crowd behavior at Asano Park one of many such episodes, or was it a rare, isolated occurrence? When the thousands of refugees were evacuating the flaming target areas, were they so terror stricken that they were unable to control maladaptive impulses? or did they generally tend to maintain a fairly high level of ego control and act in a way that maximized their chances of survival? Were trapped disaster victims frequently abandoned by terror-stricken fellow survivors at times when they could easily have been saved? or did such abandonment occur only when extreme danger was so imminent as to preclude any possibility of successful rescue effort?

As is all too apparent from the laborious review of the fragmentary evidence, we simply do not have the answers to these questions of historical fact. If a tentative conclusion were to be drawn in the light of the meager information available, it would be the following: It is probable that overt panic and extreme disorganized behavior occurred in some local circumstances during the two atomic disasters, but it is unlikely that such behavior was widely prevalent among the hundreds of thousands who survived the atomic explosions.

SUMMARY

1. At both Hiroshima and Nagasaki the populace was caught completely by surprise. The absence of warning and the generally unprepared state of the population probably augmented the emotional effects of the A-bomb disasters.

2. Practically all survivors in the target cities experienced personal exposure to physical danger, accompanied by sudden, sharp awareness of the threat to personal survival. The incidence of "narrow-escape" experiences was extremely high.

3. A large proportion of the survivors initially believed that it was their own houses or their own immediate neighborhoods that

had been directly hit by a bomb. In most cases, there was no realization of the magnitude of the disaster until after various escape actions had been taken.

4. There were three outstanding disaster events which were perceived by the vast majority of survivors: the flash of the explosion, the blast effects, and the presence of large numbers of casualties.

5. A substantial proportion of the survivors reacted automatically to the brilliant flash as a danger signal. Some who were not located near ground zero took prompt action, such as falling to a prone position, which minimized exposure to the blast and secondary heat waves. In other cases, the opportunity to minimize the danger was missed because the individual remained fixed or because the action which was taken proved to be inappropriate.

6. Severe blast effects probably played a primary role as the danger stimuli evoking strong emotional excitement. In this respect the traumatic impact resulting from the atomic explosion does not appear to differ from that of other types of explosions and bombings.

7. The perception of large numbers of burned, cut, and maimed bodies was a major source of emotional trauma. Many survivors located only a short distance from the center of the explosion appear to have undergone a double emotional shock—the first, from the physical impact of the explosion and, the second, after they ran out into the streets and saw large numbers of casualties. Among those at the periphery who escaped the full physical violence of the explosion, the initial emotional impact seems to have occurred when they saw the streams of injured victims pouring out of the destroyed areas. Apparently it was not simply the large numbers of casualties, but also the specific character of the injuries, particularly the grossly altered physical appearance of persons who suffered severe burns, that produced emotional disturbances among those who witnessed them.

8. Acute fear was a dominant reaction among the survivors during the crisis phase of the atomic disasters. At least in a small percentage of cases, the emotional excitement reached such a high level that there was temporary loss of inhibitory control over primi-

tive, automatic manifestations of acute anxiety. In some cases, the emotional disturbance took the form of acute depressive reactions. In general, however, the acute symptoms among the A-bombed survivors do not appear to differ from those observed among the British, Germans, and Japanese subjected to exceptionally severe air attacks.

9. There was at least one incident of overt panic behavior among a sizeable crowd of survivors. In addition, at least a small proportion of terrified survivors behaved impulsively, and perhaps irrationally, for a brief period of time. But the meager, fragmentary evidence available on overt behavior does not provide substantial support for claims that overt panic, disorganized activity, or anti-social behavior occurred on a mass scale during the two A-bomb disasters.

CHAPTER 3
AFTERMATH OF THE ATOMIC DISASTERS

Does an atomic disaster give rise to delayed psychological effects that are qualitatively different from those caused by other types of wartime disasters? Are there any unusual syndromes—comparable to the delayed biological effects—that characterize the psychological state of the survivors after an atomic explosion? The material on postdisaster reactions to be presented in this chapter provides an empirical basis for formulating some tentative answers to these questions.

In the last chapter we have seen that there was relatively little that was unique about the immediate reactions of the A-bombed survivors. It was noted that there was an exceptionally high incidence of narrow-escape experiences and of disturbing perceptions of the casualties; nevertheless, the emotional effects of such exposures do not appear to differ from those seen in persons exposed to heavy bombardment or incendiary attacks. The symptoms of acute emotional shock observed in a small proportion of the A-bombed survivors apparently were the same as those seen in other types of disasters. The widespread feelings of fear and apprehensiveness seem to have been typical "objective" anxiety reactions of the sort to be expected whenever people are exposed to sudden danger. From the fragmentary evidence, it seems that overt panic was not of frequent occurrence and was probably evoked only when survivors were trapped in the presence of rapidly approaching fires or were caught in other special circumstances where they were helpless in the face of imminent danger.

The possibility remains, however, that there may have been some unique postdisaster reactions. Insidious, delayed effects might have shown up in the form of unusually persistent anxiety reactions, prolonged apathy, or other sustained symptoms that are indicative of a failure to re-establish normal emotional equilibrium. Conceivably, the exceptionally intense stress of an atomic disaster might even have had the effect of weakening psychological stamina to the point where acute psychoses, traumatic neuroses, or other forms of chronic mental disorder would be prevalent. Or perhaps the atomic disasters had a profoundly demoralizing effect, giving rise to extreme changes in the social and political attitudes of the survivors.

Such possibilities will be examined in our survey of the observations on postdisaster reactions. As will be seen, the evidence points to some fairly severe psychological sequelae; but, again, none of the effects appears to differ from those which have been noted among the English, German, and Japanese people who were exposed to "conventional" air attacks.

SUSTAINED FEAR REACTIONS

After the acute danger phases of the atomic disasters had come to an end, the sources of emotional stress had by no means subsided. The A-bomb shattered the normal pattern of community life and left the survivors in an extremely deprived state. For many days there was practically no medical aid for the tens of thousands suffering from acute burns, lacerations, and other severe injuries. Injured and uninjured alike were homeless, without adequate clothing or shelter. Food was in such scarce supply that starvation and malnutrition became widely prevalent.[1]

In addition to the extreme physical deprivations, there were many other sources of emotional stress. With the economic and social life of their community so completely disrupted, the survivors faced a bleak and insecure future. Moreover, during the postdisaster period most survivors experienced grief over the death of relatives or close friends and many were continually worried about those who were missing, seriously injured, or unexpectedly afflicted with radiation sickness. Under such conditions, emotional recovery from the

---

[1] USSBS Report, *The Effects of Atomic Bombs on Health and Medical Services in Hiroshima and Nagasaki*, U.S. Government Printing Office, Washington, D.C., 1947.

traumatic events of the disaster could hardly be expected to proceed rapidly.

Various sources of information indicate that severe anxiety persisted among some of the survivors for many days and possibly weeks after the bombings. One of the most frequent types of sustained emotional disturbances appears to have been a phobic-like fear of exposure to another traumatic disaster. This reaction consisted in strong feelings of apprehensiveness accompanied by exaggerated efforts to ward off new threats.

A vivid description of anxiety states evoked by minimal signs of potential danger has been given by Dr. T. Hagashi, a physician in Hiroshima, who was one of the special informants on postdisaster reactions interviewed by USSBS investigators:

> "Whenever a plane was seen after that, people would rush into their shelters. They went in and out so much that they did not have time to eat. They were so nervous they could not work. . . .
>
> ". . . Most of the people were very, very uneasy and afraid that another bomb would be dropped. They lived in that condition for days and days."[2]

Hersey describes a few illustrative incidents, such as the following:

> It began to rain. . . . The drops grew abnormally large, and someone [in the evacuation area] shouted, "The Americans are dropping gasoline. They're going to set fire to us!"[3]

That sustained fear reactions occurred at Nagasaki as well as Hiroshima is indicated by some of the statements in the USSBS morale interviews. For example:

> ". . . after that atomic bomb I was constantly afraid." [Domestic worker in Nagasaki]
>
> "There are no words that can describe the terror it caused. . . . We were so scared that another would fall that we stayed in the woods for two days wondering what to do next." [Housewife in Nagasaki]

---

[2] These quotations and similar ones are taken from the original protocols of the USSBS interviews in Hiroshima, Nagasaki, and the towns surrounding those two cities.

[3] John Hersey, *Hiroshima,* Alfred A. Knopf, New York, 1946.

"I later heard it was an atomic bomb, but didn't venture out of the house for a week or so because we were told it was dangerous." [Housewife in Nagasaki]

"[I left because] I had the fear of another atomic bomb at Nagasaki." [Housewife in Nagasaki]

Further indications of sustained apprehensiveness among the populace comes from the anxiety-laden rumors which are reported to have been widely circulated during the postdisaster period. Both Siemes[4] and Hersey[5] state that there were rumors that American parachutists had landed in the vicinity of Hiroshima shortly after the A-bomb attack. The latter author also reports that several weeks after the disaster stories were circulating to the effect that "the atomic bomb had deposited some sort of poison on Hiroshima which would give off deadly emanations for seven years; nobody could go there all that time." Brues[6] reports similar exaggerated fears of lingering danger at Nagasaki. He states that there was a widely circulated rumor that Nagasaki would remain uninhabitable for years to come and that this rumor was still creating concern when his party of investigators visited the city several months after the disaster.

In several of the eyewitness accounts from Nagasaki there are allusions to such rumors. For example, one woman reports:

I heard that people who had not been wounded and seemed to be all right would begin feeling out of sorts and all of a sudden drop dead. It made me panicky. Here I was bustling around now, but I might go off myself. . . .

The story was going around that the ruins of Urakami ran for two miles from north to south and that if you walked through them you would get diarrhea and if you tried to take care of many of the dead you would come down with some terrible disease, and sometimes you would start coughing up blood. Was this

---

[4] Father Siemes, "Hiroshima—August 6, 1945," *Bull. Atomic Scientists,* Vol. 1, May, 1946, pp. 2–6.

[5] *Op. cit.*

[6] A. M. Brues, "With the Atomic Bomb Casualty Commission in Japan," *Bull. Atomic Scientists,* Vol. 3, June, 1947, pp. 143–144.

going to happen to me too? I wondered. [Fujie Urata Matsu-
moto's story in *We of Nagasaki*.][7]

Dr. Nagai claims that directly after the explosion the damaged area
actually was so powerfully radioactive that people who merely
walked around in it developed acute enteritis with diarrhea and
those who worked in the ruins came down with incapacitating or
fatal attacks of blood disease.

To some extent, fear rumors may have been touched off or reinforced by the unexpected appearance of many cases of radiation
sickness. During the weeks following the atomic explosion numerous unusual signs of organic pathology began to appear among
survivors: loss of hair, high fever, excessive fatigue, hemorrhagic
spots under the skin, and other severe symptoms of radiation sickness.[8] A number of the morale interviews contain references to the
surprising occurrence of severe illness and sudden death among the
ranks of seemingly intact survivors. For example:

> "Next evening, my son, who was burned—his face, hands, and
> legs—came home on foot. . . . At first he seemed all right and
> I never thought he was going to die as he used to eat three times
> a day. But after two weeks his teeth began to loosen and his hair
> started falling out and three weeks later he died." [Housewife in
> Hiroshima]

> "Six more of my men died a month later. They were well at first,
> but their hair started coming off about twenty days later and their
> teeth; their gums started bleeding, and another two or three days
> later they finally died." [Mechanic in Nagasaki]

> "This friend of mine was well when we worked together helping
> the other people, but after a few days he said he lost his appetite.
> Then his hair started falling out and the next day he just fell over
> dead. There were many people who just dropped dead as the days
> went on. I suppose it was due to the concussion." [Electrician in
> Nagasaki]

---

[7] T. Nagai, *We of Nagasaki: The Story of Survivors in an Atomic Wasteland*,
Duell, Sloan and Pearce, Inc., New York, 1951.

[8] Los Alamos Scientific Laboratory, *The Effects of Atomic Weapons*, U.S. Government Printing Office, Washington, D.C., 1950; USSBS, *The Effects of Atomic Bombs
on Health and Medical Services in Hiroshima and Nagasaki*.

"Some of the folks when they came seemed normal. But about one month later their hair all dropped off and they died. Death was caused by gas. The people that were [?] over—their faces were beyond description. If you haven't seen it for yourself, it couldn't be understood. The children, two or three years of age, even if they were living at our place, were dead with the hair on their heads all falling off. . . . The people even after they have recovered—their faces are all disfigured so it is really a pitiful sight." [Female high school student in Hiroshima]

From descriptions such as these, it is apparent that over a long period of time the survivors were likely to see the human damage caused by the violent release of nuclear energy; such experiences probably augmented the sustained emotional disturbances created by the disaster.

With respect to overt avoidance behavior, there is one well-established fact from which some inferences can be made. Within twenty-four hours after the mass flight from Hiroshima, thousands of refugees came streaming back into the destroyed city. According to one of the USSBS reports, road blocks had to be set up along all routes leading into the city because there were so many people who wanted to search for missing relatives or to inspect the damage.

The strong motivation to return to the destroyed city is illustrated in several of Hersey's case studies. For example:

. . . Mrs. Nakamura, although she was too ill to walk much, returned to Hiroshima alone. . . . All week, at the Novitiate, she had worried about her mother, brother, and older sister, who lived in the part of town called Fukuso, and besides, she felt drawn by some fascination, just as Father Kleinsorge had been.[9]

Although both Hiroshima and Nagasaki required almost complete rebuilding and lacked an adequate food supply, the inhabitants gradually returned to live in improvised shacks. Within three months the population in each city was back to about 140,000.[10]

The fairly prompt return of large numbers of survivors to the target cities is itself a noteworthy postdisaster reaction. This be-

---

[9] Hersey, *op. cit.*

[10] Report of British Mission to Japan, *The Effects of the Atomic Bombs at Hiroshima and Nagasaki,* His Majesty's Stationery Office, London, 1946.

havior points up the obvious fact that despite whatever potential radiation hazards might persist after an atomic explosion, there are no immediate, impressive signs of lingering danger that impel people to stay away. From what happened at Hiroshima, it is apparent that special problems of disaster control are likely to arise in connection with keeping unauthorized persons out of stricken or contaminated areas (unless avoidance tendencies have been built up by public information about the dangers of radioactivity). Apparently there were strong "approach" motives among the survivors: to search for the missing, to salvage possessions, or to satisfy curiosity. Of central importance to our present inquiry is the inference that such motives were capable of overriding reluctance to return to the scene of the disaster. From the material presented earlier, we know that apprehensiveness about another attack may have been prevalent immediately after the disaster and, later on, fear of contamination may have developed; but evidently such fears were generally not so intense as to prevent resettlement in the target cities. In any case, the fact that such large numbers of survivors returned to the target cities during the days and weeks following the disasters implies that the A-bomb did not produce a unique mass avoidance of the disaster locale.

DEPRESSION AND APATHY

Among some of the survivors, severe reactions of guilt and depression are known to have occurred during the postdisaster period. Dr. Nagai gives a vivid description of his own guilt feelings.[11] Despite being injured, he had worked assiduously during the disaster rescuing people and rendering medical aid until he collapsed from loss of blood and utter fatigue. Nevertheless, he blamed himself for numerous shortcomings: by remaining at the hospital with the members of his first-aid squad, he was neglecting his own wife and children, as well as his injured neighbors who were expecting him to care for them; while devoting himself to directing the rescue

---

[11] Nagai, op. cit.

work of patients, he was aware of the "selfish" motive of wanting to achieve social recognition for his heroism; several nurses who subsequently succumbed to radiation sickness had complained to him of feeling weak, but, not recognizing the early symptoms, he had forced them to keep going; later on, while lying ill and exhausted, he experienced intense fear of another bomb attack and could not get up the nerve to cut across the shelterless wastes to the ruins of his neighborhood, where his wife lay dead.

In the context of reporting his personal reactions, Nagai develops the general thesis that practically all survivors were affected in the same way:

> We of Nagasaki, who survive, cannot escape the heart-rending, remorseful memories. . . .
>
> We carry deep in our hearts, every one of us, stubborn, unhealing wounds. When we are alone we brood upon them, and when we see our neighbors we are again reminded of them; theirs as well as ours.

Nagai believes that persistent "survivor-guilt" is an inevitable consequence of atomic bombing, because most survivors could not avoid behaving negligently in one way or another: people who were in the heart of the city were able to survive only by running away from the fires without stopping to rescue others; people who were in a position to give aid could not simultaneously perform all the duties and obligations of rescuing the wounded, rushing to their own families, assisting neighbors, carrying out their civil defense assignment, saving valuable materials at the office or factory where they worked, preserving treasured household articles, etc.

Although there are independent observations which indicate that some survivors experienced temporary guilt reactions following the A-bombings, there is no satisfactory evidence to support the claim that such reactions persisted in large numbers of survivors or that, four years after the war, the "rents in the ties of friendship and love . . . seem to be getting wider and deeper." Nagai is able to cite a few examples of persistent guilt feelings in the eyewitness accounts he collected from his neighbors. The translators of his book, however, inform us that: "In his editing, Nagai has preserved entirely the plain, unsophisticated character of the narratives, while focusing each one in such a way as to point up the theme that a spiritual wreckage, more vast than the material, must result from atomic war." Moreover, it is doubtful that Nagai had the opportunity to observe the postwar behavior of very many of his fellow survivors inasmuch as he had been continuously confined to his home, bedridden due to chronic leukemia.

Other sources of information provide no substantial basis for concluding that persistent guilt or depressive reactions were an inordinately frequent consequence of the atomic bombings.

Some of the evidence cited in the preceding chapter indicates that at least a small percentage of the survivors felt depressed during or immediately after the disaster. But in the entire sample of USSBS morale interviews, there were found only a few cases who made comments suggesting that they had experienced feelings of guilt, sadness, hopelessness, or apathy during the postdisaster period.

At the time of the interviews, three months after the bombings, a very small percentage expressed attitudes of pessimism or gloom. In discussing their future, most of the survivors described fairly concrete plans for increasing their economic security. Although practically all of them were deeply concerned about the food shortage and other economic difficulties, very few voiced feelings of resignation or despondency. In response to the question, "Do you feel you are better or worse off now than you were during the war?" only 20 per cent of the Hiroshima cases stated "worse off now." The comparable figure cited by the USSBS morale report for Japan on a whole is almost the same: 17 per cent.[12] (Only the Hiroshima sample was used in the present analysis of pessimistic responses; the impression received from reading the Nagasaki interviews was that negative responses, e.g., "worse off now," occurred even less frequently in the Nagasaki interviews than in those from Hiroshima.)

---

[12] USSBS Report, *The Effects of Strategic Bombing on Japanese Morale*, U.S. Government Printing Office, Washington, D.C., 1947.

From a detailed examination of answers to all relevant questions, it was found that about one-half of the Hiroshima cases expressed some degree of concern about the future. Only 11 per cent, however, expressed clear-cut pessimism. Directly comparable percentages are not available for other urban areas in Japan, but the USSBS morale report gives the following information:

> Three months after the surrender, fifty-three per cent of the Japanese people gave pessimistic answers to the question: "Now that the war is over, how do you think you and your family will fare in the next two or three years?" Only twenty-five per cent reported fair satisfaction with their prospects. It is apparent, again, that the majority of the Japanese people were exceedingly depressed in the post-surrender period. Typical responses were: "We have no plan." "We are living from day to day."[13]

From this statement, it would appear to be highly improbable that there was a significant difference between Hiroshima and other Japanese cities with respect to the relative incidence of interview responses expressing pessimistic attitudes about the future.

Although the interview data provide little evidence of widespread gloom, despondency, or hopelessness among the A-bombed survivors, there are some independent observations which have been interpreted as indicating a high degree of overt lethargy. USSBS investigators in the Medical Division visited Hiroshima three months after the bombing and noted that the city still had not recovered to the point where adequate shelter and essential utilities were available: Only a few shacks had been constructed for homeless people; there was no garbage or sewage collection; leaking water pipes all over the city remained unrepaired; etc. In the Medical Division's report the slow and haphazard restoration of Hiroshima is interpreted as indicating an absence of initiative among the populace. The same sort of apathy is reported at Nagasaki:

> At the time the Allied Military Government entered Nagasaki, about 1 October, the population was found to be apathetic and profoundly lethargic. Even at this time the collection of garbage and night soil had not been reestablished, restoration of

---

[13] *Ibid.*

other public utilities was lacking and the hospital facilities were inadequate.[14]

The claim that there was widespread apathy or lethargy among the A-bombed survivors is evidently based solely on the fact that the restoration of housing, public utilities, and hospital facilities had proceeded at a very slow rate. However, when a city has been almost totally destroyed, with over half its population killed or injured, the rate of restoration probably is not an adequate indicator of the motivational state of the remainder of the city's population. Restoration would undoubtedly depend to a large extent on the amount of aid received from the rest of the country.

It should also be borne in mind that apathy and absence of co-operative activity have been reported by the USSBS Morale Division as characteristic of the entire Japanese nation after the war was terminated by the unexpected surrender, which came shortly after the A-bomb attacks.

> The war left Japan with its cities laid waste, its industrial system disorganized, and its merchant fleet almost obliterated. Millions of Japanese were unemployed, underfed, homeless. Countless others were casualties from bombing or had been displaced in evacuation. The nation as a whole had suffered the extreme hardships of the war and tasted the bitterness of defeat. It had been disillusioned about its leaders and left uncertain about its own future.
>
> . . . recognized common goals and accredited common leadership were lacking. The cement that held the nation together during the war lost its grip, and the people, in many places, became a disorganized mass, split among themselves, seeking individual solutions to their desperate personal problems and conscious only of the immediate day-to-day task of staying alive.[15]

When the factors mentioned in the above excerpts are taken into account, together with the other findings from the morale surveys, it appears unwarranted to conclude that the A-bombs produced an

---

[14] USSBS, *The Effects of Atomic Bombs on Health and Medical Services in Hiroshima and Nagasaki.*

[15] USSBS, *The Effects of Strategic Bombing on Japanese Morale.*

exceptionally high degree of apathy or depression among those who survived at Hiroshima and Nagasaki.

PSYCHIATRIC CASUALTIES

In Chapter 5, it will be seen that chronic psychopathological disorders were rarely produced by heavy bombing attacks, although emotional shock reactions occurred with considerable frequency among those who had undergone direct personal involvement. Does this conclusion apply equally to atomic bombings? Or are there indications that the severe stress of an atomic disaster gives rise to psychiatric effects which are different in some ways from those produced by other types of wartime disaster?

It has already been mentioned that typical symptoms of acute emotional shock—anxiety states, apathy, depression—occurred temporarily in A-bombed survivors immediately after the destructive impact of the explosion. From the fact that large numbers of survivors had undergone harrowing danger experiences and had suffered direct personal loss, it might be predicted that in many people the emotional disturbances would persist for months after the disaster. The scanty observations described in preceding sections indicate that symptoms of acute emotional disturbance probably persisted for several days, and perhaps for a number of weeks in some cases. But the information is too incomplete to permit an adequate estimate of the incidence of such reactions. The available evidence serves only to exclude extreme possibilities: it indicates that postdisaster disturbances were neither wholly absent nor inordinately widespread.

Unfortunately, no psychiatric studies of the A-bombed survivors have been reported. In the USSBS Medical Division's report,[16] there is only one incidental allusion to a possible emotional disorder among A-bombed survivors. In the discussion of changes in reproductive functions, evidence is cited which shows that during the

---

[16] USSBS, *The Effects of Atomic Bombs on Health and Medical Services in Hiroshima and Nagasaki.*

months after the atomic bombings there were marked increases in
(1) aspermia among men; (2) menstrual difficulties among adult
women; and (3) miscarriages, abortions, and premature births
among pregnant women. We are told that although these symptoms
were probably due to physiological changes produced by gamma
radiation, precise evidence on the causes is lacking. The report
points out that other factors such as "poor living conditions" and
"emotional disturbances" may have played an important role, particularly in connection with the extraordinarily high incidence of
miscarriages. Hence, the possibility should not be overlooked that
some of the pathological effects on reproductive processes might
have been psychogenic in origin. Nevertheless, there is no substantial evidence to indicate that the reproductive disturbances were
psychosomatic disorders arising from emotional stress. Nor is there
any evidence in the USSBS reports that is relevant to any other psychosomatic or neurotic symptoms that might have been evoked by
the atomic disasters.

We are left in the dark not only with respect to the incidence of
sustained symptoms of emotional shock, but also with respect to the
possible outbreak of more serious types of psychiatric disorder,
e.g., traumatic neuroses and acute psychoses. A single instance of
possible psychotic breakdown is alluded to in one of the eyewitness
accounts from Nagasaki: A woman is described who "went out of
her mind . . . and acted like a lunatic" when her child died four
days after the bombing; she was seen wandering around carrying
the child's body, laughing hysterically.[17]

In the absence of any other information, it is worth while to look
into the morale interviews for whatever psychiatric leads they may
contain. After examining the interviews from Hiroshima and Nagasaki, one is left with the impression that there were at least a few
cases who suffered from sustained neurotic symptoms which were
caused or precipitated by atomic-disaster experiences. This impression, however, is based only on very fragmentary indications of the
following sort:

---

[17] Nagai, *op. cit.*

Case 1. A fifty-year-old carpenter in Nagasaki alluded to difficulties which suggest a neurotic fatigue reaction. He reported that he had been uninjured during the disaster and had been extremely energetic in his attempts to save his three children, all of whom subsequently died. Although more than three months had elapsed since the disaster, he complained that he was still excessively fatigued: "I have not regained my energy yet."

Case 2. A twenty-seven-year-old housewife in Nagasaki described a symptom which suggests conversion hysteria. In a highly emotionalized account of her disaster experiences she mentioned that she was "not hurt" by the bombing but a few days later certain parts of her body had felt sore and stiff. During the months that followed she was free from any such complaints. Then two days before the interview, the symptom reappeared: the soreness and stiffness returned in exactly the same regions of her body that had previously been affected.

Case 3. Another housewife in Nagasaki, forty-five years of age, evidently experienced an unusually severe anxiety attack during the disaster and thereafter appears to have developed a persistent phobia. More than three months later, according to her statements, she could not stand the sight of any of the damaged areas in the bombed city.

It should be emphasized that these three cases represent the most extreme instances of postdisaster disturbances culled from more than 100 interviews. Very few respondents made any explicit reference to suffering from emotional upset, and none mentioned being incapacitated in any way because of psychological symptoms. Altogether, there were only a handful of cases who referred to complaints that could be construed as possible signs of neurosis or psychosomatic illness.

In evaluating the interview evidence, it is necessary to take account of possible selective factors affecting the morale-survey sample: Very severe psychiatric casualties, by virtue of their incapacities, might have been excluded from the group of survivors who were interviewed. Nevertheless, if the incidence of gross psychopathology were extremely high, one would expect signs of behavioral disturbance to appear in any group of 100 survivors, particularly when the group had been selected according to sampling criteria designed to provide a cross section of the bombed population.

There are several specific features of the interviews which imply an absence of severe emotional disorders among the vast majority of the respondents. First of all, the interviewers kept a record of overt expressive behavior exhibited by the respondents. Evidently, none of the survivors displayed extraordinary affective outbursts at any time during the interviews. There are frequent notations to the effect that a respondent "wept" or "had tears in his eyes" while describing feelings about the Emperor's announcement of the surrender, but there are practically no notations about emotional manifestations when A-bombing experiences were being described. (As a matter of fact, the emotionally toned language used by the respondents, as well as the interviewers' notations, suggests that memories of the surrender announcement were more painful than memories of the atomic disaster.)

A second indication of emotional control at the time of the interviews is the relative absence of impulsive or excessive verbalization about disaster experiences. Very few respondents spontanously brought up their personal bombing experiences until asked to discuss them, near the end of the lengthy interview. So far as the interview records go, there is no evidence that any of the respondents displayed a hysteria-like tendency to gush forth with dramatic details at the slightest opportunity. Nor are there any signs of repetitiveness or overelaboration that would suggest persistent, obsessive rumination about disaster experiences.

In general, the accounts of the bombings were coherent and fairly well organized, containing a few elaborated details. Explicit complaints about being unable to remember the disaster events were very rare and, from the fairly adequate answers given to the interviewers' question, there is no basis for suspecting that any of the respondents had developed retroactive amnesia. It should also be mentioned that the interviews contain no bizarre verbalizations or delusional ideas suggestive of psychosis. On the whole, the character of the interview responses is such as to indicate that the respondents were able to talk about the harrowing experiences they had undergone, to discuss their personal feelings about a wide variety of topics, and to describe their current beliefs and expectations without manifesting any obvious signs of psychopathology.

The tentative conclusions to be drawn from the interview data tend to support the generalizations derived from other types of wartime disasters. The most severe types of psychiatric disorder appear to have been of rare occurrence following the A-bomb attacks. While there are no signs of psychosis or of grossly incapacitating neurosis among the survivors, there are some indications that a few individuals may have developed minor neurotic symptoms, such as excessive fatigue, recurrent bodily complaints, and persistent phobias. The more transient symptoms of emotional shock described earlier probably were the predominant psychiatric effects of the atomic disasters.

MORALE EFFECTS AMONG THE SURVIVORS

It is to be expected that such a shattering event as an A-bomb disaster would have a powerful effect on morale. Study of beliefs, expectations, and morale attitudes of the survivors indicates that pronounced changes occurred as a result of the atomic bombings. Nevertheless, the A-bombs did not give rise to any different kind of morale effects than those produced by other types of heavy air attack. This is the conclusion reached by USSBS investigators in Japan, on the basis of their extensive morale survey.[18]

The morale of the people in and around Hiroshima and Nagasaki did not fall below that of the rest of Japan. For example, only 27 per cent of the respondents in the A-bombed areas reported that before the surrender they had felt victory was impossible; the corresponding figure for the rest of Japan was 26 per cent. On other indicators of wartime morale ("personal willingness to continue the war" and "confidence in victory"), a significantly *larger* percentage of people in the A-bombed areas expressed high morale.

---

[18] USSBS, *The Effects of Strategic Bombing on Japanese Morale.*

In general, the amount of defeatism at Hiroshima and Nagasaki was less than in other Japanese cities. When compared with respondents elsewhere in Japan, the attitudes of the A-bombed population were found to resemble those of people in the lightly bombed and unbombed cities rather than in the heavily bombed cities. Of the sixty cities and towns in which the USSBS morale survey was conducted, Nagasaki ranked tenth highest on an over-all morale index and Hiroshima ranked thirty-second highest.

The comparatively high morale of the survivors in the two A-bombed cities has been explained as being due to the fact that morale was initially higher than average: prior to the A-bomb attacks they had not been exposed to heavy bombing, whereas most other cities had been subjected to destructive B-29 raids. Apparently the A-bomb attacks produced no greater drop in morale among the Japanese survivors than would be expected from a single heavy raid (employing incendiaries or high explosives) of the type carried out during the massed B-29 campaign against other Japanese cities.

There was one unique characteristic of the interview responses of the A-bombed survivors, but it was a relatively unimportant one. A comparatively low proportion of respondents in Hiroshima and Nagasaki (as compared with other cities in Japan) expressed defeatist attitudes; among those who did express such attitudes, the A-bomb was frequently mentioned as the reason. In other cities, those who expressed defeatism were much more likely to mention the B-29 attacks, reflecting the sort of bombing to which they had been subjected.

Relatively little hostility toward the United States was expressed by the respondents in Hiroshima and Nagasaki. According to the USSBS report, this may have been due, in part, to factors introduced by the interviewing situation: politeness, timidity, or retrospective distortion. However, such factors probably would not account for significant differences between Hiroshima-Nagasaki respondents and civilians elsewhere in Occupied Japan.

In response to the question, "When American planes bombed Japan, on which side did you feel the responsibility lay?" a significantly greater percentage of the A-bombed survivors stated that neither side was responsible—that it was an inevitable consequence of war.

Evidently there was some tendency to turn hostility against Japanese war leaders, since a sizeable minority (35 per cent) stated that it was Japan's fault. But this was not an unusual reaction, because 46 per cent of the people in the rest of Japan gave the same response.[19]

It is possible that immediately following the atomic disasters there was much more hostility toward the United States than is apparent in the postwar interviews. According to a police chief in Hiroshima, who was interviewed by USSBS investigators:

> "At the time of the bombing, they felt 'what a terrible thing the Americans had done!' and they were bitter. After the surrender, they turned on the Japanese military. They felt that they had been fooled and wondered if the military knew the bomb was coming and why they did not take steps."

In a few of the interviews from Nagasaki there are indications that some resentment was directed toward the Japanese government for withholding information about the bomb and for failing to prepare the population after the Hiroshima disaster had made the danger clearly apparent. For example:

> "I wondered why Japan wouldn't know of such a thing as the use of atomic energy and why we weren't told of it. The Hiroshima report was not in detail. They tried to hide as much of the destructive damage as possible." [Newspaper reporter in Nagasaki]

> "Before this we had heard of the atomic bomb experience that had happened in Hiroshima. But if the newspaper and radio had given a clearer picture of the strength and told us what to do, Nagasaki would have been spared a little of this misery. When I think of this I get furious with disgust." [Industrial worker in Nagasaki]

Whether or not there had been an earlier shift in the target of aggression, the fact is that there is no evidence suggesting that at the time of the interviews the survivors retained a residual attitude of resentment toward the United States. Despite their economic hardships, the majority expressed favorable attitudes toward the

---

[19] *Ibid.*

U.S. Military Government. Less than 10 per cent made critical comments, most of which pertained to minor aspects of occupation
policies. In contrast, about 50 per cent made critical or hostile
remarks about Japanese war leaders. With respect to the A-bomb,
about one-fifth of the survivors characterized it as a cruel, inhuman,
or barbarous weapon, and only 2 per cent explicitly criticized the
United States for having used it. Again, it is impossible to know
to what extent these interview results are distorted because of the
suppression of true feelings; but, so far as the evidence goes, it
indicates that the A-bomb attack itself generated very little persistent
hostility toward Americans.

From the USSBS data, it appears to be very probable that the
same factors found to be responsible for lowering morale among
civilians exposed to "conventional" air attacks apply equally to the
effects of the A-bomb. The inverse relationship between personal
involvement and morale, which will be discussed in Chapter 7, has
been found to hold for the A-bombed population:

> Hiroshima and Nagasaki respondents were divided into two
> groups on the basis of having been physically affected by the
> bomb. In the first group were placed all those who were knocked
> down, injured, or wounded in any way by the bomb. In the
> second were placed those who merely saw the effects of the
> bomb. The two groups were significantly different in respect to
> several indices of morale.
>
> In a group of questions designed to measure confidence in vic-
> tory, the physically affected group was much lower in morale
> than the unaffected group. . . .
>
> In the Morale Index, thirty-one per cent of the physically unaf-
> fected group fell into the highest of the four morale index cate-
> gories, while seventeen per cent of the affected group fell into
> this category.[20]

In this connection, it is worth noting that certainty of defeat and
other attitudes indicative of low morale were more prevalent at
Hiroshima, where the area of devastation and the casualties were
greater, than at Nagasaki.

---

[20] *Ibid.*

MORALE EFFECTS ELSEWHERE IN JAPAN

The potential morale effects of the A-bomb were undoubtedly curtailed to a considerable degree by the Japanese surrender, which occurred before most of the population outside the target cities had learned about the A-bomb. Almost no publicity was given to the new weapon prior to the surrender. As would be expected, therefore, the psychological effect of the bombs dropped on Hiroshima and Nagasaki was found to be comparatively slight in the rest of Japan.[21]

According to the USSBS report, when the people in other communities first learned about the new destructive weapon, the most common reaction was apprehensiveness. Of those interviewed throughout Japan, 57 per cent reported having felt fearful upon hearing about the A-bombs and their effects. But over the islands as a whole, the proportion who expressed a personal fear of being killed by an A-bomb was only half as great as among persons who had been more directly exposed to the bomb's effects.

The effects on morale attitudes appear to have been even more attenuated. Only about 10 per cent of the Japanese people mentioned the A-bomb in explaining their reasons for defeatist attitudes (certainty that Japan could not win; personal unwillingness to go on with the war). Military losses were mentioned twice as frequently and the general air attack three times as frequently as the A-bomb.

There is some evidence which suggests that certain of the morale effects may have varied inversely with the distance from the target areas. The cities in which the morale survey had been conducted were arranged in four groups according to the distance from Hiroshima and Nagasaki. It was found that as the distance increased there was a progressive decline in the proportion of the population who mentioned the A-bomb as one of their reasons for defeatist attitudes. Only in the cities within sixty miles of the targets was there a substantial proportion who referred to the A-bomb as a factor that influenced their personal beliefs.

---

[21] *Ibid.*

The USSBS report points out that the above findings on morale effects outside the target cities probably do not give an adequate picture of the demoralizing potentialities of the atomic weapon:

> . . . the lack of understanding of the meaning of the new weapon in areas away from the target undoubtedly limited its demoralizing effect. . . .

> . . . Were the channels of mass communication as readily available to all the population as they are in the United States and had the use of the bomb received anything like the intensive coverage it had here, the effect on continued support of the war would probably have been greater.[22]

Thus, from the standpoint of predicting responses to subsequent A-bomb attacks, the findings are of limited value because the destructiveness of the A-bomb remained unknown to the vast majority of the Japanese population. It should also be borne in mind that at the time the A-bomb was used the population was already suffering severe wartime hardships. Among a substantial proportion defeatist attitudes had already developed because of military losses, the food shortage, and the concentrated incendiary and high-explosive attacks on Japanese cities. Furthermore, even if the A-bomb attacks had been immediately publicized, the surrender came so soon after the two bombs were dropped that there was no opportunity for delayed reactions of defeatism to develop.

According to USSBS investigators, the surrender itself cannot be regarded as being mainly due to the A-bomb attack. A powerful faction of the Japanese government was already prepared to surrender unconditionally and the A-bomb appears to have speeded up this action primarily by providing an obvious "face-saving" excuse.[23]

SUMMARY

1. Fear reactions persisted among a sizeable proportion of the population for many days and possibly weeks after the atomic bomb-

[22] *Ibid.*
[23] *Ibid.*

ings. One of the most frequent types of emotional disturbance noted during the postdisaster period consisted in sustained feelings of apprehensiveness accompanied by exaggerated efforts to ward off new exposures to danger.

2. During the weeks following the atomic disasters, the distressing symptoms and sudden deaths from radiation sickness, as well as the presence of people suffering from intractable burns and other sustained, visible injuries, produced strong emotional reactions among some of the survivors and may have augmented or reinforced the emotional disturbances evoked by the original disaster experience.

3. Anxiety-laden rumors circulated among the survivors during the postdisaster period. In both target cities, there were rumors which exaggerated the lingering dangers of contamination.

4. Although apprehensiveness about another attack and fears of contamination may have been fairly frequent, such fears evidently were not so intense as to prevent resettlement in the target cities. From the fact that very large numbers of survivors promptly returned to the destroyed areas, it appears that avoidance of the disaster locale did *not* occur on a mass scale.

5. Among a small percentage of the survivors, there were sustained reactions of depression during the postdisaster period. But the available evidence does not support the claim that the A-bomb produced an unusually high incidence of severe guilt feelings or of apathy among those who survived at Hiroshima and Nagasaki.

6. Although no adequate psychiatric observations are available, some highly tentative conclusions emerge from indirect sources of information which tend to bear out the findings from other types of wartime disasters. Psychoses, traumatic neuroses, and other severe psychiatric disorders appear to have been a rare occurrence following the A-bomb attacks. A small percentage of survivors probably developed some minor neurotic symptoms that were evoked or precipitated by disaster experiences, such as, excessive fatigue, recurrent bodily complaints, and persistent phobias. Although most cases of reproductive disorders following the atomic bombings are probably attributable to the physiological effects of gamma radiation, there is some possibility that the high incidence of menstrual difficulties

and miscarriages among female survivors may have been due, in part, to emotional stress engendered by atomic-disaster experiences. In general, the more transient symptoms of acute emotional shock seem to have been the predominant psychiatric effect of the atomic disasters.

7. The morale of the people in and around the target cities did not fall below that of the rest of Japan. Apparently the A-bombing at Hiroshima and at Nagasaki produced no greater drop in morale than would be expected from a single raid of the type carried out during the massed B-29 campaign against other Japanese cities.

8. Relatively little sustained hostility against the United States was observed among survivors of the A-bomb attacks.

9. Some of the residents of Hiroshima and Nagasaki subsequently blamed their own war leaders for the bombing of Japan, but this reaction did not occur to a greater extent than in other Japanese cities. In Nagasaki, there appears to have been some resentment toward the Japanese government for withholding information about the Hiroshima disaster and for failing to prepare the population for the A-bomb attack.

10. The inverse relationship between personal involvement and postdisaster morale, observed following other types of air attack, was also found to hold for the A-bomb attacks.

11. Outside the target areas, the A-bombs had very little effect on the morale of the Japanese population. The absence of publicity about the bomb, the rapid termination of the war, and other special factors probably prevented the demoralizing potentialities of the atomic weapon from materializing in the rest of Japan.

PART II
EFFECTS OF AIR WAR

CHAPTER 4
SCOPE OF THE INQUIRY

The core of existing knowledge concerning disaster reactions resides in the recorded experience of World War II. In contrast to the sparse reports on human reactions to floods, conflagrations, hurricanes, industrial explosions, and other peacetime catastrophes, the literature on psychological effects of high-explosive and incendiary raids is voluminous. From their recent wartime observations, many social scientists, psychologists, psychiatrists, and psychoanalysts have given detailed accounts of the way civilians felt and behaved when their community was subjected to attack from the air. Shortly after the end of the war, a group of American social psychologists in the Morale Division of the United States Strategic Bombing Survey conducted large-scale surveys of civilian attitudes among cross sections of the bombed populations of Germany and Japan. In addition, the extensive files of official intelligence reports dealing with civilian reactions to the air war were examined and analyzed. Other USSBS divisions also collected relevant behavioral data on psychiatric casualties, absenteeism, crime, subversion, etc.

No attempt has been made, as yet, to piece together all the disparate source materials for the purpose of discerning recurrent patterns of disaster behavior. As an initial step toward accomplishing this task, the following four chapters will present a systematic survey of available observations on psychological effects of bombing.

The primary aim is to arrive at a set of empirical generalizations which are warranted by the evidence at hand. The scope of the inquiry is limited, however, to one general type of problem, that of specifying the relationship between each major type of reaction and the environmental conditions characteristic of bombing disasters. In other words, attention will be directed mainly to the effects of *situational factors* and the role that such factors play in determining emotional responses, attitudes, and behavior.

Predispositional factors, such as socio-economic status, age, sex, personality traits, will not be discussed in detail. Actually there is relatively little evidence that can be drawn upon for predicting how different types of persons differentially react to wartime disasters. If one were to work on this problem, it would be necessary to rely on inferences from studies of other types of danger situations, particularly military combat. The present inquiry, however, will make no attempt to specify the influence of predispositional factors, except in limited contexts where they are directly pertinent to problems concerning the effects of situational factors. Most of the generalizations to be presented simply make the assumption that when predispositional factors are held relatively constant, certain changes in the environment produced by air attacks will regularly evoke certain reaction tendencies. Some of the descriptive conclusions, however, such as those dealing with the relative incidence of psychopathological symptoms, are probably applicable only to populations which have approximately the same distribution of personality traits as obtains among the samples from which the evidence is derived.

In order to extract sound generalizations, it is essential to give considerable weight to replications of specific findings. Only if a number of independent British investigators report the same general observation can one feel any degree of certainty about drawing a conclusion on the behavior of British civilians. The same stricture applies to reports on any other civilian population. It is generally necessary to be highly skeptical about any single observer's statements for the simple reason that the vast majority of reports present observations of unknown reliability. Often the reports contain only impressionistic, unsystematic accounts of civilian reactions without describing the procedures used to obtain the evidence, the number of cases studied, or the composition of the sample on which the observations were based.

Replication among different national populations is another important requirement for sound empirical generalizations. The available evidence on civilian reactions comes almost exclusively from only three countries: Britain, Germany, and Japan. Is it safe to assume that the conclusions derived from such evidence are applicable to the populations of the United States, Soviet Russia, and other countries?

If a conclusion is based solely on observations of the British, it would be rather risky to make use of that conclusion in predicting the behavior of any other national group. One could not exclude the strong possibility that the conclusion is merely a statement of characteristically British behavior, i.e., an indication of the distribution of certain predispositions (or "national character" traits) among the British population. On the other hand, if the same conclusion is supported by evidence not only from Britain but from Germany and Japan as well, it becomes much more probable that the conclusion is applicable for predicting the behavior of any other roughly comparable national population.

Undoubtedly, there are some common reaction tendencies elicited by exposure to severe danger conditions which are characteristic of the entire species of Homo sapiens and some that are limited only to that large sector of mankind who share the general culture patterns of western civilization. Still other mass reactions may be restricted to small local populations. From the type of evidence currently available, it is usually impossible to ascertain how far one may generalize. But cross-national replication, particularly when populations as diverse in their political and social behavior as the British, the Germans, and the Japanese are included, provides at least a rough basis for assuming that a given conclusion is probably applicable to other national groups. Consequently, the empirical generalizations on which attention is primarily focussed are those for which supporting evidence is derived from more than one country.

No use will be made of those findings from different countries which are divergent. When there is lack of agreement among observations made in different countries, the findings are highly ambiguous, even if one can assume that all the observations are accurate. The fact that the British behaved in one way and the Germans in another, when confronted with the same type of bombing, offers little useful information because it is generally impossible to estimate whether this is due to differences (1) in the distribution of relevant predispositional factors among the two populations; (2) in unique features of the air attacks to which the two populations were subjected; or (3) in specific deprivations such as food shortages or other special conditions which might affect responses to wartime stress. For this reason, conclusions from comparable observations made in different countries will be drawn only when the observations are in agreement.

From the above discussion, it is obvious that definitive conclusions cannot be expected from a survey of the existing data on reactions to bombing. Certain of the generalizations which emerge appear to be fairly well supported by the evidence already at hand, but, in view of the nature of the evidence, even the best of them should be regarded as tentative.

In addition to the empirical generalizations, numerous hypotheses dealing with underlying psychological processes are presented as preliminary theoretical explanations of the general findings. Most of the explanatory hypotheses, particularly those on adjustment mechanisms in Chapter 8, are supported only by suggestive but highly inconclusive evidence. Such hypotheses are intended primarily to serve as guides for further research on personal adjustment to danger situations.

In general, an attempt has been made to summarize the cogent evidence in such a way that the reader may make his own evaluation of the degree to which each of the major conclusions is supported by empirical observations. The observations of reactions at Hiroshima and Nagasaki described in the preceding chapters will not be repeated, however, although they often lend additional support to the conclusions derived from the studies of "conventional" bombing.

It will become apparent that the latter studies tend to bolster the presumption that the dominant psychological effects resulting from the A-bomb disasters generally did not differ in any unique way from those produced by other types of bombing disasters. Accordingly, it seems probable that the material to be presented in the next four chapters will be useful for predicting the psychological consequences of atomic warfare.

CHAPTER 5

PSYCHIATRIC DISORDERS

Civilians who are exposed to air attacks are likely to undergo a wide variety of intense emotional stresses. During an air raid every person in the community is under almost constant threat of sudden danger, not only to himself, but also to those persons and objects to whom he is most deeply attached. Defensive and control measures, as well as personal losses occurring during periods of air warfare, frequently entail severe hardships and require basic alterations in habitual patterns of everyday life.

Traumatic neuroses and other types of psychiatric disorders represent the most extreme form of emotional and mental disturbance that occurs in response to intensely fearful and deprivational circumstances. Such reactions, if widespread, present an acute social problem to the local community and to the nation at large. So long as incapacitating symptoms persist, the persons affected are unable to participate effectively in productive occupations and in civilian defense activities. Furthermore, their maladjusted behavior often tends to demoralize others who are in contact with them. Consequently, an examination of the frequency and character of civilian psychiatric casualties during World War II may be expected to provide some over-all indication of the emotional impact of wartime disasters.

CHRONIC PSYCHOPATHOLOGICAL DISORDERS

One of the most widely reported findings on civilian reactions to air attacks is the low frequency with which obvious psychiatric casualties occurred. This finding, however, applies only to the major chronic forms of psychopathology: psychoses, traumatic neuroses, prolonged depressive states, and other *persistent* disorders. As will be seen in the following section, there are some indications that transient, acute behavioral disturbances were a fairly frequent consequence of disaster experiences. But the available reports from Britain, Germany, and other countries are highly consistent in indicating that the bombing disasters to which civilians were exposed in World War II did not produce a marked increase in chronic mental disorder.

The scanty empirical material available prior to the war already pointed in this direction. In their review of the literature on war neuroses, published early in 1940, Wittkower and Spillane[1] summarized the psychiatric observations made during World War I:

> . . . Most German writers stress the infrequency of psychological disorders in severely bombarded French villages, but no confirmatory French observations can be traced. According to Redlich (1915), in refugees from invaded areas the resistance and capacity for adaptation were remarkable.

> . . . An inquiry made at various London hospitals about the behavior of patients during air raids showed the absence of any marked reaction. Similarly, according to Hoche in Germany and, more recently, Mira (1939) in Spain, the civilian population stood up surprisingly well to the terrifying experiences of repeated air attacks. . . .[2]

Beginning with the earliest reports from England during World War II, the relatively low frequency of psychiatric air-raid casualties has been reiterated. Gillespie[3] asserts that the psychiatric out-patient department of a major hospital (located in the heart of a heavily bombed area in London) recorded very few cases of neuroses attributable to air-raid experiences. Glover[4] refers to the "almost monotonous regularity" of reports which state that the incidence of bomb neuroses was "astonishingly small." He adds, as supporting evidence,

---

[1] E. Wittkower and J. P. Spillane, "A Survey of the Literature of Neuroses in War," Chap. 1 in E. Miller (ed.), *The Neuroses in War,* The Macmillan Company, New York, 1940.

[2] *Ibid.*

[3] R. D. Gillespie, *Psychological Effects of War on Citizen and Soldier,* W. W. Norton & Company, New York, 1942.

[4] E. Glover, "Notes on the Psychological Effects of War Conditions on the Civilian Population," Part III, "The Blitz," *International J. Psychoanal.,* Vol. 23, 1942, pp. 17–37.

that the number of "bomb neuroses" treated in the London Emergency Region averaged little more than two per week during the first three months of the air blitz and that only one "genuine case" was reported from the practices of fifteen psychoanalysts at a meeting held several months after the blitz had begun.

On the basis of data obtained from a number of medical psychologists, Vernon[5] concludes that although air-raid strain was a factor leading to mental breakdown in numerous cases, many of the preparations made by hospitals and clinics for dealing with psychiatric casualties were not needed. He cites some typical statistical findings on the low frequency of such casualties: Only 1.4 per cent of the 1100 persons treated by a medical service (in London public shelters) showed obvious signs of psychological disorders; a general hospital in a heavily raided area of London reported that only 2 out of the 578 civilian casualties admitted to the hospital were primarily psychological cases; the staff of a London mental hospital estimated that only 2.5 per cent of the 200 admissions received over a six-month period were attributable, at least to some degree, to the heavy air raids which had occurred during that period.

Stokes[6] reports that admissions to London psychiatric observation wards were not significantly increased after a period of heavy bombing; total admissions to mental hospitals in 1940 were slightly *less* than in 1938, and there was a further decrease in 1941. Gross trends of this sort, as Stokes indicates, are subject to various sources of error, but they nevertheless point to the unlikelihood of any significant rise in the incidence of severe mental illness.

Several years after the end of the European war, Titmuss[7] examined all the available wartime evidence on psychiatric admission rates in Britain. He concluded that there is no evidence to suggest any marked increase in neurotic illness or mental disorder during the war: the air raids of 1940–41 did not lead to a rise in the

---

[5] P. E. Vernon, "Psychological Effects of Air Raids," *J. Abnorm. Soc. Psychol.*, Vol. 36, 1941, pp. 457–476.

[6] A. B. Stokes, "War Strains and Mental Health," *J. Nervous Ment. Disease*, Vol. 101, 1945, 215–219.

[7] R. M. Titmuss, *Problems of Social Policy*, His Majesty's Stationery Office, London, 1950.

number of psychiatric patients admitted to hospitals and clinics, nor was there any increase in the incidence of suicides or alcoholic intoxication. For most indicators of mental disorder, the statistics show a decrease rather than an increase. For example, cases of attempted suicide among women (recorded by the police in England and Wales) decreased by 32 per cent during the year of the air blitz (1941), as compared with the prewar rate. Figures on juvenile delinquency, on the other hand, registered a rise during the war years, but, according to Titmuss, these data are not a suitable index of either juvenile or adult neurosis.

The findings cited by the various British writers are based on material obtained from a large number of psychiatrists and medical psychologists, including observers with widely different clinical and theoretical approaches to psychiatric problems. Their methods of investigation ranged from brief psychiatric examinations for purposes of large-scale statistical tabulation to intensive case studies of small groups of patients. Despite the diversity of diagnostic criteria used, there is high agreement that the type of air attacks to which London and other English cities were subjected during World War II did not produce a sizeable increase in major psychiatric disorders.

The available information on psychiatric air-raid casualties among German civilians is consistent with the British findings. At the end of the war in Europe, the Medical Team of the USSBS sent a questionnaire to German psychiatrists and directors of psychiatric institutions. The "universal reply" to the questionnaire was that "neither organic neurologic diseases nor psychiatric disorders can be attributed to nor are they conditioned by, the air attacks."[8]

A parallel survey of relevant specialists on psychosomatic disorders in Germany revealed some definite wartime trends (which will be discussed later in this chapter), but what is relevant here is the general conclusion: ". . . in view of the tremendous exogenous stimuli which offered a fertile ground for the development of psychosomatic complaints, the relative infrequency of the development

---

[8] USSBS Report, *The Effect of Bombing on Health and Medical Care in Germany*, U.S. Government Printing Office, Washington, D.C., 1945.

of these disorders among the population is striking."[9] There was no observable increase in addiction to alcohol, to sedations, to pick-up drugs, or to other narcotics, although there was an increased tendency for people to smoke excessively. As in England, a general rise in juvenile delinquency was observed, but, according to German police records, delinquency and looting never reached "alarming proportions" after destructive air raids. Following periods of bombing, there was a slight rise in the German suicide rate, but the increase was not statistically significant.

One of the few bits of information available on psychological disorders in Japan is some similar statistical material on suicide.[10] The rate increased substantially during the last year of the war when heavy air assaults against the Japanese home islands were being carried out. The average number of suicides for seven cities in 1943–44 was 11.7 per 100,000, while in 1944–45 it rose to 18.7 per 100,000. From the findings that are presented, however, one cannot rule out the possibility that the change in suicide rates might be an artefact, merely reflecting changes in the composition of the urban population. For example, the majority of those who evacuated were young mothers with their children, a group less likely to be suicide-prone than the age groups who stayed in the cities. Even if it is assumed that there was a genuine trend, the findings still leave open the question of antecedent causes. A month-by-month analysis of the data from six cities showed that there was no consistent relationship between suicide rates and the occurrence of air attacks. In four of the six cities, the most marked rise occurred in August, 1945, and the rate remained high in September, 1945. This suggests that the increase may have been associated with the Japanese surrender. Hence, it cannot be concluded that the air raids, as against other factors, were responsible for the rise in suicide rates.

The only material on Japanese psychiatric casualties in the USSBS medical report consists of some highly ambiguous data on hospital

---

[9] *Ibid.*

[10] USSBS Report, *The Effects of Bombing on Health and Medical Services in Japan,* U.S. Government Printing Office, Washington, D.C., 1947.

admissions for diseases of the nervous system. The statistics from several cities suggest that during periods of bombing there may have been a slight increase in the number of cases with organic and functional psychosis, but this trend is not consistently borne out. Detailed results are presented from only two psychiatric hospitals. One of the hospitals, in Yokohama, showed that there was a *marked increase* in the number of admissions for schizophrenia, general paresis, and other psychoses during May, 1945, the month during which the city received its most severe bombing. The other psychiatric hospital, in Kobe, showed that during the months of severe bombing attacks there was a *decline* in the number of admissions for psychosis and for all other neuropsychiatric disorders. Although some of the Japanese hospital statistics lend themselves to interpretations about possible causal factors, the evidence is not adequate for ascertaining whether bombing produced any significant changes in the incidence of neuropsychiatric cases. In general, the statistical data from Japan do not contradict the observations reported from England and Germany.

The absence of psychiatric casualties following the one air raid on American territory—the Pearl Harbor attack on December 7, 1941—has been described by Weatherby.[11] On the day of the attack, no patients with war neurosis were brought to the hospital that normally served a majority of American troops stationed at Oahu. During the two weeks following the attack, the number of psychiatric admissions was no greater than during the two weeks preceding the attack.

In evaluating the evidence on psychiatric effects of air warfare, it is necessary to recognize that the information is far from complete and that many of the observations are unsystematic and impressionistic in character. Moreover, the statistical studies of psychiatric casualty rates have been criticized on various grounds as underestimating the actual number of psychiatric casualties to be expected among a civilian population exposed to heavy air raids. Vernon[12]

---

[11] F. E. Weatherby, "War Neuroses after Air Attack on Oahu, Territory of Hawaii, Dec. 7, 1941," *War Med.*, Vol. 4, 1943, pp. 270–271.

[12] *Loc. cit.*

calls attention to the fact that approximately half of the people in the heavily blitzed areas of London had been evacuated and that those who remained consisted of persons who were least susceptible to psychological disturbances. Glover[13] asserts that a large number of cases with psychopathological reactions evoked by air raids were treated as cases of organic illness or were never treated; he estimates that if all such cases were included, the official psychiatric statistics for London would be at least double.

Nevertheless, despite the shortcomings of the available evidence, the numerous reports for many different samples of bombed communities show such a high degree of consistency that it appears to be safe to accept the following general conclusion: air attacks of the type employed against civilian communities during World War II produced only a very slight increase in chronic psychopathological disorders.

Even those writers who are most critical of the available evidence on psychiatric casualty rates tend to accept this conclusion—although some of them call attention to the possibility that the pathogenic consequences of wartime-disaster experiences might not show up in the form of overt symptoms until many years later. Most clinical investigators regard the low incidence of chronic emotional disorders resulting from air attacks as a reflection of the primary importance of basic personality structure in determining adjustment to severe environmental stress. Vernon's retrospective statements emphasizing the role of underlying personality factors are typical of the views expressed by many psychiatrists and psychologists: "Perhaps we ought to have anticipated the small incidence of harmful psychological effects, since it is generally agreed that neuroses and psychoses are due far more to unconscious conflicts within the personality than to conscious strains."[14]

Commenting on the general features of traumatic neurosis, Hadfield[15] points out that the precipitating factors and the physiological

---

[13] Loc. cit.

[14] Vernon, loc. cit.

[15] J. A. Hadfield, "Treatment by Suggestion and Hypnoanalysis," Chap. 7 in E. Miller (ed.), op. cit.

shock or fatigue which often accompanies the traumatic experience appear to be of far greater significance than the predisposing factors. But he goes on to say that whenever there is an opportunity to analyze such cases more deeply, it is discovered that an important determinant is *psychoneurotic predisposition,* whether due to native constitution (temperament) or to the nuclear conflicts and precarious defensive processes acquired from earlier experiences.

In psychiatric discussions, it is increasingly recognized that the concept of "psychoneurotic predisposition" has often been employed in an extremely loose and vague fashion, sometimes as a pseudo-explanation or as a mere label for unknown causes of mental disorders. Furthermore, much of the evidence on psychoneurotic predisposition has been obtained retrospectively, from interviews of individuals who had already displayed their vulnerability to stress. Such findings are especially likely to suffer from various sources of distortion which tend to exaggerate the incidence of predispositional characteristics. Nevertheless, the findings from studies of many different types of danger situations provide a tentative empirical basis for assuming that certain personality types are more vulnerable to environmental stress than others.

There are a number of clinical reports which indicate that chronic traumatic reactions to air raids tend to occur predominantly among persons with pre-existing psychoneurotic tendencies. According to Glover,[16] the most severe reactions were seen in persons who had previously displayed emotional instability, lack of working capacity, or other obvious manifestations of neurosis. Fraser, Leslie, and Phelps[17] observed the same relationship in a follow-up study of 94 uninjured air-raid victims who had been brought to First-Aid Posts in an English city. They found that persistent emotional symptoms were less likely to occur among formerly stable personalities than among those with personality defects. Case histories of patients at the Royal Edinburgh Hospital are described by Stengel[18]

---

[16] *Loc. cit.*

[17] R. Fraser, I. M. Leslie, and D. Phelps, "Psychiatric Effects of Severe Personal Experiences during Bombing," *Proc. Roy. Soc. Med.,* Vol. 36, 1943, pp. 119–123.

[18] E. Stengel, "Air-raid Phobia," *Brit. J. Med. Psychology,* Vol. 20. 1944, pp. 135–143.

to illustrate the generalization that there is usually a history of previous neurotic disorders in those persons who develop sustained symptoms of traumatic neurosis. Many more reports of this kind could be cited, all of which point to pre-established psychoneurotic tendencies as a predisposing factor.

The conclusions from such studies are often formulated in such a way as to lend themselves to overgeneralization and misinterpretation. Although some of the findings may be suggestive of broad and elaborate theoretical implications, the empirical generalization supported by the findings is a relatively simple one: severe traumatic reactions of long duration tend to occur disproportionately from among the ranks of persons who have previously displayed neurotic symptoms. This generalization applies only to *chronic* disorders of traumatic onset; it does not necessarily apply to acute "emotional-shock" reactions of the sort to be discussed later in this chapter.

As yet, we know very little about the specific role of psychoneurotic tendencies in adjustment to wartime conditions. Apparently, *not* all types of psychoneurotics are affected adversely by being exposed to the dangers of air warfare. From a review of available evidence on British patients who had displayed neurotic trends before the heavy raids began, Vernon[19] reports the following conclusions about their reactions to bombing: roughly one-half of the psychoneurotic cases showed no change in symptoms; one-quarter became worse; one-quarter spontaneously improved.

Clinical reports by therapists, who worked intensively with psychoneurotic patients during the air blitz, contain a few suggestive leads as to specific predispositional factors that determine whether exposure to the stresses of air attack will be beneficial, harmful, or without effect:

1. Improvement was observed mainly in cases for whom the threat of real danger served to relieve certain secondary sources of anxiety. Chronically timid and shy psychoneurotics may have benefited from the opportunity for courageous self-sacrifice and social

---

[19] *Loc. cit.*

participation.[20]   Some reassurance was gained by psychoneurotics
who previously had been highly concerned about their deviations
from normality: the discovery that their own fear and tension was
no longer markedly different from that displayed by apparently
normal people may have increased their self-esteem.[21,22] Another
important factor may have been the opportunity for gratifying unconscious self-punitive needs in a socially acceptable way. Some
patients with strong masochistic tendencies (that formerly could
be satisfied only by neurotic symptoms) apparently were able to
improve because of the objective opportunities for undergoing in-
conveniences and for risking their lives.[23]

2. Heightened anxiety and exacerbation of neurotic symptoms
were noted in patients who had previously overreacted to threats
of violence or danger. Schmideberg[24] describes two specific types of
psychoneurotic patients who were adversely affected by air raids:
The first were those who had previously developed specific phobias
to loud noises, darkness, fire, or other signs of external danger.
During bombing attacks, these patients were unable to avoid perceiving the phobic stimuli and experienced a revival of childhood
fears. The second type of patient reacted with excessive fear to
the threat of danger because of unconscious masochistic tendencies,
evoked by the temptation to gratify self-punitive impulses. These
two types of phobic patients, according to Schmideberg, experienced
a genuine increase in anxiety as a result of bombing, in contrast to
those psychoneurotics who superficially appeared to be excessively
afraid of air raids but for whom such fears were merely a new
rationalization (or displaced content) for pre-existing anxieties.
According to Glover,[25] the threat of air raids evoked more severe
symptoms mainly in cases suffering from chronic anxiety states; but

[20] R. D. Gillespie, "Résumé of His Addresses before the New York Academy of
Medicine," So. J. Med., Vol. 41, 1941, pp. 2346–2349.

[21] F. Brown, "Civilian Psychiatric Air-raid Casualties," Lancet, Vol. 1, 1941,
pp. 686–691.

[22] Glover, loc. cit.

[23] M. Schmideberg, "Some Observations on Individual Reactions to Air Raids,"
International J. Psychoanal., Vol. 23, 1942, pp. 146–176.

[24] Ibid.

[25] Loc. cit.

patients with pronounced psychosexual inhibitions, perversions, or excessive narcissism also showed an increase in psychopathologic manifestations. Although patients with manifest psychotic symptoms generally displayed no change during periods of air attack, those with paranoid delusions and those with latent psychotic tendencies were likely to be adversely affected.

3. The large proportion of psychoneurotics who showed no essential change may have been incapable of reacting to environmental events because of exclusive preoccupation with the self. Brown[26] describes cases with obsessional fears of murder, neurotic inhibitions, and conversion symptoms who were relatively free from air-raid anxieties: "External happenings such as bombs were trivial compared with the internal conflicts." During periods of air-raid danger, obsessive-compulsives were especially likely to be free from manifest anxiety,[27,28] as has been noted in clinical studies of other types of danger situations. In such cases, the well-practiced (neurotic) defenses against affect seem to be successful in warding off feelings of anxiety that would normally be aroused by a threat of external danger.

One of the obvious implications of these clinical reports is that we cannot regard the entire class of psychoneurotics as in any sense homogeneous with respect to their disposition to respond favorably or unfavorably to the environmental changes that occur when a community is exposed to the threat of disaster. It is to be noted, for example, that there seems to be one particular subtype of psychoneurotic who is able to overcome social inhibitions, enjoy increased self-esteem, and develop healthier interpersonal relationships. These patients are probably able to benefit from the new opportunities that arise for engaging in useful work and for participating with others in collective efforts to mitigate external danger. Although there are only occasional indications of this sort, the clinical observations bring into focus the need for more refined research on the

---

[26] *Loc. cit.*
[27] *Ibid.*
[28] Glover, *loc. cit.*

emotional impact of objective danger among persons with different types of maladjustment.

TRANSIENT EMOTIONAL DISTURBANCES

Persons who have been exposed to a traumatic event, e.g., bombardment, an automobile accident, a plane crash, an earthquake, or some other disaster, generally display varying degrees of emotional shock. When brought to a hospital after a harrowing danger experience, they may be in a state of delerious agitation or they may suffer from gross sensory, motor, and mental inhibitions. These acute states tend to subside spontaneously; over a period of days and weeks, there is a gradual return to normality. Characteristic initial symptoms are jitteriness, sensitivity to noise, excessive fatigue, trembling of the hands, and terrifying nightmares in which the traumatic situation is re-experienced. Although there is considerable variation in the specific symptoms which develop during the post-trauma period, most of the behavioral disturbances form a general pattern consisting of two main components: (1) blocking or inhibition of various ego functions and (2) spells of uncontrollable emotion, especially anxiety and rage.

Kardiner,[29] who has made a careful clinical study of several hundred cases of traumatic neurosis following World War I, claims that the acute reactions to a severe traumatic event are essentially the same in all persons, irrespective of the pre-existing personality structure, whether psychoneurotic or normal. The difference between a predisposed personality and a normal one lies solely in the *failure of recuperation.* In the predisposed, according to Kardiner, the anxiety reactions persist and become overlayed with defensive inhibitions, giving rise to typical chronic symptoms, such as persistent irritability and diminished capacity for work. It is this failure to recover from a traumatic event that constitutes a traumatic neurosis, "a type of adaptation in which no complete restitution takes

---

[29] A. Kardiner, *The Traumatic Neuroses of War,* Paul B. Hoeber, Inc., New York, 1941.

place but in which the individual continues with a reduction of resources or a contraction of the ego."[30]

The fact that air attacks did not produce a high incidence of traumatic neurosis by no means precludes the possibility that many nonpredisposed persons exposed to traumatic bombing experiences may have developed acute symptoms from which they were able to recover. From the theory of traumatic neurosis, as put forth by Kardiner and other clinical investigators, one would expect to find a sizeable incidence of acute reactions with transient symptoms that could be characterized as a "temporary traumatic neurosis."

In general, the available observations tend to support the hypothesis that predispositional factors primarily determine the duration of psychological incapacitation. Although there are no precise data on the incidence of acute symptoms among civilians who were exposed to heavy air attacks, numerous reports suggest that transient behavioral disturbances occur with a far higher frequency than chronic psychopathologic reactions. Glover[31] points out that the "mass neurosis myth" current in medical and administrative circles prior to World War II is being replaced by the opposite myth that *no* neurotic reactions are produced by air raids, which is equally fallacious. He maintains that only a very small proportion of the population in any raided area in England experienced severe traumatic conditions and that the majority of cases of emotional shock never reached the emergency hospitals. On the basis of observations made at several welfare centers, he speculates that there were at least five times as many cases of "minor psychopathological shock" as major ones and that the incidence of the latter is much greater than the official statistics indicate.

Most of the cases who did not come under psychological or medical observation were people with sporadic symptoms that sometimes affected working capacity for many weeks but that generally did not preclude a fairly normal, though restricted, routine of daily activity. Sensory and motor disturbances, emotional agitation, mental inhi-

---

[30] *Ibid.*
[31] *Loc. cit.*

bition, and irritability were characteristic symptoms. In a "typical" case described by Glover, the patient's work efficiency was below normal for several weeks, but she was able to help her family put their affairs in order. Her overt symptoms consisted of pronounced stammering, mild attacks of trembling, and frequent crying spells. Subjectively, she experienced feelings of unreality and sensations of bodily rigidity. She also complained of feeling excessively fatigued and of lacking self-control. She had difficulty in concentrating and her memory was impaired. These symptoms, which closely resemble those seen in chronic traumatic neurosis, spontaneously cleared up within a few weeks and, apart from her marked startle reactions to noise, she experienced no further discomfort.

In addition to unrecorded psychiatric casualties of this type, there were some cases who showed no obvious symptoms of acute shock, but who nevertheless displayed signs of pronounced emotional disorder in the form of disturbed interpersonal relations or reduced social capacities. In these cases the heightened emotional tension could be inferred from behavioral manifestations such as increased passivity or excessive resentment and aggression.[32]

Acute Anxiety Symptoms

Dunsdon[33] claims that bombings frequently produced acute anxiety symptoms among British adults and that the sufferers often absented themselves from defense jobs on the grounds of over-fatigue, because they were ashamed to admit their symptoms. On the basis of independent sources of information, Vernon also bears out Glover's assertion that many cases of minor emotional shock occurred but were never recorded:

> Psychologists and laymen such as wardens [in Britain] often report cases of hysterical screaming and weeping, or trembling and incoherent speech among bombed persons, but few of these ever reach the First Aid Posts.[34]

---

[32] Ibid.

[33] M. I. Dunsdon, "A Psychologist's Contribution to Air-raid Problems," Mental Health, Vol. 2, London, 1941, pp. 37–41.

[34] Vernon, loc. cit.

A large number of the acute cases, as described by Vernon, recovered spontaneously or were responsive to the simplest forms of
psychiatric first aid: rest, sympathy, and suggestion. Temporary
reactions of acute terror and confusion, similar to "shell shock,"
were fairly frequent. Many such cases were brought to First-Aid
Posts in a dazed, stuporous condition or displayed uncontrolled
emotional outbursts. But despite the severity of their symptoms,
most of these patients seemed to recover in a day or two. According
to Stokes,[35] 134 patients with fright or anxiety symptoms were seen
in a First-Aid Post during one London bombing, but all the patients were able to return home within twenty-four hours and only
six required further psychiatric treatment.

Brown[36] also reports that there were large numbers of persons
observed during air raids in Britain who recovered rapidly from
emotional shock. The acute symptoms included dilated pupils,
tremor, severe tachycardia, anxiety attacks, conversion symptoms,
or semistuporous states. These were of short duration, especially
when treated psychiatrically by supportive procedures, such as encouraging the patient to verbalize his traumatic experiences.

Several allusions to transient anxiety symptoms, presumably of
the same type, occur in psychiatric reports from Germany. In the
USSBS medical report, a general statement by Professor Mueller
of Leipzig is quoted: "Fleeting reaction symptoms in the sense of
neurohysteria were not uncommon after severe damaging attacks."[37]
Reports from numerous German psychiatrists indicate that hysterical
manifestations in front of bunkers or air-raid shelters were rare in
general, but that they did occur during heavy air raids.[38] From the
brief descriptions given, it is not clear whether the anxiety symptoms
were severe, but "normal," fear reactions during the period of
actual danger or acute psychopathological reactions which persisted
for a time after the objective danger had subsided. The latter alternative would seem to be more likely than the former, since the

[35] Loc. cit.
[36] Loc. cit.
[37] USSBS, The Effect of Bombing on Health and Medical Care in Germany.
[38] Ibid.

symptoms alluded to sound very much like certain emotional-shock reactions described by British observers. Similar reactions were seen during World War I: "In severely bombarded towns the civilian population suffered from anxiety states lasting for weeks. . . ."[39] The symptoms included disorders of sleep, auditory hypersensitivity, excessive startle reactions, and various psychosomatic complaints.

In general, then, psychiatric reports on civilian reactions to bombing indicate that heavy air attacks produce a sizeable incidence of "emotional-shock" cases with acute anxiety symptoms. Most of these cases appear to be capable of fully recovering, either spontaneously or in response to simple forms of psychiatric treatment, within a period of a few days up to several weeks.

Although many accounts of acute anxiety symptoms fail to provide information about the degree to which the behavioral disturbances are incapacitating, almost all of them specify that the conditions under which severe anxiety reactions were observed were those of an *unusually heavy* air attack. The physical magnitude of the air attack to which a community is exposed undoubtedly is a major factor in determining the incidence of acute anxiety symptoms. (This conclusion is highly plausible not only on the basis of psychiatric reports, but also because it is supported by the large-scale survey findings to be described in the next chapter.)

Mild Depression and Apathy

Another type of emotional disorder which apparently escapes being recorded in the statistics on psychiatric casualties is a comparatively mild form of depression, characterized by apathy, lethargy, retreat from social activities, and pessimistic attitudes. Harrisson first called attention to this type of air-raid reaction among the British. In the course of investigating attitudes by use of the various techniques employed in preparing "mass-observation" reports, a number of persons were observed in widely scattered towns who "caved in" after a heavy bombardment. These cases are described in the following terms: "They have not shown marked trembling or hysteria, but

---

[39] Wittkower and Spillane, *op. cit.*

an extreme desire to retreat into sleep and into being looked after, as if chronically ill."[40] Harrisson speculates that there may have been quite a large number of such cases, and that they were overlooked by medical observers because the symptoms are not as dramatic as had been expected. Gillespie discusses Harrisson's observations and suggests that the reaction is ". . . akin to the apathy resulting from various forms of frustration which I have alluded to in describing the psychoneurotic reactions of peacetime."[41]

Vernon claims that a number of investigations have shown that heavy raids produce a considerable amount of depression and temporary lowering of confidence: "There is widespread lethargy and lack of energy, even after lost sleep has been made up, and pessimistic feelings about the future."[42] Transient conditions of exhaustion with anxiety symptoms and depression of various degrees were extremely common, according to Denny-Brown.[43] In describing acute "shock" reactions, Glover mentions that some cases, instead of displaying agitated anxiety symptoms, exhibited a marked degree of mental inhibition, depression, or irritation. Some persons were seen in the East End districts of London who, upon viewing the destruction to their homes, became speechless for a time; they were unable to eat and wandered about in an aimless and apathetic way, returning every now and then to the ruins of their home or street. Such cases are described as recovering rapidly if given effective care and attention.[44] One of the features of this acute apathetic phase is marked docility and ready response to suggestion. In this connection, it should be noted that observers in Japan[45] as well as in England[46] have commented on the high incidence of excessive docility among air-raid victims, which suggests that the acute apathy described by Glover may occur fairly often.

---

[40] T. Harrisson, "Obscure Nervous Effects of Air Raids," *Brit. Med. J.*, Vol. 1, 1941, pp. 573–574 and 832.

[41] Gillespie, *Psychological Effects of War on Citizen and Soldier.*

[42] Vernon, *loc. cit.*

[43] D. Denny-Brown, "Effects of Modern Warfare on Civil Population," *J. Lab. Clin. Med.*, Vol. 28, 1943, pp. 641–645.

[44] Glover, *loc. cit.*

[45] USSBS, *The Effects of Bombing on Health and Medical Services in Japan.*

[46] Schmideberg, *loc. cit.*

Apathy reactions following air raids have been frequently observed among the German population. The USSBS medical report on Germany concludes that although marked depressive states showed only a negligible increase ". . . a greater number of people suffering from nervous exhaustion, concomitant apathy, emotional lability, and depressed attitudes . . . must be considered 'air raid victims'." Certain reactions were seen which are probably similar to the apathy-retreat symptoms described by British writers: "Over prolonged periods of aerial bombardment some patients suffered from extreme fatigability and 'chronic nervous exhaustion.' . . ."[47] Meerloo[48] also refers to frequent apathy and stupor reactions produced by the bombing raids in Germany.

There is no definite information on the incidence of depressive reactions, but from the comments of various psychiatric observers it appears to be probable that apathy, pessimistic attitudes about one's future, and other depressive manifestations tend to increase markedly following severe air attacks.

From the various descriptions of emotional-shock reactions to air raids, and from clinical investigations of psychiatric casualties in combat, it seems that depressive reactions and acute anxiety reactions are alternative forms of emotional response to intense environmental stress, the latter predominating in some cases, the former in others. Hypotheses on the psychological mechanisms underlying the development of one or the other type of reaction will be discussed in Chapter 8.

PSYCHOSOMATIC DISORDERS

Psychosomatic symptoms have frequently been observed during World War II, particularly during periods of heavy air attacks. One of the most detailed studies is described in the USSBS medical report on Germany.[49] Information was obtained from interviews of special-

---

[47] USSBS, *The Effect of Bombing on Health and Medical Care in Germany.*

[48] A. M. Meerloo, *Aftermath of Peace,* International Universities Press, New York, 1946.

[49] USSBS, *The Effect of Bombing on Health and Medical Care in Germany.*

ists in the various fields of psychosomatic medicine who had made clinical observations in hospitals, universities, and private practice. The major positive finding was that following air attacks there was a marked increase in the incidence of *peptic ulcer,* particularly among young adults. Most of the German specialists attributed this increase primarily to the anxiety and tension produced by air attacks. Clinical observations on the onset of the disorder indicated that the ulcers were formed very rapidly; in many cases the symptoms occurred suddenly during an air raid in persons who had not previously experienced gastrointestinal disorders. Few cases of ulcer formation were seen by physicians in areas not subjected to air raids.

Independent, confirmatory data are cited from the records of German government insurance groups which reveal a definite increase in the incidence of peptic ulcer during the war years, especially during periods of air attack. Little or no increase was found in those areas which were not subjected to bombing. From the various types of evidence presented, it is concluded that "the conditions brought about by war and especially by bombing contributed a psychological factor to this increased incidence."[50]

This conclusion is fairly well supported by evidence from other countries. Reports from England,[51] from France,[52] and from Russia[53] indicate that there is a general wartime rise in the incidence of peptic ulcer. That there is a sizeable increase specifically during periods of heavy air attack is borne out by reports on civilians in London,[54] Bristol,[55] and Hawaii.[56] Practically all observers are in agreement

---

[50] *Ibid.*

[51] D. N. Stewart and D. M. Winser, "Incidence of Perforated Peptic Ulcer," *Lancet,* Vol. 2, 1942, pp. 259–260; J. M. Morris and R. M. Titmuss, "Epidemiology of Peptic Ulcer," *Lancet,* Vol. 2, 1944, pp. 841–845.

[52] Lambling, *et al.,* "Le Génie évolutif de la Maladie ulcereuse avant et pendant la Guerre," *Paris Médicale,* Vol. 1, 1946, pp. 146–152.

[53] V. M. Kogan-Yasny, "Some Aspects of Peptic Ulcer during Wartime," *Am. Rev. of Soviet Med.,* Vol. 2, 1945, pp. 233–237.

[54] Stewart and Winser, *loc. cit.;* Morris and Titmuss, *loc. cit.*

[55] C. J. F. Phillips-Wolley, "An Analysis of Gastric and Duodenal Ulcers in Vancouver General Hospital," *Can. Med. Assoc. J.,* Vol. 49, 1943, pp. 113–117.

[56] F. J. Pinkerton, "Wartime Experiences in Hawaii after the Blitz on Pearl Harbor," *J. Am. Med. Assoc.,* Vol. 126, 1944, pp. 625–630.

that the increase in peptic ulcers is due, at least in part, to the heightened emotional tension produced by air attacks.

Another psychosomatic trend also attributed to bombing in the USSBS report on Germany is a definite increase in the incidence of *coronary symptoms.* Among the older-age group, coronary thrombosis occurred so frequently during air raids that German physicians called it "the shelter death of the aged."[57] Younger persons, too, suffered from various forms of coronary insufficiency. In many cases, severe anginal attacks presumably were due to severe emotional stress; usually no clinical evidence of organic coronary disease was found. In England and Wales, a general wartime increase in cerebral hemorrhage, coronary occlusion, and angina pectoris has been reported,[58] but no indication is given as to whether or not this increase was due to bombings.

Other somatic reactions found to increase among German civilians during periods of air attack were *exopthalmic goiter* (Grave's disease), *neurodermatitis* and related *skin diseases.*[59]

Minor disorders of *menstruation* (intermenstrual bleeding, amenorrhea, and painful menstruation) occurred extremely frequently among German women, particularly after bombing or evacuation, presenting a major problem to the gynecological clinics of Germany during the war.[60] According to numerous German medical authorities, menstrual disturbances were primarily "psychic" in origin, although certain nutritional factors may have contributed to their occurrence.

A high incidence of amenorrhea throughout Japan during 1944 and 1945 has also been reported.[61] Confirmatory evidence that the wartime increase in amenorrhea is attributable mainly to emotional upset produced by air raids and by other wartime stresses is provided

[57] USSBS, *The Effect of Bombing on Health and Medical Care in Germany.*

[58] P. Stocks, "Vital Statistics of England and Wales in 1941," *Brit. Med. J.,* Vol. 1, 1942, pp. 789–790.

[59] USSBS, *The Effect of Bombing on Health and Medical Care in Germany.*

[60] *Ibid.*

[61] USSBS Report, *The Effects of Atomic Bombs on Hiroshima and Nagasaki,* U.S. Government Printing Office, Washington, D.C., 1946; USSBS Report, *The Effects of Atomic Bombs on Health and Medical Services in Hiroshima and Nagasakai,* U.S. Government Printing Office, Washington, D.C., 1947.

by Whitacre and Barrera.[62] These investigators studied over 1000 women in an internment camp in Manila and found 125 cases who had developed prolonged amenorrhea after the outbreak of war. In many cases the menses stopped abruptly after the first bombing of Manila or soon after internment, before a food deficiency could have had any effect. On the basis of this evidence, the authors conclude that the widespread prevalence of amenorrhea noted in many countries during World War I was probably not due to food deficiency, as was thought at that time, but rather to severe psychic shock, worry, and fear.

Although the evidence cited in this section indicates that air raids contributed to the wartime increase in various types of psychosomatic disorder, the proportion of the bombed population displaying such reactions was probably not very large. USSBS investigators in Germany, for instance, were impressed by the relative infrequency of psychosomatic cases, as was mentioned earlier.

BEHAVIORAL DISTURBANCES AMONG CHILDREN

Only the immediate effects of exposure to air raids will be discussed in the present survey of behavioral disturbances among children. It should be noted, however, that the indirect effects of air attacks, particularly separation from parents during periods of evacuation, may prove to be by far the most pathogenic feature of wartime events.[63] As Titmuss[64] points out, the most prevalent and most marked symptom of psychological disturbance among British children during the war was not acute anxiety caused by exposure to air-raid dangers, but bed-wetting evoked by the evacuation of children without their families.

---

[62] F. C. Whitacre and B. Barrera, "War Amenorrhea," *J. Am. Med. Assoc.*, Vol. 124, 1944, pp. 399–403.

[63] F. Bodman, "Child Psychiatry in Wartime Britain," *J. Educational Psychol.*, Vol. 35, 1944, pp. 293–301; J. L. Despert, *Preliminary Report on Children's Reactions to the War, Including a Critical Survey of the Literature*, Cornell University Medical College, New York, 1942; A. Freud and D. Burlingham, *Young Children in Wartime*, George Allen & Unwin, Ltd., London, 1942; A. Freud and D. Burlingham, *Infants without Families*, International Universities Press, New York, 1944.

[64] *Problems of Social Policy.*

In general, the findings of psychiatric studies of children parallel those reported for adults. Practically all observers who have described children's reactions agree that chronic behavioral disturbances following air raids were extremely rare.[65] Nevertheless, transient symptoms of an acute nature, mainly in the form of excessive anxiety, often did occur during air attacks. Such reactions have been ascribed to the excitement and other evidences of emotional upset displayed by the child's parents or by other adults in the immediate vicinity.[66] Inability to resist the contagion of panic or excitement from the mother or other adults is often described as the main cause of children's emotional reactions to aid raids.

Freud and Burlingham[67] describe a number of cases in which "nervousness," bed-wetting, and other symptoms which persisted after air raids were attributable to the overanxious reactions of their mothers. These authors conclude that "The quiet manner in which the London population on the whole met the air raids is therefore responsible in one way for the extremely rare occurrence of 'shocked' children."

Some observations of children in the United States provide complementary findings. On the basis of individual psychiatric study and reports from nursery school teachers, Solomon[68] concludes that the most noteworthy feature in the reaction of children to the San Francisco blackouts and alerts was "the contagion of anxiety from their parents." This author claims that in every situation where the parent or adult in charge of a child displayed overt fear symptoms, the child reacted in a similar manner, usually to an exaggerated degree.

---

[65] Brown, *loc. cit.;* H. Crichton-Miller, "Somatic Factors Conditioning Air-raid Reactions," *Lancet,* Vol. 2, 1941, pp. 31–34; Despert, *op. cit.;* Freud and Burlingham, *Young Children in Wartime;* Gillespie, *Psychological Effects of War on Citizen and Soldier;* E. Mira, "Psychiatric Experiences in the Spanish War," *Brit. Med. J.,* Vol. 1, 1939, pp. 1217–1220; USSBS Report, *The Effects of Strategic Bombing on German Morale,* Vol. 1, U.S. Government Printing Office, Washington, D.C., 1947; Vernon, *loc. cit.;* Wittkower and Spillane, *op. cit.*

[66] Crichton-Miller, *loc. cit.;* Despert, *op. cit.;* Gillespie, "Résumé of His Address before the New York Academy of Medicine"; Wittkower and Spillane, *op. cit.*

[67] *Young Children in Wartime.*

[68] J. C. Solomon, "Reactions of Children to Blackouts," *Am. J. Orthopsychiat.,* Vol. 12, 1942, pp. 361–362.

From clinical reports on the causal relationship between the reactions of parents and their children, the following general conclusion is suggested: The incidence of acute emotional disturbances among young children in a community exposed to air raids will tend to vary directly with the incidence of overt excitement and emotional upset among the adults in that community.

There are some indications that responsiveness to adult reactions may not be the only major determinant of behavioral disturbances in children following air raids. Dunsdon[69] obtained reports from schoolteachers on 8000 children who were evacuated from Bristol, and it was found that there were approximately eight times as many cases of psychological disturbance among those who remained in the heavily bombed city each night as among those who were removed nightly to rock shelters on the outskirts. Apparently, the disturbances among children repeatedly subjected to heavy air attacks were not simply a matter of excessive excitement and apprehension, modeled after the fear reactions of the adults who accompanied them during the raid; rather, Dunsdon's findings reveal that pronounced apathy is a predominant symptom in the first stage of air-raid shock and is followed by other symptoms of reactive depression which set in after a period of ten days to four weeks.

Brander's report on children in Finland who were exposed to air raids[70] describes immediate reactions to violent bombing as a "general inhibition" of all activities. Following the bombings, many children exhibited marked startle reactions, severe terror states at night, and other sustained anxiety symptoms. Several reports are cited by Despert[71] in which acute anxiety symptoms, usually of a transient nature, have been noted among British children exposed to severe air raids. Excessive fear and "hysterical crying" in cellars and bunkers was a widespread reaction among German children during heavy air raids, according to testimony obtained from German teachers, doctors, psychologists, and parents.[72] The report

[69] Loc cit.

[70] T. Brander, "Psychiatric Observations among Finnish Children during the Russo-Finnish War of 1939–1940," Nervous Child, Vol. 2, 1943, pp. 313–319.

[71] Op. cit.

[72] USSBS, The Effects of Strategic Bombing on German Morale, Vol. 1.

on German morale also states that ". . . children who had to be rescued from wrecked houses often suffered a long time from shock, and wept and cried in their sleep."

From the various reports which have just been cited, it appears that when children are subjected to severe bombing, transient symptoms of acute anxiety or depression occur frequently, just as in adults. Even though such reactions in children may be mediated to some extent by "contagion" from adults, it is likely that other factors also play a major role, particularly when there has been prolonged exposure to heavy air raids.

From their clinical investigations of evacuated children who had extensive air-raid experience, Freud and Burlingham[73] discerned a number of additional determinants of anxiety in children. They noted that all children over two years of age had acquired at least some limited knowledge of the realistic dangers of air raids ("They realize that houses will fall down when bombed and that people are often killed or hurt in falling houses."). Hence, insofar as children are able to perceive and comprehend the signs of danger to which they are exposed, their fear reactions are probably determined by realistic threats to their safety. The authors caution against overrating this factor, however, because children so often display a tendency to deny the presence of potentially dangerous objects. For example, an un-exploded bomb which remained for over a week in the immediate vicinity of a residential war nursery was at first recognized to be dangerous but soon was totally ignored by the children. Nevertheless, it is probable that during the period of an actual air raid the unusual sights and loud sounds serve to reinforce the child's awareness of the actual danger which is present.

Another source of air-raid anxiety in children, according to Freud and Burlingham, is the arousal of intrapsychic conflicts as a result of witnessing physical destruction, injuries, and deaths. This form of reaction was noted mainly in young children at the age (presumably around four) when they have only recently learned to abhor destruction and to curb their own aggressive impulses.

---

[73] *Young Children in Wartime.*

. . . [the child] can only keep up this attitude when the people in the outer world do likewise. When he sees killing and destruction going on outside, this arouses his fear that the impulses which he has only a short while ago buried in himself will be awakened again.[74]

The authors claim that in younger children, who have not yet reached this stage of personality development, the destruction produced by air raids does not typically evoke anxiety, but may give rise to serious characterological disorders due to the interference with the process of educating them to control their own aggressive impulses.

The psychoanalytic observations just cited carry the same practical implication as the nonpsychoanalytic studies described earlier; namely, that behavioral disturbances in children may be minimized by removing them to areas in which they will not perceive the signs of objective threat to their own safety or the obvious destruction produced by air raids. One important limitation on this proposition should be specified, however: the net effect may be an augmentation of behavioral disturbances among young children if removal from the target area entails sudden separation from the family. The presence of the mother during periods of danger can often prevent traumatic reactions among very young children; as was mentioned earlier, many studies of evacuation difficulties emphasize the separation factor as a critical determinant of emotional disturbances in children.

SUMMARY

1. Air attacks of the type to which civilians were exposed during World War II produce only a very slight increase in psychoses, chronic traumatic neuroses, and other sustained psychopathological disorders in adults and in children. Prolonged, incapacitating symptoms are likely to occur only in markedly predisposed personalities.

2. Under conditions of severe bombing there is a marked incidence of temporary emotional shock, presumably even among persons

---

[74] *Ibid.*

who were previously emotionally stable. Such reactions may take the form of excessive anxiety symptoms or of mild depression and apathy. Most cases are capable of recovering within a period of a few days up to several weeks.

3. Following heavy air attacks there is a slight but definite increase in psychosomatic disorders. From the observations made during World War II, it appears that the most frequent form of such disorder is peptic ulcers, which often develop suddenly during air raids. Coronary insufficiency is another psychosomatic reaction which is likely to be evoked. Menstrual difficulties frequently occur among women during periods of air warfare; this minor form of psychosomatic disorder may reduce the work efficiency of large numbers of women, not only because of the physical discomfort, but because of the secondary anxiety aroused by disturbances of bodily functions.

4. In children, emotional disturbances following air raids are most likely to occur: (*a*) if their parents and other adults exhibit overt signs of emotional upset in their presence; (*b*) if the children are exposed to the obvious signs of immediate danger; and (*c*) if they perceive the destruction or casualties the raid produces. To the extent that these conditions are present in a community exposed to severe air attacks, a high incidence of emotional-shock reactions may be expected among children. Their anxiety or depressive reactions may persist for months after exposure to an air attack. Psychiatric problems among young children may be prevented by removing them from target areas before perceptible signs of danger and destruction have occurred, without separating them from their mothers.

CHAPTER 6
FEAR AND EMOTIONAL ADAPTATION

CHARACTERISTIC FEAR REACTIONS

Many of the psychopathological symptoms discussed in the preceding chapter may be regarded as an extreme form of emotional reaction to objective conditions of danger. Acute anxiety states and reactive depression are, in effect, intense emotional reactions which present a psychiatric problem because they persist after the danger has subsided. At least for a short time, they affect the person's entire life adjustment, markedly incapacitating him in his work and in his social relationships.

Much more widespread are the severe fear reactions which do not result in obvious maladjustment. Schmideberg,[1] in describing the reactions of British civilians, claims that "When it was said of someone that he was not afraid of the raids, what was meant as a rule was that he got over the fright in a few minutes or hours, usually by the next morning." The same point is emphasized by Fraser, Leslie, and Phelps,[2] and is based on their interviews of approximately one thousand British civilians who were exposed to the air blitz. According to these authors, the usual reaction was acute fear with somatic symptoms of emotional tension. This "normal" reaction, however, was characterized by a high degree of *appropriateness to the danger situation.* Usually the symptoms were elicited only by signs of immediate danger, such as the sound of bombs exploding. Although the warning signal of planes overhead frequently evoked apprehensiveness, the somatic symptoms of fear usually did not build up if there was merely a "quiet" alert. Whenever a dangerous raid occurred,

---

[1] M. Schmideberg, "Some Observations on Individual Reactions to Air Raids," *International J. Psychoanal.*, Vol. 23, 1942, pp. 146–176.

[2] R. Fraser, I. M. Leslie, and D. Phelps, "Psychiatric Effects of Severe Personal Experiences during Bombing," *Proc. Roy. Soc. Med.*, Vol. 36, 1943, pp. 119–123.

however, acute symptoms developed and persisted throughout the period of danger, generally subsiding within one-quarter of an hour after the end of the bombing attack.

Data on the incidence of subjective fear reactions are available from USSBS morale interviews[3] of a cross section of the German population: 38 per cent of the people who had undergone bombing reported having experienced severe upset, intense fear, or nervous collapse; an additional 31 per cent, temporary or less severe fright or upset. Only 22 per cent claimed to have experienced little or no fear. Confirmatory evidence of the harrowing fear produced by air raids is provided by a study of captured German mail.[4]

That widespread fear reactions occur during air attacks is further borne out by interview data from a cross section of Japanese civilians:

> . . . fright was by far the most common emotional reaction to bombing experience. Many thought that they would be killed. Others were so paralyzed that they could neither think nor act. Few claimed that they were not frightened. . . .[5]

Although overt behavior is often well controlled despite the occurrence of intense feelings of fear, the high incidence of such subjective responses may present a critical problem to a community subjected to air attack. The powerful desire to escape that is mobilized when fear is highly aroused may sometimes lead to irrational action, especially if there has been no prior instruction or training in appropriate ways to avoid the danger. From his interviews of Spanish Loyalist civilians who experienced the Barcelona raids, Langdon-Davies[6] cites many instances of irrational escape behavior occurring when there is widespread terror among an unprepared population; for instance, ". . . people scattered crazily in all directions, plunging into doorways, falling over and over." Haldane[7] also describes people in the Barcelona raids who ". . . lost their heads

---

[3] USSBS Report, *The Effects of Strategic Bombing on German Morale,* Vol. 1, U.S. Government Printing Office, Washington, D.C., 1947.

[4] *Ibid.*

[5] USSBS Report, *The Effects of Strategic Bombing on Japanese Morale,* U.S. Government Printing Office, Washington, D.C., 1947.

[6] J. Langdon-Davies, *Air Raid,* George Routledge & Sons, Ltd., London, 1938.

[7] J. B. S. Haldane, *A. R. P.,* Victor Gollancz, Ltd., London, 1938.

completely and tried to dig holes in the streets." Such maladaptive
actions not only give rise to unnecessary casualties, but may also
result in failure to carry out necessary disaster-control measures. The
fear and confusion among Japanese civilians during incendiary raids
has been described as resulting in mass flight, with few persons
remaining behind to combat the fires.[8]

Perhaps of even greater importance is the carry-over effect of
undergoing an intense subjective experience of fear or terror. Even
among those whose self-confidence has not been profoundly shaken
and who are able to dispel the persisting apprehension, work efficiency may be impaired because of automatic defensive reactions
acquired during the terror experience.

> The people of the bombed areas [in Japan] are highly sensitive
> to all flashes of light and all types of sounds. . . . they are fright-
> ened by noises from radios, the whistle of trains, the roar of our
> own planes, the sparks from trolleys, etc.[9]

Another serious carry-over effect is emotional sensitization to subsequent air-raid experiences. The USSBS report on German morale
asserts that:

> More than one-third of the people going through a big air raid
> suffer relatively permanent psychological effects, that is, the terror
> transcends the immediate raid to such an extent that it is rein-
> stated by the next alert.[10]

It is probable that having once undergone an intense terror experience, a person's capacity for emotional adaptation to subsequent
danger experiences is reduced. This factor is repeatedly mentioned
in reports on psychiatric casualties. Gillespie,[11] for example, despite
his strong emphasis on the proposition that severe traumatic
neuroses occur as a rule only in predisposed personalities, calls
attention to an important exception: incapacitating symptoms and
even dissociated states occur under bombing among previously

---

[8] USSBS, *The Effects of Strategic Bombing on Japanese Morale.*
[9] April, 1945, Domei Report quoted in *ibid.*
[10] USSBS, *The Effects of Strategic Bombing on German Morale,* Vol. 1.
[11] R. D. Gillespie, *Psychological Effects of War on Citizen and Soldier,* W. W.
Norton & Company, New York, 1942.

stable soldiers and civilians who have undergone "more than usually terrifying experiences."

THE MAGNITUDE OF THE AIR ATTACK

From the preceding discussion, it is clear that when we speak of "fear reactions" we are referring to many different correlated variables, including both subjective and overt forms of emotional behavior: (1) feelings of apprehensiveness; (2) excited and disorganized action during the period of danger; (3) persistent emotional upset after the danger has subsided; (4) impairment of postdanger adjustment by startle responses or by incapacitating anxiety symptoms; or (5) reduced capacity for controlling emotional responses upon subsequent exposures to danger; etc. For purposes of formulating and evaluating general hypotheses on the conditions under which a high incidence of such reactions occur, it appears to be useful to retain the term "fear reactions" to designate this entire set of intercorrelated response variables. We should recognize, however, that ultimately, as our knowledge of reactions to danger increases, our hypotheses will require more precise formulation. The evidence to be presented in this chapter deals primarily with subjective feelings of fear (type 1). Only insofar as strong reactions of this type may be assumed to be *indicators* of each of the other types, is one justified in inferring that the conclusions will apply to all types of fear reactions.

Rarely does one find in the literature on air attacks an explicit discussion of the central problem upon which our inquiry will be focused: under what conditions is an air raid most likely to evoke severe fear reactions on a mass scale? One obvious condition has previously been alluded to a number of times; namely, the *physical magnitude of the air raid*. We have already noted that emotional-shock reactions are most likely to occur following a heavy air raid. (By a heavy air raid is meant one which produces relatively high casualties and extensive destruction.) Not only does a greater proportion of the population suffer from incapacitating emotional disorders in heavier air attacks, but, among the majority who escape being psychiatric casualties, the subjective fear reactions are more severe.[12] This is, of course, precisely what one would expect on the basis of the popularly accepted principle that the greater the danger, the greater the fear. A more detailed inquiry into the specific factors involved in heavy raids will lead us to some less obvious determinants of intense fear reactions.

The experience of undergoing an air attack is one in which a person is exposed to a large number of unusual and complex stimuli, evoking a wide variety of "meanings"; it is in their unique sequences, combinations, and patternings that the stimuli produce intense emotional responses. Nevertheless, for purposes of predicting mass reactions, it is necessary to discover *which variables* play the most important role in augmenting fear.

Early in the war, Harrisson observed at first hand the widespread fear among people living in "blitztowns" and he speculated that:

> . . . the most upsetting factor is *uncertainty*. . . . First, you never know what night the raid is going to come. Secondly, you never know which plane noise or other noise is the noise which may mean your end.[13]

It is undoubtedly true that some degree of emotional tension is aroused when an air attack is anticipated. If one becomes aware of the fact that a heavy raid has begun and that the danger may be very great, tension is likely to mount. Fear increases markedly during the suspenseful period when one has not yet been affected, but the bomb explosions or incendiary fires occurring nearby clearly indicate that the threat of impending danger is rapidly materializing. Nevertheless, the available evidence from many observers does not confirm Harrisson's hypothesis that such "uncertainties" constitute "the most

---

[12] E. Glover, "Notes on the Psychological Effects of War Conditions on the Civilian Population," Part III, "The Blitz," *International J. Psychoanal.*, Vol. 23, 1942, pp. 17–37; Langdon-Davies, *op. cit.*; J. Stern, *The Hidden Damage,* Harcourt, Brace and Company, Inc., New York, 1947; USSBS, *The Effects of Strategic Bombing on German Morale,* Vol. 1; P. E. Vernon, "Psychological Effects of Air Raids," *J. Abnorm. Soc. Psychol.*, Vol. 36, 1941, pp. 457–476.

[13] T. Harrisson, "Obscure Nervous Effects of Air Raids," *Brit. Med. J.*, Vol. 1, 1941, pp. 573–574 and 832.

upsetting factor" in connection with heavy raids. The experiences involved in anticipating a heavy attack—being aware that a dangerous raid has begun and undergoing the suspense entailed by perceiving the danger approach closer and closer—probably evoke acute fear symptoms in a relatively small number of predisposed personalities. Such experiences appear to be of the type which people in Britain and in other countries were able to "take" and to which they typically became emotionally adapted (described later in this chapter).

THE "NEAR-MISS" FACTOR

There is another type of experience which has been singled out by MacCurdy[14] as the most critical factor in the emotional impact of bombing: the experience of suddenly facing danger in the immediate vicinity. After discussing MacCurdy's hypotheses we shall examine the available evidence. It will be seen that by and large his views are well supported.

When a high explosive hits a person's house or shelter and the walls come crashing down all about him; when the blast from a powerful explosion hurls him to the ground; when the incendiary fires suddenly flare up and a member of his family is burned to death—situations of this kind, according to MacCurdy, arouse the most acute and persistent fear symptoms. Emotional-shock reactions, ranging from a dazed stupor to jumpiness and preoccupation with the horrors of the air raid, occur primarily among the "near-misses"—people who undergo direct exposure to actual danger. This may involve a narrow escape from death, being wounded, witnessing the destruction of persons close by, or suffering the loss of a loved one.

In contrast to the powerful reinforcement of fear among the near-misses, there is likely to be a reduction of fear among those who do not directly experience the destructive impact of the air

---

[14] J. T. MacCurdy, *The Structure of Morale*, The Macmillan Company, New York, 1943.

attack. The "remote-misses," as MacCurdy calls them, often experience considerable tension when they perceive danger cues, e.g., a warning siren, enemy planes overhead, bombs exploding somewhere not far off. But when a raid is over, there is immense relief, a feeling that "It has happened and I'm safe." Under these conditions the experience is one of *successful escape*. Previous fearful anticipations of personal loss and destruction tend to be replaced by feelings of optimism and confidence. This benign effect is especially likely if, upon visiting scenes of destruction, the damage is found to be circumscribed and the bodies have already been removed. Hence, ". . . the proportion of fear to courage in the population will correspond to the relative sizes of the near- and remote-miss groups."[15]

The heavier the raid, the higher the proportion of the population in the community who will be near-misses. It is this simple relationship which MacCurdy singles out to explain the fact that a heavy raid, as against a light raid, will produce a marked increase in the incidence of emotional shock and other severe fear reactions. He applies this explanation to the morale of the community as well:

> If the remote-miss person has more courage after a raid than before it, if courage, like fear, is contagious, and if the near-miss group in any community is small, it follows that a light, a "token" bombing must improve morale in that community. Innumerable Home Security reports attest the truth of this conclusion as I have been told.[16]

MacCurdy's emphasis upon *the degree of personal involvement* as the major determinant of severe fear reactions was presumably based on his own clinical experience as well as on impressionistic observations of air-raid victims. There are many independent observations which, when considered together, definitely tend to support this hypothesis.

Reports on acute air-raid anxiety repeatedly mention that the reaction usually occurs in situations involving direct personal involvement in immediate danger. Glover[17] specifies, as "the most

15 *Ibid.*
16 *Ibid.*
17 *Loc. cit.*

common" clinical picture observed among psychiatric casualties during air raids, the emotional-shock reactions "following direct involvement in a bomb explosion." He goes on to discuss the "minor varieties of 'shock'," referring, presumably, to acute and sustained fear reactions which are less serious from a psychiatric standpoint. Clinical examination of such cases indicates that "even in apparently stable types, these states occur most commonly when three . . . conditions are fulfilled, viz., when the room or shelter is wrecked, when the individual suffers some physical injury and when some grave or fatal casualties are caused by the explosion." Glover also calls attention to the fact that observations of British reactions to air raids do not confirm the hypothesis that those who suffer organic injuries are relatively free from neurotic reactions. According to a recent study by Lander,[18] the anxiety-reducing effect of being wounded might hold true for combat troops in World War II as well as in World War I. With respect to civilian air-raid reactions, however, Glover[19] states that the experience of sudden physical injury appeared to be one of the important causes of neurotic reactions.

A report by the Military Mobilization Committee of the American Psychiatric Association summarizes the available material on British reactions during the early war years. This report asserts that at the beginning of the war, psychoneurotic manifestations occurred primarily among highly educated persons in positions of responsibility; whereas, during the period of the air blitz, such reactions appeared mainly among people who had been in actual danger, had been knocked down by blasts, or had been in houses wrecked by high explosives.[20]

Supporting data on the importance of the personal involvement factor are provided by Fraser, Leslie, and Phelps.[21] These investigators obtained the names of all uninjured persons admitted to First-

[18] J. Lander, "The Psychiatrically Immunizing Effect of Combat Wounds," *Am. J. Orthopsychiat.*, Vol. 16, 1946, pp. 536–541.

[19] *Loc. cit.*

[20] Military Mobilization Committee of the American Psychiatric Association, *Psychiatric Aspects of Civilian Morale*, Family Welfare Assoc. of America, New York, 1942.

[21] *Loc. cit.*

Aid Posts in one (unspecified) English city during a period of heavy bombing. This group is assumed to be fairly representative of all of those who had undergone severe personal involvement during the air raids, since it was the usual practice for A.R.P. workers to send all such cases to one of the Posts for a routine examination in order to check on possible physical injury. All traceable cases were followed up and interviewed ten months after they had been examined in the First-Aid Post. There was a small group of thirty-five people who had experienced severe personal involvement—buried beneath debris for over an hour because of a bomb explosion in the immediate vicinity. Of this group, 66 per cent developed temporary or persistent neurotic symptoms; in 40 per cent, the emotional disorder resulted in absence from work for three weeks or longer. A larger group (94 cases), which comprised all persons who had experienced direct blast effects, also showed a high incidence of neurotic symptoms, the most frequent being anxiety states and depression. The high incidence for these groups is in marked contrast to the low incidence of neurotic symptoms noted among the general population of the bombed city.

A direct comparison was made between those First-Aid-Post cases who developed clear-cut neurotic symptoms (61 cases) and those who did not (33 cases). The nonneurotic group was found to have suffered slightly less severe danger experiences than the neurotic group. Furthermore, close to 50 per cent of the neurotic group had experienced a definite personal loss from the air attack (destruction of the home or death of a close friend); whereas, among the non-neurotic group, such loss was experienced by only 4 per cent. From these and other findings, the investigators conclude that "neurosis is likely to follow severe personal air-raid experiences, which at the time upset the individual emotionally, or produced a serious upset in the pattern of his living by destroying a much-esteemed home or a close friend. . . ." Formerly stable personalities as well as those with personality defects were found to have developed neurotic symptoms following direct personal involvement. Among the latter, the symptoms were likely to persist for many months, whereas, among the former, recovery usually occurred within a few weeks.

Reports on German civilians who were exposed to extremely heavy air raids also tend to support the hypothesis that severe fear reactions occur primarily under conditions of direct personal involvement. Seydewitz, for example, gives the following impressionistic description of the aftermath of the devastating attack against Hamburg (summer of 1943), where practically all the survivors were near-misses:

> For weeks eyewitnesses were unable to report without succumbing to their nerves and weeping hysterically. They would try to speak, then would break down and cry: "I can't stand seeing it again; I can't stand it!"[22]

The USSBS report on German morale also describes such reactions among German civilians, as exemplified by the following excerpt in which a woman tells about the first big raid she experienced:

> I saw people killed by falling bricks and heard the screams of others dying in the fire. I dragged my best friend from a burning building and she died in my arms. I saw others who went stark mad. The shock to my nerves and to the soul, one can never erase.[23]

There is some quantitative evidence based on interviews of a cross section of German civilians which indicates the importance of the personal involvement factor. The increase in fear, as well as the deterioration in morale resulting from increased bomb tonnage, was found to be produced principally by the amount of personal involvement incident to the bombing.

> When personal involvement, in terms of casualties in the immediate family or property loss, is taken as a measure of the severity of raids, there is a marked decline in morale as the degree of involvement increases. There is little evidence of diminishing returns and no tendency for morale to improve at the level of greatest personal involvement. Personal involvement is clearly the most sensitive measure of the severity of raids for the individual, and is more closely related to changes in morale than the other measures reported.[24]

---

[22] M. Seydewitz, *Civil Life in Wartime Germany*, The Viking Press, Inc., New York, 1945.

[23] USSBS, *The Effects of Strategic Bombing on German Morale*, Vol. 1.

[24] *Ibid.*

Thus the evidence from the USSBS Morale Survey of German civilians definitely tends to bear out MacCurdy's assertion that morale deteriorates chiefly in the near-miss group. In the above quotation from the USSBS report, the term "morale" is used in a very broad sense to include fear reactions as well as war weariness, defeatism, and other unfavorable wartime attitudes. Among the "indices of morale" referred to were the interview responses to questions dealing with (1) fear experienced during the first big raid; (2) increased fear with successive raids; (3) anxiety about future raids; and (4) apathy and fatigue experienced under conditions of continuing raids. Presumably these four variables were found to be related to personal involvement. Unfortunately, the quantitative data on the *degree* of relationship between personal involvement and severity of fear reactions are not presented in the USSBS report. Nevertheless, the evidence reported does lend considerable weight to the general proposition that the psychological impact of heavy air raids is determined to a large extent by the proportion of people in the community who undergo a high degree of personal involvement.

That the experiences occurring in a single air raid may be a critical factor in producing persistent fear reactions is also suggested indirectly by another finding reported by the USSBS morale survey: "Frequency of raids was of much less importance in its effect upon subsequent [fear] reaction to bombing than the experience of the first raid."[25] Of those who reported having been badly frightened in their first air-raid experience, 48 per cent asserted that they continued to experience fear in subsequent raids; whereas, among those frightened a little, only 29 per cent gave this response. Although this finding could be interpreted in a number of different ways without implicating the "personal involvement" hypothesis, it is nevertheless consistent with MacCurdy's assertion that there is a powerful reinforcement of fear reactions among those who undergo, for the first time, a near-miss experience which arouses acute fear.

The findings from the large-scale survey of German civilians, when combined with the reports by independent British observers,

---

[25] *Ibid.*

provide a fairly substantial empirical basis for accepting MacCurdy's near-miss factor as a critical one in determining the high incidence of severe fear reactions produced by the heaviest air raids. Apparently, it is those survivors who directly experience the physical impact of the air attack who are most likely to exhibit severe and prolonged fear reactions.

EMOTIONAL ADAPTATION TO AIR RAIDS

MacCurdy's theory is not limited merely to the proposition that fear reactions are augmented by undergoing a near-miss experience. In describing the remote-miss reaction pattern he makes the assumption that the level of fear is actually *diminished* by exposure to an air raid in which one does not directly experience a narrow escape. In other words, MacCurdy assumes that people who are exposed to a series of air raids will tend to show increased capacity to withstand the emotional stress of subsequent air attacks provided that they do not have a near-miss experience. The available evidence on emotional adaptation tends to bear out this assumption, and it raises a number of important theoretical issues in connection with personal adjustment to objective threats of danger.

At the very beginning of World War II the vast majority of the population of England expected to be subjected to terrifying air attacks at any time,[26] but during the first year of the war these fears did not materialize. A large number of hostile aircraft frequently flew over England, making it necessary to have many air alerts. The attacks were light and sporadic, however, producing comparatively little damage. Marked changes in attitudes and in overt behavioral responses to air-raid alerts were consistently noted during this period.[27]

After the declaration of war, the government's mass-evacuation program met wide popular support: tens of thousands of women

[26] E. Klein, "The Influence of Teachers' and Parents' Attitudes and Behavior upon Children in Wartime," *Mental Hygiene*, Vol. 26, New York, 1942, pp. 434–445; MacCurdy, *op. cit.;* "Mass Observation," T. H. Harrisson and C. Madge (eds.), *War Begins at Home*, Chatto & Windus, London, 1940; Schmideberg, *loc. cit.*

[27] Glover, *loc. cit.;* MacCurdy, *op. cit.;* Harrisson and Madge (eds.), *op. cit.;* Schmideberg, *loc. cit.;* Vernon, *loc. cit.*

and children moved from London and from other metropolitan centers to the countryside. The first air-raid warnings were scrupulously observed. The great majority of the people "scurried to their shelters with little confidence of ever seeing daylight again."[28] As the months went past and few bombs fell, large numbers of evacuees returned on their own initiative to the large cities. Air-raid sirens were generally ignored. Many people refused to go to shelters or to take cover and there were strong protests against official precautions, such as the closing of shops during alerts. Little public support was given to A.R.P. activities. The excitement and fright which characterized the earlier air-raid alerts were replaced by indifference, mild irritation, or boredom.[29]

The most obvious factor in explaining the transformation among the British population during the first year of the war is that they experienced a large number of air-raid alerts in which little or no objective danger occurred. MacCurdy emphasizes this point in his explanation of the extinction of fear among those who escaped direct exposure to danger: ". . . arbitrary signals for taking precautions, such as sirens, are obeyed only if experience confirms the association of danger with the signal."[30]

Matte[31] gives a similar explanation and points out that a succession of false alarms and light raids provides a favorable condition for the gradual development of psychological defenses for overcoming terrifying expectations of danger. In addition, he calls attention to the fact that fear responses to the air-raid siren were evoked in earlier alerts, not only because of its meaning as a warning signal, but also because it was a very loud and unpleasant auditory stimulus. Vernon[32] also describes the siren as a "gruesome wail" which frightened people initially. These observations suggest that with successive exposures to relatively nondangerous alerts there may have been

[28] MacCurdy, op. cit.

[29] Glover, loc. cit.; MacCurdy, op. cit.; I. Matte, "Observations of the English in Wartime," J. Nervous Ment. Disease, Vol. 97, 1943, pp. 447–463; Schmideberg, loc. cit.; R. M. Titmuss, Problems of Social Policy, His Majesty's Stationery Office, London, 1950; Vernon, loc. cit.

[30] MacCurdy, op. cit.

[31] Loc. cit.

[32] Loc. cit.

desensitization to the intense auditory stimulus as well as a change in expectations of danger.

Although a series of false-alarm alerts or very light raids produced a marked decline in apprehensiveness among the British, there was a marked increase in emotional tension as soon as heavy air attacks began. British observers report that during the early days of the air blitz (summer of 1940) there was a noticeable increase in irritability, concern about bomb damage, excitement during air raids, and other overt signs of fear.[33]

There is no evidence one way or the other to indicate whether the preceding experience of having undergone emotional adaptation had the effect of diminishing initial fear reactions to the heavy raids. But one important point which emerges very clearly is that *there was a definite decline in overt fear reactions as the air blitz continued, even though the raids became heavier and more destructive.*[34] With successive dangerous raids, the bombed population displayed more and more indifference toward air attacks. Warning signals again tended to be disregarded unless attacking planes were overhead.

For example, a survey in two target areas (Islington and Southwark) carried out by the Ministry of Home Security showed that by April, 1941, very little notice was taken of an air alert without noise.[35] In London, as well as in other target cities, little concern or interest was shown in bomb damage. Cautions about staying away from unexploded bombs were frequently ignored, and, in general, bombings came to be regarded with a degree of detachment that approached the usual attitude toward peacetime traffic dangers. Among a large proportion of the British population, exposure to a series of relatively dangerous raids during the air blitz evidently produced a gradual extinction of fear reactions, just as occurred in the earlier period when the population experienced a series of relatively nondangerous alerts.

---

[33] Glover, *loc. cit.;* Schmideberg, *loc. cit.;* Vernon, *loc. cit.*

[34] R. D. Gillespie, "Résumé of His Addresses before the New York Academy of Medicine," *So. J. Med.,* Vol. 41, 1941, pp. 2346–2349; MacCurdy, *op. cit.;* J. M. Mackintosh, *The War and Mental Health in England,* Commonwealth Fund, Division of Publication, New York, 1944; Matte, *loc. cit.;* Schmideberg, *loc. cit.*

[35] Titmuss, *op. cit.*

There was seldom a day in five years of war when bombs or rockets were not dropping on some part of Britain.[36] Even when the presence of raiders was not signalled, there was always the threat of bombing attacks and of new, unsuspected weapons. Nevertheless, the continual uncertainty and suspense to which the entire population in the target areas was exposed apparently did not play a major role in augmenting fear reactions.

It is likely that emotional adaptation was also manifested during the later period of V-1 and V-2 attacks. In agreement with reports by numerous foreign correspondents who were in Britain at the time, Woltmann[37] states that people frequently did not seek shelters or display overt signs of fear during robot-bomb attacks. He claims that American soldiers stationed in Britain exhibited more disturbed behavior than did British civilians and that this difference was due to the fact that the latter had been through the earlier "blitz."

The British observations on widespread emotional adaptation to heavy air attacks, when considered together with the observations cited in the preceding section on the occurrence of severe emotional reactions following direct personal involvement, definitely tend to support MacCurdy's theory that fears are extinguished by remote-miss experiences and are reinforced by near-miss experiences.

USSBS reports indicate that emotional adaptation to heavy air attacks occurred among at least a substantial minority of the bombed populations of Japan and Germany. According to the report on Japanese morale:

> Urban people who experienced more continuous bombing and therefore represent the better test on the question of adaptation, clearly indicate that they became better adapted as their bombing experience increased, while rural people, who had less direct and less frequent experience, became more afraid.[38]

Among the Germans, 36 per cent of a cross section of the bombed population reported that they had felt less afraid with successive air

---

[36] *Ibid.*

[37] A. G. Woltmann, "Life on a Target," *Am. J. Orthopsychiat.*, Vol. 15, 1945, pp. 172–177.

[38] USSBS, *The Effects of Strategic Bombing on Japanese Morale.*

attacks; 30 per cent reported no change; and 28 per cent reported increased fear.[39] The fact that a sizeable proportion of Germans reported having experienced emotional adaptation, even though they were subjected to far more destructive attacks than were the British, is consistent with the hypothesis that among a population exposed to severe air attacks fear reactions will be reinforced among some persons but extinguished among others, depending on the personal experiences they have during the raids. In this connection, it is important to note that one of the items which was correlated with direct personal involvement among bombed German civilians was the question dealing with emotional adaptation to successive air attacks.[40] Apparently, those who were *not directly involved in danger,* despite exposure to extremely heavy air attacks, were the ones who were most likely to feel *less afraid* as the raids continued. (This statement is implied by the material presented in the USSBS morale report, although the specific data are not reported.)

From the various sources of evidence, it seems fairly safe to conclude that a sizeable proportion of the civilian population exposed to successive air attacks during World War II displayed a gradual decline in fear reactions. Insofar as the air attacks represent typical situations of external danger, the findings carry the obvious implication that among people in our culture there may be a general tendency toward emotional adaptation under conditions of repeated danger exposures. This implication is likely to be grossly misleading, however, unless one takes into account other reaction tendencies that are also evoked by recurrent danger experiences—tendencies which would operate in the direction of counteracting or preventing the development of emotional adaptation.

Of critical importance is the decline in the individual's capacity to withstand emotional stress as a consequence of near-miss experiences. There are also other factors associated with prolonged stress which might produce a similar impairment in protective "ego" functions. Numerous studies have been made among military personnel who were repeatedly exposed to combat situations that were comparable

[39] USSBS, *The Effects of Strategic Bombing on German Morale,* Vol. 1.
[40] *Ibid.*

in some important respects to the recurrent air attacks to which civilian populations were subjected. From such studies, it is apparent that emotional adaptation is by no means the dominant tendency when there is a high degree of personal involvement. Morale surveys of combat ground troops in the United States Army show that with increased duration of front-line duty, there is a marked rise in the incidence of anxiety symptoms.[41] Similarly, among combat flying personnel there is a definite increase in symptoms of chronic tension and anxiety as the number of missions flown are increased.[42]

Clinical investigations of war neurosis highlight the loss of control over primitive emotional impulses that comes from repeated exposure to combat. From descriptions of the cumulative stresses of combat, it is clear that psychological resistance was gradually weakened by a complex set of factors, including prolonged fatigue, hunger, and other incessant deprivations. What is most often singled out as the primary source of emotional stress, however, is a type of traumatic event that corresponds closely to the near-miss experiences described in connection with air-raid reactions. For instance, in Garner's description of the reaction of ground troops to artillery bombardment, the differential effects of near-miss and remote-miss experiences are sharply delineated:

> The explosion of shells at some distance, aside from the general tension produced, seldom leads to acute symptomatology. Short or prolonged stress, such as that produced by a barrage of shells in the immediate vicinity of the individual, or being "pinned down" for prolonged periods by constant shelling, is the frequent immediate cause for an acute psychologic disturbance. Terrifying situations will cause some of the most severe psychologic disturbances; such situations may be the landing of a shell within a few feet of a foxhole, being caught in a cellar from which escape is cut off while the enemy fires point blank from a tank-borne artillery of men nearby. The possible number of traumatic situations which may produce explosive reactions is extremely large; but all the

---

[41] R. M. Williams and M. B. Smith, "General Characteristics of Ground Combat," Chap. 2 in S. Stouffer, et al., The American Soldier: Combat and Its Aftermath, Vol. 2, Princeton University Press, Princeton, N.J., 1949.

[42] I. L. Janis, "Objective Factors Related to Morale Attitudes in the Aerial Combat Situation," Chap. 8 in ibid.

situations have in common an overwhelming threat to life and an inability to cope with it, or a strong identification with someone who has been mutilated or killed.[43]

In general, clinical reports on emotional breakdown in combat consistently point to the experience of undergoing a series of *repeated narrow escapes* as an outstanding pathogenic factor. As Kardiner puts it, "one little traumatic neurosis predisposes to another, much more severe."[44] The most extreme symptoms among ground troops were seen in men who had been "blown up" six or seven times.

So far as the personal involvement factor is concerned, the studies of war neurosis are in essential agreement with the observations of civilian reactions to air attacks. But there are only a few fragmentary observations on the effects of successive remote-miss experiences in combat. The relevant cases for studying emotional adaptation would have been the men who consistently experienced a relatively low degree of personal involvement during a series of combat exposures. Perhaps there was little opportunity for such cases to occur, because of the high casualty rates and the extreme danger conditions that characterized the usual tour of combat duty. When ground units and air crews were in sustained or recurrent combat situations, the individual's chances of undergoing at least one severe near-miss experience may have been so great that any general tendency toward emotional adaptation would have been obscured.

At any rate, in the absence of the relevant observations, it remains an open question whether the progressive loss of fear reactions observed among civilians during periods of air warfare was paralleled by a similar trend among those men whose combat experience was consistently remote-miss in character. Nevertheless, the observations of combat reactions call attention to the need for formulating the limiting conditions necessary for the occurrence of emotional adaptation. At the very least, they serve as caution against overgeneralizing from the observations of civilian reactions in bombed com-

---

[43] H. H. Garner, "Psychiatric Casualties in Combat," *War Med.*, Vol. 8, 1945, pp. 343–357.

[44] A. Kardiner, *The Traumatic Neuroses of War*, Paul B. Hoeber, Inc., New York, 1941.

munities. Obviously, when a population is exposed to recurrent danger, widespread manifestations of emotional adaptation can be expected *only if there is a relatively low incidence of near-miss experiences.* The gradual loss of fear reactions and the decline in conformity to protective measures noted among the civilians in bombed communities were probably consequences of the remote-miss character of their air-raid experiences.

Emotional adaptation would probably be a rare occurrence in a target city subjected to atomic bombing or to a series of "conventional" attacks that entailed a high incidence of direct personal involvement. Under such conditions, an increase in fear reactions rather than a decrease would be the expected trend. Probably there would also be a progressive increase in fear reactions insofar as the danger exposures give rise to severe deprivations, unremitting fatigue, and other cumulative stresses of the sort which weaken the psychological stamina of combat troops. Consequently, emotional adaptation cannot be regarded in any sense as the "typical" reaction to successive air attacks. Rather, it is a reaction tendency that can easily be submerged or counteracted, becoming a dominant trend in a community only under relatively limited disaster conditions.

DETERMINANTS OF EMOTIONAL STRESS

From the discussion of the differential effects of near-miss and remote-miss experiences, it is possible to single out certain specific features of an air attack which are likely to be major determinants of the emotional impact upon the bombed community. Of primary importance in predicting the incidence of severe fear reactions is the number of persons who become directly involved in immediate danger. Typical indices of this factor might be the number of non-fatal casualties, the number of public air-raid shelters damaged, and the number of homes and buildings damaged in neighborhoods where public shelters were lacking or were not used.

A second predictive factor is the number of persons who suffered some degree of personal loss, whether or not they had been directly involved in personal danger. The number of families in which one or more fatalities occurred, the number of persons made homeless, and a variety of similar indicators might be used to estimate the incidence of personal loss. A third factor is exposure to the sight of the dead, the dying, and the wounded. The extent to which the population witnesses such disturbing sights is determined by the total number of casualties in the community and by the promptness with which casualties are removed to emergency centers before large numbers of people emerge from their homes or shelters.

A number of other situational factors which interfere with emotional adaptation and increase the incidence of severe fear reactions remain to be considered.

Spacing of Air Attacks

In a discussion of emotional adaptation among the British, Vernon points out:

> People whose houses have been demolished or who have undergone an unusually intense "Blitz" very often regress for a time and show less habituation and more nervousness during the next few raids. A reversion occurs also when there is a long spell of immunity from raids.[45]

This excerpt again points to personal involvement as a factor which counteracts the development of emotional adaptation, but it also refers to another interfering factor. According to Vernon, people generally found a succession of raids less trying than sporadic ones because they became "disadapted" during the quiet intervals. Glover refers to some confirmatory observations:

> . . . many observers have reported how, after people had gained some immunity to raid conditions, a temporary evacuation to the country led, as Ritchie Calder aptly put it, to their "losing their sea legs."[46]

As was mentioned earlier, USSBS investigators in Japan[47] found that urban people who experienced more continuous bombing indi-

---

[45] Vernon, *loc. cit.*
[46] Glover, *loc. cit.*
[47] USSBS, *The Effects of Strategic Bombing on Japanese Morale.*

cated that they became better adapted as their bombing experience increased, whereas rural people who had less frequent experience became more afraid. Consequently, it appears that among the Japanese, as well as among the British, a regular succession of raids had a less disturbing effect than sporadic ones.

This conclusion should be modified, in the light of the material on the near-miss factor presented earlier, so as to exclude those cases who experienced a narrow escape or direct personal loss during the series of air attacks. Schmideberg[48] asserts that "near escapes" proved to be most disturbing when they came in rapid succession; more widely spaced raids allowed time for recuperation. This observation, however, is not incompatible with the British and Japanese observations which imply that when dangerous air raids are widely spaced, there is a loss in emotional adaptation among those who do not undergo near-miss experiences. The latter observations suggest that spontaneous recovery of fear reactions may occur under conditions similar to those under which spontaneous recovery has been observed in experiments on human and animal conditioning.

Adequacy of Civilian Defense Measures

The ability of a community to minimize the disorganizing and fear-arousing effects of air raids is dependent largely on the availability and efficiency of rescue organizations, medical facilities, and social-service and welfare organizations. Glover[49] points out that severe emotional reactions are often aggravated, and in some cases precipitated, by lack of adequate social organization during the period following a heavy air raid, e.g., delay in rescue work, disruption of social services, inadequate welfare arrangements, etc. Suggestive evidence along similar lines comes from the USSBS survey of the bombed population of Germany: it was found that those Germans who felt that air-raid shelters, antiaircraft barrages, and relief measures were inadequate had poorer scores on a com-

---

[48] Loc. cit.
[49] Loc. cit.

bined index of fear and morale than those who considered defensive measures adequate.[50]

Lack of adequate shelters or insufficient time to get to shelters is likely to have the effect of exposing large numbers of persons to actual danger and to a variety of fear-eliciting stimuli. When one is not able to get to a shelter which is known to be fairly safe, anxiety is likely to mount. Glover[51] reports that insecurity among Londoners was at its height when "sneak" raids began. The combination of helplessness and surprise elicited by bombs falling suddenly without alerts gave rise to strong feelings of anxiety during the raid, followed by anger and exasperation toward the local authorities after the raid was over. The absence of antiaircraft barrages had a similar effect, after the population had had sufficient experience to discriminate between the sound of their own defensive weapons and those of the enemy bombs. During the first few air raids, however, the sheer intensity of loud sounds from all sources tended to augment fear reactions because the ability to discriminate among the various sound cues had not yet developed.

The setting up of flak installations in areas subject to air raids probably tends to have a favorable effect on a threatened population, but under certain conditions may arouse insecurity. For example, the people of Wuerzburg, Germany, are reported to have regarded new flak installations with mixed feelings, viewing them more as a point of attraction for enemy planes than as a protection for the city which, up until that time, had been spared a heavy attack.[52]

Night versus Day Raids

The vast majority of a cross section of German civilians reported that they were more frightened by raids occurring at night than by those occurring during daylight.[53] When bombing was light, however, there was a slight tendency to fear either day raids or night raids, depending on which kind was experienced more often. In

---

[50] USSBS, *The Effects of Strategic Bombing on German Morale*, Vol. 1.
[51] *Loc. cit.*
[52] USSBS, *The Effects of Strategic Bombing on German Morale*, Vol. 1.
[53] *Ibid.*

general, the vast majority of those who experienced both day and night raids considered the latter much worse. Parallel results are reported by the USSBS survey of a cross section of Japanese civilians.[54] One of the most common reasons for fearing night raids is that it is more difficult to get away from the fires and destruction at night when orientation is more difficult. Interview comments indicate that "in the darkness the flashes and sound of bombs are psychologically exaggerated and produce more fear."[55] Glover[56] also mentions that among the British, night raids evoked more sensational reactions but that these were usually dispelled the next morning if there was little visible evidence of widespread destruction.

Similar observations have been reported in connection with other types of danger situations. For example, it has been noted that frontline combat troops also tend to be more fearful at night than during the day.[57] As Sullivan points out, "terror is far more commonly experienced in darkness than in daylight and in fog than in clear weather."[58] Thus, the observations on augmented emotional reactions among civilians exposed to night raids can be subsumed under a more general proposition: in any danger situation, anything interfering with clear visual perception tends to diminish feelings of security. Darkness reduces the opportunity for sensory discriminations and thereby interferes with the individual's ability to evaluate the dangerous and safe features of his environment. Under these conditions, the fear-evoking effects of loud noises and of other salient danger cues tend to be augmented.

Lack of Purposeful Action

It is a generally accepted principle that people who face danger tend to feel less fearful if they are able to engage in some form of useful overt activity. Perhaps it is because this principle is so banal

---

[54] USSBS, *The Effects of Strategic Bombing on Japanese Morale.*
[55] *Ibid.*
[56] *Loc. cit.*
[57] Garner, *loc. cit.*
[58] H. S. Sullivan, "Psychiatric Aspects of Morale," *Am. J. Sociology,* Vol. 47, 1941, pp. 277–301.

that there is so little data pertinent to the effects of various types of assigned tasks and to overt activities on reactions to air raids. Although the general proposition is indeed a banal one, relatively little is known about the psychological mechanisms involved or about the specific conditions under which activity is maximally effective when large numbers of people are exposed to a common disaster situation. Only a few fragmentary observations have been reported.

Langdon-Davies[59] noted that in the raids on Barcelona in May, 1938, during which there was widespread terror, the people who were working at their jobs tended to bear up better initially than others. It appeared, however, that working as usual "was an antidote for fear for at best a very short time." Unfortunately, Langdon-Davies does not describe enough of the situation, nor do observers of other civilian populations provide sufficient relevant material, to enable us to discern even tentative answers to such obvious questions as: Is the activity of working on one's job effective only during the period when the danger is minimal or is it successful even when there is awareness of imminent personal danger?

Gillespie[60] suggests that there may be a critical period in which having an assigned occupation is extremely effective in avoiding anxiety symptoms, i.e., during the weeks immediately following a severe air attack. He claims that if there is extensive opportunity for rumination during this period, neurotic symptoms are more likely to develop. The only evidence he cites, however, is the fact that in one study a large number of cases were observed who did not develop neurotic symptoms until two or three weeks after the actual bombing—the symptoms appeared "only after the individuals concerned had finished rearranging themselves and their affairs and had time to sit down and consider the situation."

One particular type of activity that has been emphasized by several observers as being effective in reducing air-raid anxieties is the performance of tasks which require responsibility for others (children, members of the family, groups of shelterers) during the period

---

[59] Op cit.
[60] Gillespie, *Psychological Effects of War on Citizen and Soldier.*

when the raid is going on.[61] Although there may be a gain in self-confidence and in motivation to control one's own emotional responses among some people who are assigned a socially responsible task, there are others for whom the conflicts engendered by such responsibilities may increase the chances of neurotic breakdown.[62]

In the absence of reliable observations on the effectiveness of alternative types of actions, no specific conclusions can be drawn as to the conditions under which the fear-reducing value of activity is enhanced or diminished. In general, the air-raid literature contributes very little information beyond adding a few more examples which suggest that the opportunity to engage in some form of useful overt action is sometimes effective in reducing the severity of fear reactions.

Type of Bomb

The specific type of bomb used in an air attack is likely to make a difference in the amount of fear aroused. Among the Japanese, it was found that although incendiary attacks actually caused the largest number of casualties, most civilians who had been exposed to air raids had a greater fear of high explosives.[63] The reasons most frequently given by those interviewed were that it is more difficult to escape injury or death from high explosives and that little can be done to limit the damage produced by a high explosive. The frightening effects of the explosion itself, particularly the noise, were also commonly mentioned. As one Japanese housewife put it, "Every time I heard an explosion I thought I would die." The minority who feared incendiaries more than explosives usually asserted that they would prefer to be killed instantaneously rather than to be burned to death.

It is possible that certain weapons are capable of evoking such a high degree of anticipatory anxiety that the emotional impact is more severe than that produced by ordinary heavy explosives. Meer-

[61] Langdon-Davies, *op. cit.;* Schmideberg, *loc. cit.;* Vernon, *loc. cit.*

[62] Glover, *loc. cit.;* Schmideberg, *loc. cit.*

[63] USSBS, *The Effects of Strategic Bombing on Japanese Morale.*

loo[64] claims that the long warning of the flying V-1 bomb aroused more fear among British civilians than the sudden explosive burst of the V-2 rocket. The V-1 apparently elicited a high degree of tense expectation before the dangerous explosion actually occurred. The sudden explosion of the V-2, on the other hand, was probably less feared because people came to realize that one did not hear the noise until after the damage had already been done ("If you hear it you are safe!").

SUMMARY

1. The incidence of severe fear reactions tends to increase with increased physical magnitude of the air raid. In heavier air attacks there is not only a higher incidence of incapacitating symptoms of anxiety or depression, but there is also a higher incidence of intense fear reactions among those who do not become psychiatric casualties.

2. Severe and prolonged fear reactions are most likely to occur among those who undergo near-miss experiences, i.e., direct exposure to the physical impact of the air attack (knocked down by blast, injured, home destroyed, etc.). It is primarily because a higher proportion of the population undergoes direct personal involvement that a very heavy raid, as against a light raid, produces a marked increase in the incidence of severe emotional reactions.

3. In contrast to the powerful reinforcement of fear reactions which occurs among those who are near-misses, the level of fear is *diminished* among the remote-misses, i.e., those who are exposed to an air raid in which they do not directly experience a narrow escape or direct personal loss. People who are exposed to a series of air raids tend to show increased capacity to withstand the emotional stress of subsequent air attacks, provided they do not have a near-miss experience.

4. The high degree of uncertainty and suspense characteristic of periods when air attacks are expected probably elicits acute fear

---

[64] A. M. Meerloo, *Aftermath of Peace*, International Universities Press, New York, 1946.

symptoms in only a relatively small proportion of the population. The fact that emotional adaptation occurred in the vast majority of remote-misses implies that, in the long run, such factors are not generally effective in producing intense and prolonged fear reactions.

5. When a population is exposed to a series of *false alarms or light raids* in which there is little or no objective danger, fear responses tend to extinguish and air-raid precautions are generally ignored. From the experience of the British, it appears that two major factors may be involved in the emotional adaptation which occurs when there are successive exposures to relatively nondangerous alerts: (*a*) a change in the "meaning" of air-raid alerts so that terrifying expectations of danger tend to be eliminated and (*b*) psychophysical adaptation to the intense auditory stimulus used as a warning signal.

6. When a population is exposed to a series of *heavy and relatively dangerous* raids, fear responses again subside and precautionary measures tend to be gradually disregarded (except when near-miss experiences counteract emotional adaptation).

7. Various specific features of the air-raid situation have the effect of increasing the incidence of severe emotional reactions:

   a. Variable and wide intervals between successive raids tend to have a more disturbing effect than regular, short intervals. During prolonged quiet intervals between dangerous raids, there tends to be a loss of emotional adaptation (or "spontaneous recovery" of former fear reactions).

   b. Inadequate civilian defense measures, before and during a raid, produce widespread insecurity and expose the civilian population to fear-eliciting stimuli. Following a raid, the lack of adequate rescue organizations, medical facilities and welfare organizations tends to aggravate emotional disturbances produced by the raid.

   c. In general, night raids produce more acute fright reactions than day raids.

   d. Engaging in some useful form of overt activity sometimes tends to reduce air-raid anxieties. (The conditions under which assigned tasks and spontaneous activities have a beneficial or detrimental effect upon emotional adjustment during air attacks are, as yet, unknown.)

e. High explosives usually arouse more fright than incendiaries. Weapons which evoke an unusually high degree of tense expectation, such as the flying V-1 which emitted a loud warning noise before it exploded, may arouse more fear than ordinary high explosives.

f. From the findings on near-miss reactions, it may be inferred that the following additional features of an air raid are relevant factors for predicting the incidence of severe emotional reactions: (1) the number of nonfatal casualties; (2) the number of survivors who are in public shelters or in homes that are damaged during the attack; (3) the number of families in which a fatality occurs; (4) the number of homeless people; and (5) the number of *visible* casualties (not removed before the populace emerges from shelters).

CHAPTER 7
AGGRESSION AND WARTIME MORALE

Insofar as air attacks evoke severe fear reactions, they also tend to have unfavorable effects upon wartime morale. Although the conditions which produce fear are often quite different from those which lower morale, there is a certain degree of continuity between the two types of reactions. The arousal of intense fear generally heightens the motivation to escape further attacks and, in extreme cases, may result in defeatist attitudes, willingness to surrender, and personal demoralization. Moreover, there is probably a close functional relationship between fear and aggression. When a community is subjected to dangerous and harrowing disaster conditions, many people display fear reactions at first which later give way to intense irritation and anger. If aggressive responses are directed toward community leaders or toward fellow citizens, there is likely to be a serious impairment in group morale. However, such aggression directed toward outsiders, notably the enemy, may improve group morale.

Obviously, one of the major problems in evaluating the morale effects of air war is that of determining the *targets* toward whom aggressive feelings are directed. The first three sections of the present chapter will be concerned primarily with this problem. The next three sections will deal with various air-raid conditions in relation to morale attitudes. In the section on "Disruptive Behavior Following Air Attacks" (page 147), overt aggressive behavior and various forms of disruptive action that are indicative of "behavioral" morale will be examined.

INTRAGROUP HOSTILITY

Only one outstanding generalization pertaining to aggressive reactions is to be found in existing reports on civilian morale during

World War II. Formulated in varying ways by different writers, the gist of what is repeatedly said is the following: The hostility aroused by air attacks frequently was directed not toward the enemy, but toward home authorities and fellow citizens. This proposition is intended to apply to aggressive *attitudes* and *feelings* as subjectively experienced and communicated to others. Overt aggressive *actions* occurred very rarely in bombed communities, as will be seen later.

That British civilians did not respond to air raids with a marked increase in hatred toward the enemy is suggested by several surveys, including a Gallup poll.[1] These surveys showed that the most heavily bombed people were not the ones who were most likely to demand reprisals. The aggressive "Bomb Berlin" policy was favored primarily by those who had *not* experienced heavy air attacks.

A number of independent observers report that during the raids, early in 1940, aggression was directed mainly against the home authorities and, to a lesser extent, against "scapegoats," such as foreigners and refugees in England.[2] Vernon,[3] asserts that there was scarcely any resentment against the Germans, but very widespread criticisms of the home authorities during the first air raids. He interprets this reaction as a sign of emotional upset even though many criticisms of civilian defense activities may have been justifiable. During later phases of the air war, according to Vernon, resentment was usually directed only against those authorities who really had shown negligence; concomitantly, there was increased hatred of the bombers and the enemy. But Glover[4] cites some evidence indicating that the widespread resentment against the local authorities in the early stages of the blitz—which had an element of

---

[1] R. H. Thouless, "Psychological Effects of Air Raids," *Nature,* Vol. 148, 1941, pp. 183–185; P. E. Vernon, "Psychological Effects of Air Raids," *J. Abnorm. Soc. Psychol.,* Vol. 36, 1941, pp. 457–476.

[2] E. Glover, "Notes on the Psychological Effects of War Conditions on the Civilian Population," Part III, "The Blitz," *International J. Psychoanal.,* Vol. 23, 1942, pp. 17–37; M. Schmideberg, "Some Observations on Individual Reactions to Air Raids," *International J. Psychoanal.,* Vol 23, 1942, pp. 146–176; Thouless, *loc. cit.*

[3] *Loc. cit.*

[4] *Loc. cit.*

reality-justification because of the poor organization of civilian defense—persisted long after conditions had been greatly improved:

> Control observations made at some of the same areas at a later period, when air defenses and rescue organizations were much more effective, showed that, although diminished in quantity, the quality and to a large extent the direction of these social responses remained unchanged. Resentment was again directed primarily at home authorities; but the onus of criticism was not exclusively upon the lack of care, foresight or effective defense; criticism spread to such matters as the political and military conduct of the war or alleged incapacities of the Government on the domestic and industrial fronts. Even when, as was often the case, such criticisms were already current, they were strongly reinforced after raids.[5]

Other investigations, carried out in many different cities, indicated that people in the heavily raided areas were more critical of the government than those in unbombed areas.[6] As in the case of fear reactions, resentment was most marked among people who had been subjected to a number of heavy raids with long periods of calm in between.

It should be noted that these observations on resentment, reported by British social psychologists and psychiatrists, tend to be at variance with the well-publicized conception of high British morale as presented by many journalists during the Battle of Britain. Nevertheless, there were some correspondents who did not share the popular view; e.g., Ralph Ingersoll[7] claims that if the air blitz had continued for only a few more weeks, it would have produced a serious breakdown in British internal morale. One of the USSBS reports claims that Morale Division investigators who had examined the available evidence on British morale concluded that "its alleged rise was more propaganda than fact."[8] In the absence of systematic data, however, it would be unsafe to assume that the resentment

---

[5] *Ibid.*
[6] Thouless, *loc. cit.*
[7] R. Ingersoll, *Report on England,* Simon and Schuster, Inc., New York, 1940.
[8] USSBS Report, *The Effects of Strategic Bombing on Japanese Morale,* U.S. Government Printing Office, Washington, D.C., 1947.

stimulated by air attacks had any considerable effect on British cohesiveness and morale in general.

In Germany, the heavy air attacks to which civilians were subjected had the effect of increasing aggression against home-front authorities, according to the USSBS morale report:

> Bombing did not stiffen morale. The hate and anger it aroused tended to be directed against the Nazi regime which was blamed for beginning air warfare and for being unable to ward off Allied air attacks. . . .[9]

Typical of the evidence cited is the finding that hostile feelings toward national leaders were related to bombing experience. For example, 62 per cent of the people in unbombed towns expressed trust in the leaders, as against 48 per cent in heavily bombed towns. When describing their air-raid experiences, one out of every eight of the respondents spontaneously told of feeling resentful toward Nazi leaders during a raid (e.g., "I felt we have only the Nazis to thank for this."). Additional evidence that heavy raids on German cities had the effect of increasing resentment against fellow Germans will be cited below.

The USSBS survey of Japanese civilians[10] also indicates that residents of the heavily bombed cities were more likely than those in lightly bombed communities to express critical attitudes toward their leaders and toward fellow citizens. Various captured Japanese documents, as well as the morale-survey results, are cited in support of the conclusion that the Japanese people often directed their resentment for the bombing not at the Americans, as had been expected, but against Japanese government officials, military leaders, and other domestic targets.

HATRED OF THE ENEMY

Although the evidence from England, Germany, and Japan consistently indicates that the bombed population often directed their

---

[9] USSBS Report, *The Effects of Strategic Bombing on German Morale,* Vol. 1, U.S. Government Printing Office, Washington, D.C., 1947.

[10] USSBS, *The Effects of Strategic Bombing on Japanese Morale.*

resentment toward persons and groups within their own country, it remains an open question as to whether this type of reaction in any way *reduced* the amount of hostility directed against the enemy. It is certainly unwarranted to draw the naïve inference that the harrassed survivors of a destructive air assault become so intent upon blaming people in their own country that they begin to develop less enmity toward those who have inflicted the damage. In fact, from what has been reported on the effects of air attacks during World War II, one cannot be at all sure that more resentment was directed against the home front than against the enemy.

Certain statements in the USSBS reports, such as the following, might lead one to surmise that bombing produced relatively little hatred toward the Allies:

> The popular notion that bombing stiffens the resistance of a people finds little confirmation in the facts of German experience. It creates some anger and hatred and at times a temporary increase of determination, but the aggressive emotions of rage and anger have no ready outlet against the enemy. They *tend to be directed against the Nazi leaders* or to be dissipated and replaced by dejection and apathy.[11]

> . . . only a small proportion [of the Japanese people], 8 percent and 10 percent respectively, blamed the United States. Interviews with informed government officials reiterated this point: "The people began to hate the militarists more and more as a result of the bombing. They did not hate the United States but rather the military. Despite the military propaganda, people did not hate the United States nor blame them for the bombing."[12]

When the evidence is examined carefully, however, there appears to be little basis for drawing any definite conclusion about the amount of anti-enemy hostility that was produced by air attacks in Germany and Japan.

Much of the USSBS data on attitudes toward the enemy comes from a single question which provided only a very limited opportunity for indicating aggressive feelings. In the morale interviews, the respondents were simply asked to state whether or not they felt

[11] USSBS, *The Effects of Strategic Bombing on German Morale*, Vol. 1.
[12] USSBS, *The Effects of Strategic Bombing on Japanese Morale*.

that the Allies were responsible for the bombings. In Germany, the proportion who "blamed" the Allies was higher in lightly bombed communities than in unbombed communities. Contrary to the excerpts cited above, this isolated finding suggests that bombing may have stimulated anti-enemy sentiment to some degree. The evidence is ambiguous, however, because the communities that had been subjected to medium or heavy bombing did not differ from unbombed communities. In Japan also, there was no consistent difference between bombed and unbombed communities. Moreover, as is repeatedly emphasized in the USSBS reports, the majority of the people in both countries said that they did not blame the Allies, whereas a relatively high proportion attributed the responsibility to their own leaders.

A qualitative examination of the interview protocols suggests that the answers given to the "responsibility" question might not reliably indicate the way in which resentment was directed. Many respondents seemed to interpret the question in a rather narrow sense, considering only the inadequate defensive strength of their own country without attempting to discuss "moral" blame. Some respondents who said that the enemy was not responsible for the bombings nevertheless verbalized extremely hostile attitudes toward the Allies elsewhere in their interviews. Thus, it is not at all surprising to find in the responses given to another question in the Japanese morale interviews evidence of strongly hostile feelings toward the United States during the war:

> In spite of an understandable tendency to refuse to answer or to hedge on the question, "How did you feel about the Americans during the war?" (one-fourth of the people gave no answer), 40 percent spoke in terms of hatred, anger, or contempt; and in spite of an understandable wish not to offend the conquerors, only 11 percent answered that they had no ill feelings toward the Americans. In about the same ratio, Americans were conceived of as "the enemy"—cruel, barbaric, savage, hateful, sadistic, egotistical.[13]

---

[13] *Ibid.*

Unfortunately, the USSBS report does not include any cross-tabulations for this question in relation to bombing experience from which inferences might have been made as to whether or not such reactions were augmented by air attacks. But it is a noteworthy fact that a substantial proportion of a representative cross section of the population admitted having felt hostile toward Americans.

The actual incidence of anti-enemy sentiment was probably underestimated by the morale-survey findings in both Germany and Japan, since the interviews were conducted by Americans at a time when the two countries were under military occupation. In Germany, for example, the respondents received an official summons to report to a government building where they were interviewed by men in uniform. During this period, military authorities were actively engaged in large-scale investigations of former Nazis and, at the same time, Allied-controlled newspapers and radio stations were emphasizing the theme of Germany's war guilt. Under such conditions, it would be surprising if there was not a certain amount of deliberate distortion, particularly in answering questions concerning attitudes held toward the former "enemy." As is pointed out by the USSBS reports, some of the respondents may have withheld their true feelings because of fear, politeness, or a calculated effort to make a good impression.

There may also have been some unintentional or unconscious distortion due to the fact that the attitudes held at the time of the interview were different from those held during the war. There are indications that during the first months after the war many Japanese and Germans altered their stereotyped conceptions of Americans and genuinely changed their personal opinions with respect to war guilt.

It is apparent that numerous grounds exist for assuming that the bombing attacks against Germany and Japan may have generated much more hostility toward the enemy than is indicated by the USSBS reports. This evaluation does not necessarily imply that there was a corresponding overestimation of the amount of intragroup aggression stimulated by the bombings. On this point the interview evidence is fairly consistent and is well supported by a variety of wartime intelligence reports from inside the two countries. Independent sources of information consistently point up the unexpectedly high incidence of resentment against home-front authorities evoked by Allied air attacks.

If we now attempt to add up all the accumulated evidence from Britain, as well as from Germany and Japan, at least one fairly certain generalization emerges: that anger, resentment, or hostile feelings, in one form or another, were widespread reactions to bombing. Undoubtedly such feelings were frequently focused upon home-front authorities, but there may also have been a simultaneous increase in hatred toward the enemy. Certainly the evidence does not warrant the assumption that bombing reduced the amount of hostility directed against the enemy.

TARGETS OF AGGRESSION

When one examines the morale interview protocols, the case study materials, and various reports on individual reactions to air attack, it becomes apparent that postdisaster aggression was often relatively diffuse and labile. The assumption that the reaction would be disjunctive in character, that resentment would be necessarily directed *either* toward the enemy *or* toward the home front, does not seem to be warranted. Many instances are found of persons who felt angry toward all authorities—their own leaders and the enemy alike. Air-raid victims have been observed to curse indiscriminately, castigating the Prime Minister and the Fuehrer, the Luftwaffe and the R.A.F., the neighborhood air-raid warden who has blocked off an unsafe street, and the aircrew whose bomb did the damage. After the initial reaction of acute anger subsides, there is often a prolonged state of generalized irritability that seems to be capable of being discharged against any readily available target.

Obviously, the bitter protest, animosity, and discontent that arises under conditions of emotional stress cannot be expected to represent dispassionate intellectual judgments concerning the causes of the disaster. It is true that anyone near at hand who is perceived to be in any way responsible for the present distress is apt to become the momentary target of hostile feelings; but this does not mean that when there is no one who can be blamed, or when there is no point in blaming anyone, the feelings will not be there.

Experiences of danger, suffering, and privation are likely to touch off deep, primitive sources of rage and hostility in the human personality. Following any large-scale disaster in peacetime, including unavoidable "natural" catastrophes, a high incidence of resentment and irritability (among those who are directly affected) seems to be a regular occurrence. In this respect, the psychological impact of air war is far from unique. Numerous observations of unexpected peacetime disasters attest to the upsurge of intense aggression that is often manifested in stricken communities, sometimes irrationally directed against the very people who are attempting to mitigate suffering. Psychiatric observers who witnessed the behavior of survivors of the Cocoanut Grove fire shortly after they were brought to a large Boston hospital were impressed by the "furious hostility" directed against physicians, surgeons, and nurses. Among those who had undergone suffering or bereavement in the disaster, heated condemnation and suspicions of foul play were ready to burst forth in all interpersonal contacts.[14]

The intense, diffuse aggression evoked by disaster experiences probably arises, in part, from a temporary breakdown of certain types of social identifications which are essential for maintaining superego restraints. The change in behavior may be attributable to altered anticipations with respect to the "protectiveness" of authority figures and of other sources of emotional support in the community. Clinical observations indicate that in many persons there are unconscious attitudes surviving from early childhood which tend to equate danger, distress, and privation to parental punishment or withdrawal of affection. A latent attitude of this sort may underlie many characteristics of postdisaster behavior, as has been suggested in a report prepared by a group of British psychiatrists on psychological problems of displaced persons:

[14] E. Lindemann, "Symptomatology and Management of Acute Grief," *Am. J. Psychiat.*, Vol. 101, 1944, pp. 141–148.

Food, warmth, and security from physical danger are not merely essential to satisfy bodily needs. Their presence are for most of us a reassuring significance as indication that the world is not entirely against us, and indeed approves of us. When people have undergone real privation in the physical sense, they often tend to feel that this in some way means more than appears on the surface, and to regard experiences of this kind as overwhelming evidence that the world is a permanently hostile place.[15]

If it is true that experiences of danger and privation are commonly interpreted as an act of punishment emanating from parent-surrogates (or from the social environment in general), one can readily understand why wartime disasters would evoke strong feelings of resentment toward home authorities, even though the enemy is consciously recognized to be responsible for inflicting the punishment. Irrespective of the underlying psychodynamics, however, there is one general feature of human aggression which would lead one to expect a certain amount of variability. Whenever a person experiences intense feelings of hostility, whether evoked by danger experiences or by any of the usual frustrations of everyday life, he is in a state of emotional tension that is capable of being discharged in a variety of ways. The target against whom the person directs his hostile thoughts or actions is often selected spontaneously, in a more or less unreasoning way, under the influence of particular circumstances of the moment; extraneous events that have little or nothing to do with the original cause for anger will often cue off one or another of the person's habitual patterns of aggressive behavior. The essential point is that, except in the mentally ill, the content of hostile thoughts depends to a considerable degree on the *situational factors* that are present at the time that aggression is aroused.

Returning specifically to postdisaster behavior, we find that there is some empirical basis for assuming that intragroup aggression does not necessarily occur under all conditions of air attack. That bombing may sometimes *reduce* rather than augment intragroup

---

[15] UNRRA (Special Committee), *Psychological Problems of Displaced Persons*, London, 1945. (Mimeo.)

aggression is suggested by two official intelligence documents dealing with reactions at Karlsruhe and Dortmund.[16] According to
these official German reports, there was a noticeable decline in
quarreling and in "petty" criticism following major air raids. A
similar phenomenon was noted by Schmideberg[17] among her small
group of psychiatric patients: when the blitz started, a number of
them ceased criticizing their own country and displayed a marked
reduction in everyday manifestations of hostile attitudes. She attributes this change to the increased opportunity for symbolic gratifi-
cation of unconscious aggressive impulses. Schmideberg also reports
that among civil defense workers there was often less bickering and
complaining during periods of actual air attack than during the lulls
when the raids had abated.

As yet, very little is known about the conditions under which the
hostile feelings evoked by wartime disasters tend to be directed
toward the enemy, toward the home authorities, toward fellow citizens, or toward "scapegoat" groups. Only a few scattered clues
are to be found in the extensive reports on civilian reactions to wartime disasters. Without attempting to specify all the sources from
which the fragmentary evidence comes, the discussion which follows
will merely summarize the most suggestive leads in the form of
three tentative hypotheses.

1. When air attacks occur with a high degree of regularity, as
an expected and predictable feature of wartime existence, there is
less likelihood of resentment against the enemy than when the attacks
occur irregularly and unexpectedly. In Chapter 6, it was noted
that emotional adaptation breaks down when the attacks become
sporadic or widely spaced. Under the same conditions, along with
the reappearance of fear reactions, there seems to be more hostility toward the enemy. This relationship suggests that one of the
components of emotional adaptation is the development of a "deper-
sonalized" attitude toward wartime disasters—a tendency to take
bombing by the enemy for granted, regarding it in the same way as

---

[16] USSBS, *The Effects of Strategic Bombing on German Morale,* Vol. 1.
[17] *Loc. cit.*

recurrent natural disasters produced by impersonal physical forces. In any case, whenever there is a shift in the expected pattern of bombing—a change from night to day raids, from high explosives to incendiaries, or from regular intervals between raids to irregular intervals—there is likely to be an increase in hostile feelings against the enemy. Presumably this hypothesis would apply to any startling (unconventional) weapon, even if the actual amount of damage were the same as that produced by the kind of bombing that had already been experienced.

It remains uncertain whether the same conditions result in a parallel decline in hostility toward the home-front authorities. Perhaps when people have been expecting violence but are surprised by the way it is inflicted, they become angry, not only at the perpetrators, but also at those responsible for their protection.

2. If there are strong demands for retaliation against the enemy which remain unsatisfied, the target of hostile feelings tends to shift from the enemy to the war leaders in the home country. German intelligence reports indicate that one of the dominant forms of anti-enemy reaction evoked by heavy raids was a vociferous demand for vengeance, a strong desire to see the enemy population suffer in the same way. But when the Luftwaffe, and later on the V-weapons, failed to achieve any spectacular annihilation of British cities, the Nazi government was bitterly criticized for failure to retaliate and for other shortcomings that ordinarily were ignored. Whether the same sort of reaction occurred in England, among the comparatively small group who demanded retaliation, cannot be ascertained from the information that has appeared so far.

3. In a community subjected to air attack, any obvious lack of defensive preparation sets off resentment against domestic authorities. Apparent neglect is undoubtedly one of the major determinants of intragroup animosity.

In England, the most intense exasperation against the home government was observed in districts where there had been a failure to sound a warning signal before the bombs were dropped. In the early days of the air blitz, there was widespread discontent in the bombed cities of England because of inadequate shelters, weak antiaircraft barrages, and defects in the warning system. During the later phases of the war, whenever insufficient protection became apparent, there was a resurgence of indignant protests. Throughout the air war against Germany, similar complaints were by no means rare. According to internal intelligence reports, there was a marked growth of resentment against the German government as the inadequacy of air-raid defenses became more and more apparent. A parallel development evidently occurred among the urban Japanese, despite their deeply ingrained tradition of compliance to political authority. Numerous sources of information indicate that much of the criticism of the home government during the last months of the war was focused on the failure of the Japanese air force to offer any effective resistance to the massive B-29 assaults.

To a large extent the intragroup aggression displayed during World War II may have been due to inadequate defensive preparation for air war. Britain, Germany, and Japan were not well prepared to cope with civil defense problems engendered by the attacks to which their civilians were exposed. Moreover, in the early phases of the war, people of Germany and of Japan were repeatedly told by their leaders that they would be protected against air assaults. When the raids actually began, more false promises were given by the government.[18] This basic condition of physical and psychological unpreparedness may have been the most important single factor in determining the direction of mass aggressive responses.

BOMBING EXPERIENCE IN RELATION TO MORALE

The unfavorable morale effects of heavy air attacks were by no means limited to an increase in intragroup hostility. According to USSBS reports, bombing of civilians was found to have been a major factor, if not the critical factor, in causing a large sector of the population of Japan and of Germany to lose faith in ultimate victory

---

[18] J. Henry, "Initial Reactions to the Americans in Japan," *J. Soc. Issues*, Vol 2, 1946, pp. 19–25; USSBS, *The Effects of Strategic Bombing on German Morale*, Vol. 1; USSBS, *The Effects of Strategic Bombing on Japanese Morale*.

AGGRESSION AND WARTIME MORALE

and to feel unwilling to continue the war.[19] In general, it was among those who had undergone severe air attacks that war weariness was most prevalent.

Before examining specific aspects of bombing experience which give rise to a deterioration in wartime morale, it will be useful to consider once more the relationship between fear and morale. The expectation that some of the major factors which produce a high incidence of severe fear reactions will also give rise to adverse morale effects is borne out by the evidence to be described later, particularly with respect to the importance of the personal involvement factor. Nevertheless, it cannot be assumed a priori that deterioration in wartime morale is determined by exactly the same set of factors which influence fear reactions. Community deprivations and a variety of wartime frustrations, directly or indirectly brought about by air war, often have relatively little effect upon fear reactions but may be extremely important in producing war weariness, lack of faith in national leaders, and other unfavorable morale attitudes. Conversely, certain danger conditions might cause widespread fear without necessarily affecting morale. This is well illustrated by the outbreak of trekking that occurred in London during the spring of 1941. Because they had become so fearful of bombing, thousands of London workers left the target city every evening. Nevertheless, according to Titmuss,[20] there was no apparent decline in their morale. The amount of time they lost from work did not increase, even though their apprehensiveness had mounted to the point where they were devoting considerable energy to precautionary dispersal.

Evidence of a low correlation between fear reactions and morale attitudes is presented in the USSBS report on German morale.[21] The people in bombed cities who reported having experienced the most intense fear during air attacks did not consistently express the most unfavorable morale attitudes. Of thirty-six statistical com-

[19] USSBS, *The Effects of Strategic Bombing on German Morale,* Vol. 1; USSBS, *The Effects of Strategic Bombing on Japanese Morale.*

[20] R. M. Titmuss, *Problems of Social Policy,* His Majesty's Stationery Office, London, 1950.

[21] USSBS, *The Effects of Strategic Bombing on German Morale,* Vol. 1.

parisons between various indices of morale attitudes and emotional reaction to bombing, only three indicated a substantial relationship.

Accordingly, in order to arrive at sound conclusions concerning the morale impact of air warfare, it is essential to re-examine the factors that were found to influence fear reactions and, in addition, to investigate a number of other salient factors.

The first one to be considered is the physical magnitude of the air attack. In the USSBS report on Japanese morale, civilians in heavily bombed towns are compared with those in lightly bombed or unbombed towns with respect to various morale attitudes which they had developed prior to the end of the war.[22] It was found that those who had been subjected to the heaviest attacks were more likely than others to have felt that (1) Japan could not win; (2) their leaders were not conducting the war properly; (3) there was inequality of wartime hardships within Japan; (4) the everyday conduct of their fellow citizens had become rude and offensive; (5) they personally suffered a marked loss in their own working capacity; and (6) they were personally unwilling to continue the war. On many of these morale indices, however, there was only a very slight difference between residents of very heavily bombed towns and residents of less severely bombed towns. The main results of the Japanese survey, therefore, indicate that heavy air raids tend to produce a deterioration in morale attitudes; but the comparisons between bombing strata suggest that the effects may not have been directly proportional to the physical magnitude of the air attack.

These conclusions are strongly supported by parallel results from the USSBS morale survey of German civilians.[23] Willingness to surrender, lack of trust in leaders, and a variety of other unfavorable morale attitudes were found to be more widespread as bomb weight increased. The greatest deterioration in morale attitudes, however, was noted when towns subjected to a total average bombing of about 500 tons were compared with unbombed towns. A further decline was found for towns subjected to an average of 6000 tons.

---

[22] USSBS, *The Effects of Strategic Bombing on Japanese Morale.*

[23] USSBS, *The Effects of Strategic Bombing on German Morale,* Vol. 1.

Those towns which were most frequently and most severely hit (an average of 30,000 tons) showed very little further deterioration and, on certain attitudes (such as lack of trust in leaders), showed a slight improvement.

Parallel findings were obtained when estimates of bomb damage were used as the index of physical magnitude of air attacks. A rapid rise in the proportion of people showing low morale was found when undamaged German cities were compared with those suffering 1 to 19 per cent destruction. The morale attitudes investigated included the following: war weariness; trust in leaders; listening to Allied broadcasts; doubts about Germany's ability to win the war; desire to continue the war; willingness to surrender; and a combined "index of high morale." Most of these morale indices showed a further deterioration when the destruction reached the 20 to 39 per cent level; but from this point on there were only slight and inconsistent changes in morale attitudes as the damage increased.

Apparently there are diminishing returns so far as the morale effects of increased magnitude of air attacks are concerned. The USSBS report on German morale claims that one of the implications of this finding is that the maximum deterioration of morale produced by a given weight of bombs will occur when there is widespread bombing of many different communities with relatively light loads; in other words, the over-all morale effects are less pronounced when heavy loads are concentrated on a limited number of areas. This implication, however, is not satisfactorily established, since the empirical data from which it is derived are ambiguous in a number of respects. The USSBS report points out that a considerable number of people in heavily hit cities were evacuated, including many who had suffered the most severe consequences in the first raids. Such persons were likely to have lower morale than those who remained. Consequently, their subsequent absence from the heavily bombed cities might have obscured the deterioration in morale produced in areas which had been exposed to the heaviest bombing.

There is another reason for questioning the allegedly greater effectiveness of widespread light bombing as against concentrated heavy bombing: comparatively light raids are sometimes found to have had a favorable effect on morale in the target area. A case in point is the Doolittle raid on Tokyo, which resulted in increased popular support for civil defense preparations and enabled Japanese authorities to correct weaknesses in their air defenses.[24] A single saturation raid, on the other hand, may give rise to exaggerated rumors which spread rapidly to other cities, reducing morale among the unbombed population. For example, according to an official German report cited by USSBS investigators, large numbers of persons who survived the heavy raid on Hamburg in the summer of 1943 migrated to other cities and spread grossly exaggerated accounts of the destruction, together with huge overestimates of the number of casualties produced by the raid.

Indirect evidence presented in the USSBS report on German morale suggests that heavy raids often depressed morale in unbombed towns as well as in places actually bombed. People in unbombed communities expected that sooner or later they would be hit and they learned a great deal about the devastating consequences of raids from the evacuees in their midst.[25] A similar spread of unfavorable morale effects apparently occurred among the Japanese:

> Those of the more than 8,500,000 people who left the heavily bombed cities went to live with their friends and relatives in rural and other urban areas scattered throughout Japan, and told of the terrible destruction caused by bombing. Often their experiences, admittedly bad, were exaggerated in the telling. All of this led to widespread rumors about bombing, over which little control could be exercised by the police and government officials. These rumors reached the ears of almost everyone in Japan.[26]

In view of such observations, it is necessary to be skeptical about the alleged morale impact of diffused light bombing. The following alternative hypothesis, presented by MacCurdy, may well prove to be correct:

> The more complete is any destruction the better the story it makes. . . . The untouched have not had their fear reactions

---

[24] USSBS, *The Effects of Strategic Bombing on Japanese Morale.*
[25] USSBS, *The Effects of Strategic Bombing on German Morale,* Vol. 1.
[26] USSBS, *The Effects of Strategic Bombing on Japanese Morale.*

extinguished and rumor will reinforce them. It is sound psychological policy not to hit until you can hit hard.[27]

Another factor which has been singled out in the USSBS report as playing some role in the relationship between morale and physical magnitude of the air attack is an increase in political apathy.[28] The percentage of the population expressing apathetic attitudes was found to be proportional to the increase in bomb tonnage. The failure of the heaviest bombing attacks to produce a further deterioration in morale may have been due, in part, to the fact that the most heavily bombed communities had become more apathetic and hence less critical of the German war effort.

The apparent leveling off of the morale curve under conditions of heaviest bombing noted by USSBS investigators in Germany does not appear to be due to increased aggression directed against the enemy. As was mentioned earlier, resentment against the Allies was found to be slightly greater in bombed towns than in unbombed towns; nevertheless, increased bomb weight did not produce a corresponding increase in hostility toward the enemy. The fact that extremely heavy bombing failed to produce any discernible increase in resentment toward either the enemy or home-front leaders is consistent with the "apathy" hypothesis. When inordinately devastating attacks occur, the feelings of hostility ordinarily evoked by bombing may tend to give way to depression and preoccupation with immediate personal problems.

To the extent that increased apathy was produced by the heaviest raids, the conclusion that there are diminishing returns from increased magnitude of air attack requires modification. Those who have become extremely apathetic may be more "manageable" politically, but their passivity is likely to have serious consequences with respect to both job performance and participation in essential defense activities.

Although there is some evidence that the heaviest air attacks produced increased apathy, there is insufficient evidence for assum-

---

[27] J. T. MacCurdy, *The Structure of Morale*, The Macmillan Company, New York, 1943.

[28] USSBS, *The Effects of Strategic Bombing on German Morale*, Vol. 1.

ing that this tendency accounts fully for the diminishing returns in the relationship between morale attitudes and physical magnitude of air attacks. The factor which appears to be most important is the one which has already been discussed as a critical determinant of emotional reactions to air raids—the personal involvement factor.

PERSONAL INVOLVEMENT

USSBS investigators in Japan carried out an extensive study of morale factors in relation to personal involvement.[29] Those Japanese civilians who had been physically affected by bombs dropped nearby were found to have been more strongly critical toward their home-front and military leaders and to have somewhat lower morale in general than those who were unaffected. Practically none of the people who had undergone aerial bombardment indicated that their experience heightened their desire to carry on the war against the United States.

The USSBS report on Japanese morale mentions that the over-all index of direct bombing experience was more closely related to unfavorable morale attitudes than any of its specific components— such as damage to the home, personal injury—some of which failed to show consistent relationships. Not enough data are reported, however, to evaluate the possibility that some of these results may have failed to support the personal involvement hypothesis.

From an extensive analysis of interview data, the USSBS report on German morale concludes that "morale changes resulting from a given weight of bombs are produced principally by the amount of personal involvement incident to the bombing."[30] Degree of personal involvement was evaluated on the basis of the following direct effects of air raids: personal injury, casualty in the immediate family, property damage, impaired physical health, and sleep disturbances. It was found that the greatest deterioration in morale attitudes occurred among those German civilians who had undergone the

[29] USSBS, *The Effects of Strategic Bombing on Japenese Morale.*
[30] USSBS, *The Effects of Strategic Bombing on German Morale,* Vol. 1.

greatest degree of personal involvement. Bodily injuries apparently had a much more serious effect on morale attitudes than property damage.

It is probable that the diminishing morale effects with increasingly heavy raids can be explained, in large part, by the fact that the amount of serious personal involvement did not increase in proportion to the physical magnitude of the air attack: "This pattern of diminishing increase in personal involvement as bomb weight mounts parallels closely the pattern of change in morale with increasing bomb tonnage."[31] Further analysis of the German morale data revealed that severe personal losses (i.e., being injured, losing a member of the family), even in a lightly raided town, depressed morale so greatly that the added effects of moderate raids were relatively slight.

The findings which have been summarized, together with other relevant evidence presented in the USSBS reports, point to the personal involvement factor as a key determinant of adverse morale effects. Many of the specific psychological hypotheses concerning the relationship between personal involvement and severe fear reactions, previously discussed in Chapters 3 and 6, probably apply equally to the relationship between personal involvement and morale.

COMMUNITY DEPRIVATIONS

In addition to the increased incidence of direct personal involvement produced by a heavy air attack, there is, of course, a considerable amount of disruption in the life of a community. A variety of deprivations are inflicted upon the populace which may affect morale. Only a few investigations of these indirect effects have been reported. Unfortunately, the results do not serve to illuminate the psychological factors involved; they are limited to the mere demonstration that there is some relationship between postdisaster

---

[31] *Ibid.*

deprivations and deterioration in morale attitudes of the populace.

One of the USSBS investigations classified German people according to the amount of deprivation they had suffered during periods of air attack.[32] Inadequate food, lack of transportation, poor sanitary facilities, and the breakdown of public utilities and services (gas, water, electricity, heat supply, etc.) were taken into account. In general, morale was found to decline as the amount of deprivation increased. However, the changes in morale attitudes were not so pronounced or so consistent as was the case with personal involvement.

A separate USSBS study of the effects of disruption of public utilities and services in bombed communities showed that the breakdown of transportation had the most marked effect upon morale. Electricity was next in importance, then water, then gas.[33]

An analysis of captured German documents indicated that in some working-class areas food shortages may have been "the last straw" in leading to overt threats of refusal to work.[34] This observation is in accord with other reports on the effects of severe food shortages. It is this type of deprivation which seems to have the greatest potential for fulminating overt rebellion and countermores behavior. Food shortages have been emphasized as an important factor in the deterioration of behavioral morale among Japanese civilians.[35]

Other forms of deprivation following air raids, such as overwork, "red tape" in connection with securing compensation for air-raid losses, and lack of government assistance for reconstructing homes, have also been described as factors which produce adverse morale effects.[36]

---

[32] Ibid.

[33] USSBS Report, Over-all Report (European War), U.S. Government Printing Office, Washington, D.C., 1945.

[34] USSBS, The Effects of Strategic Bombing on German Morale, Vol. 1.

[35] USSBS, The Effects of Strategic Bombing on Japanese Morale.

[36] J. M. Mackintosh, The War and Mental Health in England, Commonwealth Fund, Division of Publication, New York, 1944; M. Seydewitz, Civil Life in Wartime Germany, The Viking Press, Inc., New York, 1945; USSBS, The Effects of Strategic Bombing on Japanese Morale.

DISRUPTIVE BEHAVIOR FOLLOWING AIR ATTACKS

Although there was a marked deterioration in morale attitudes among the Germans and the Japanese, there appears to have been relatively little disruptive behavior, even during periods of very heavy bombing.[37]

Following air raids, there was an increase in absenteeism and a decrease in working capacity in both Germany and Japan. But it is impossible to make a sound estimate of the extent to which the decline in adequate working performances was due to morale factors as against unavoidable interferences such as injury, sickness, the need to give aid to the family, or disruption of local transportation services.

In England, extensive studies of absenteeism were carried out in many raided areas by the Research and Experiments Department of the Ministry of Home Security.[38] All of their investigations showed that absence from work for personal reasons was directly related to the amount of house damage. No other factor was found to be important. Workers whose houses were completely destroyed lost an average of six days from their jobs. As Titmuss points out, this does not seem to be an excessive amount of time to spend finding a new dwelling and establishing a new household for one's family.

So far as sabotage and other overt acts of opposition are concerned, the scanty evidence from Germany and Japan indicates that under conditions of repressive and coercive control exercised by the totalitarian governments, these obvious forms of subversive activity were extremely rare.[39] Nevertheless, what little subversive activity did occur may have been stimulated to some extent by heavy air attacks. In one USSBS investigation, the principal cities in Germany were ranked in order of amount of subversive behavior (underground activity, sabotage, etc.) on the basis of interviews with local

[37] USSBS, *The Effects of Strategic Bombing on German Morale*, Vol. 1; USSBS, *The Effects of Strategic Bombing on Japanese Morale*.

[38] Titmuss, *op. cit.*

[39] USSBS, *Over-all Report (European War)*; USSBS, *The Effects of Strategic Bombing on German Morale*, Vol. 1; USSBS Report, *The Effects of Strategic Bombing on German Morale*, Vol. 2, U.S. Government Printing Office, Washington, D.C., 1947; USSBS, *The Effects of Strategic Bombing on Japanese Morale*.

leaders and authorities; the cities were also ranked according to the amount of bombing to which the population was exposed.[40] The rank-order correlation was found to be 0.59. While this finding indicates that subversive activity is related to bombing, the question remains as to whether or not air raids played a causal role in producing subversive activity. One of the USSBS reports states that the heavier bomb loads were dropped on the larger cities, in which there was a disproportionately high percentage of anti-Nazi elements.[41] Consequently, the correlation may be due, at least in part, to the spurious factor of city size.

The relationship between bomb load and minor forms of disruptive behavior (hoarding, black-market activity, riots, looting, delinquency, and petty crimes) was studied in the same way. The rank-order correlation with magnitude of bombing loads was found to be 0.44, but once again the size of the city is an uncontrolled variable. It was the larger cities which received the heaviest bomb loads, and the larger cities are also characterized by a comparatively high incidence of disruptive and criminal behavior even when there are no air raids.[42]

Although the quantitative results just described are ambiguous, they do lend some weight to the following hypothesis, which is also supported by other evidence: air raids are a contributing factor in the wartime increase of petty criminal activity (looting, black-market activity, and juvenile delinquency).

On the basis of criminality statistics from four metropolitan areas in Germany, the USSBS report on German morale concludes that looting was the type of crime most likely to occur following air raids.[43] There was a marked increase in looting and thefts in all four areas during a period of increased air activity.

Supplementary information derived from police records as well as from interviews of various local officials throughout Germany provide additional support for the conclusion that petty crimes

[40] USSBS, *The Effects of Strategic Bombing on German Morale*, Vol. 2.
[41] *Ibid.*
[42] USSBS, *The Effects of Strategic Bombing on German Morale*, Vol. 1.
[43] *Ibid.*

increased following air attacks.[44] A number of prosecuting attorneys and local leaders asserted that looting and similar offenses occurred even among "decent" middle-class people who ordinarily do not engage in such behavior. Several informants stated that people who suffered personal loss or severe deprivation from air raids tended to develop an attitude of indifference toward the law and toward government regulations in general.

Some fragmentary evidence from Britain points to a similar tendency. In summarizing the observations reported by a group of psychologists, Vernon[45] states that during periods of air attack a "good deal of what might be termed 'vagrancy' arises, accompanied by a deterioration in people's sanitary and moral standards." Schmideberg[46] asserts that looting often occurred following air raids: "I was told that Civil Defense workers very frequently took things on the spur of the moment, for which they often had no use at all." She claims that guilt feelings were sometimes counteracted by the rationalization that the looted objects would be lost to their owners anyhow, or by the feeling that amid so much destruction the small objects taken were of very little importance. Schmideberg offers the hypothesis that the increased tendency to indulge in petty criminal acts is due to a particular unconscious attitude toward bombings, namely, the feeling that the authorities have failed to prevent the unlawful behavior of the bombs and therefore one need not be so concerned about his personal conformity to the law.

As yet there is insufficient evidence to warrant acceptance of this hypothesis. But the available observations on minor forms of disruptive behavior, together with the material on hostility toward leaders presented earlier in this chapter, does appear to bear out Schmideberg's[47] descriptive generalization: "Destruction on a big scale encouraged an expression of aggression on a smaller scale."

---

[44] USSBS Report, *The Effect of Bombing on Health and Medical Care in Germany*, U.S. Government Printing Office, Washington, D.C., 1945; USSBS, *The Effects of Strategic Bombing on German Morale*, Vol. 2.

[45] *Loc. cit.*

[46] *Loc. cit.*

[47] *Ibid.*

SUMMARY

1. During World War II, aggressive attitudes and resentment aroused by air attacks frequently tended to be directed against the home authorities or toward fellow citizens, rather than exclusively toward the enemy. Although the evidence from England, Germany, and Japan is consistent in indicating a tendency toward intragroup aggression following air attacks, it remains an open question as to whether this tendency in any way reduced the amount of hostility directed against the enemy. There are some observations which suggest that bombing may evoke an over-all increase in the general level of hostility directed against both the enemy and the home country.

2. A heightening of intragroup aggression does not necessarily occur under all conditions of air attack. Among the factors that may influence the way in which aggressive feelings will be channelized are (a) regularity and predictability of the raids; (b) failure to retaliate; and (c) visible lack of defensive preparation. To a large extent, the intragroup hostility generated among the bombed populations during World War II may have been due to poor physical and psychological preparation for air war.

3. Deterioration in wartime morale attitudes occurred most markedly in those communities which had been exposed to the heaviest bombing attacks. The incidence of unfavorable morale attitudes, however, was not directly proportional to the physical magnitude of the air attacks. Detailed data from Germany indicate that the sharpest drop in morale occurred in towns subjected to relatively light raids— an average bomb load of 500 tons, or less than 20 per cent destruction. With increased bomb loads or with increased destructiveness, there were diminishing returns with respect to adverse morale effects.

4. It is unsafe to infer that the maximum deterioration of morale produced by a given weight of bombs will occur when there are widespread light bombing attacks on many different communities rather than when very heavy loads are concentrated upon a few communities. There is some evidence which suggests that the converse may be true. For example, a single saturation raid may give rise to

exaggerated rumors that are spread to other cities, reducing morale among the unbombed population as well as in the target area.

5. Evidence from Germany indicates that as the physical magnitude of air attacks increases, there is a corresponding increase in the incidence of apathetic attitudes. The apparent diminishing returns in the morale effects of increasingly heavy bombings may be due, in part, to the fact that the most heavily bombed people tend to become apathetic and hence less assertive in their criticisms of the war effort.

6. As in the case of severe fear reactions, the increase in unfavorable morale attitudes produced by an air attack is due, in large part, to the amount of personal involvement incident to the bombing. The greatest deterioration in morale occurs among those who suffer most directly from the destructive impact of the raid (personal injury, casualties in the immediate family, home or property damage, etc.). It is probable that the diminishing morale effects with increasingly heavy raids can be explained, to some extent, by the fact that the incidence of serious personal involvement does not increase in proportion to the physical magnitude of the air attack.

7. In general, morale attitudes tend to decline when air raids produce severe community deprivations. Inadequate food supplies, poor sanitary facilities, lack of transportation, and a breakdown of public utilities and services may have some effect upon morale. Food shortages following air raids seem more likely than any other type of community deprivation to induce overt rebellion and countermores behavior.

8. During World War II, sabotage and active opposition to the war effort rarely occurred, even during periods of extremely heavy bombing. The scanty evidence available suggests that air raids may have produced, at most, only a very slight increase in overt subversive activity.

9. Air raids gave rise to an increase in absenteeism and a decrease in working capacity. It is impossible to estimate the extent to which the decline in adequate working performances was due to psychological disturbances and morale factors as against obvious interferences such as physical injury or lack of transportation.

10. Air raids are probably an important contributing factor in the wartime increase of certain forms of petty criminal activity: looting, black-marketeering, and juvenile delinquency.

11. In general, the accumulated evidence on aggressive reactions and wartime morale is consistent with the psychodynamic principle that disaster experiences produce a temporary loss of internalized ("superego") restraints, resulting from altered personal anticipations concerning the protectiveness of the social environment.

CHAPTER 8
ADJUSTMENT MECHANISMS

Mental breakdown, panic, and mass demoralization—the triple psychological threat that dominated so much of the thinking in official quarters—rarely materialized during World War II. The bombed populations of Europe and Asia stood up to bombing far better than had been anticipated. From the preceding chapters, it is apparent that the dire predictions made by many self-styled "experts" on mass behavior failed to take account of the psychological stamina of the average civilian. Bombing had little effect on the incidence of chronic mental disorder; outbreaks of mass panic were rare; behavioral morale was maintained at a relatively high level. Although emotional shock did occur on a sizeable scale, most cases recovered fairly rapidly.

By and large, the effective emotional stresses of air war arose primarily from direct personal exposure to the destructive impact of bombing. The strong apprehensiveness that was originally aroused by the first air raids tended to subside with successive exposures to air attack. In the absence of any traumatic bombing experience, there was a gradual development of emotional adaptation.

How were people able to avoid becoming overwhelmed by anxiety? What were the psychological processes that enabled them to keep going in the face of recurrent threats of extreme danger, without becoming emotionally disorganized?

With advancing knowledge of the human personality, we begin to see in dim outline the adjustive capacities of normal adults. Complex mental mechanisms have been discerned which help to explain the way people meet the acute disappointments, frustrations, and interpersonal threats that arise in everyday life. But what mechanisms are set in motion when people find themselves facing inescapable signs that point to the threat of physical danger, annihilation,

153

or mutilation? At present, despite an abundance of theoretical speculation, there is a dearth of reliable empirical data. Relatively little is known concerning the basic psychodynamics of danger reactions.

In the absence of intensive, systematic investigations, it is worth while to examine carefully the sporadic observations of spontaneous changes in behavior which were displayed by people exposed to air attack. Such observations provide tentative empirical support for a number of plausible hypotheses about adjustment mechanisms.

Six types of spontaneous behavior patterns have been consistently noted in the civilian population during World War II, particularly among the British:

1. Curiosity about bomb damage,
2. Discrimination of danger cues,
3. Increased communicativeness,
4. Avoidance of social isolation,
5. Fatalistic attitudes, and
6. Taboos, rituals, and superstitions.

In the sections which follow, each of these behavior patterns will be discussed in terms of its possible role in facilitating emotional adjustment. A more general formulation of the psychodynamics of disaster reactions will be presented in the section on "Feelings of Invulnerability," page 171.

CURIOSITY ABOUT BOMB DAMAGE

One form of behavior consistently noted among the British was a high degree of curiosity about what happens during air attacks, focusing especially on the damage produced.[1] On the day after a night raid, groups of "curious-minded" people were observed mak-

---

[1] E. Glover, "Notes on the Psychological Effects of War Conditions on the Civilian Population," Part III, "The Blitz," *International J. Psychoanal.*, Vol. 23, 1942, pp. 17–37; I. Matte, "Observations of the English in Wartime," *J. Nervous Ment. Disease*, Vol. 97, 1943, pp. 447–463; M. Schmideberg, "Some Observations on Individual Reactions to Air Raids," *International J. Psychoanal.*, Vol. 23, 1942, pp. 146–176; P. E. Vernon, "Psychological Effects of Air Raids," *J. Abnorm. Soc. Psychol.*, Vol. 36, 1941, pp. 457–476.

ing extensive tours of damaged areas. At times the police were obliged to issue appeals to the public to desist from "sightseeing" because they interfered with rescue work and created traffic problems.[2] Similar forms of curiosity have been noted following air raids in Spain and in other countries.[3]

Glover suggests that the motivation is an "appetite for sensations" and a desire "to celebrate at the same time their comparatively uneventful escape from the trials of the night before."[4] He states that positive pleasure in scenes of devastation was by no means rare.

Although sightseeing may have provided vicarious gratifications of aggressive impulses, it is likely that other motives were also involved. Matte[5] claims that the facial expressions of people, as they stood in front of damaged buildings, seemed to reflect an emotional "working-through" of air-raid experiences, perhaps resulting in increased understanding and acceptance of the realities of the threat. One of his hypotheses is that viewing the destruction stimulates a *gradual* realization of the possibilities of one's own death and thereby minimizes the traumatic effects of a *sudden* confrontation with the realities of air-raid dangers. At the same time, the heightened awareness of the danger may have enhanced self-respect ("I am able to take it."). Among those who were initially inclined to ignore or to deny the existence of danger, the adjustment process described by Matte might be expected to have considerable value as a form of psychological preparation for withstanding the emotional impact of increasingly severe air attacks. Some of the persons who were initially apprehensive also might have benefited from viewing bomb damage. Numerous observers mention that there was considerable relief among the British when they discovered what the raids were really like. They had expected the attacks to be far more devastating than they actually turned out to be.[6] The satisfaction of curiosity about the destruction produced by a raid is probably one

---

[2] Schmideberg, *loc. cit.*

[3] G. Cox, "Eyewitness in Madrid," *Harper's Magazine*, Vol. 175, 1937, pp. 27–30.

[4] Glover, *loc. cit.*

[5] Matte, *loc. cit.*

[6] Glover, *loc. cit.*; J. T. MacCurdy, *The Structure of Morale*, The Macmillan Company, New York, 1943; Schmideberg, *loc. cit.*; Vernon, *loc. cit.*

of the ways in which grossly exaggerated expectations and fantasies are brought into line with reality.

Viewing the destruction following a raid would not be expected to have a favorable effect on emotional adjustment, however, if the damage turned out to be far worse than was expected. As will be described later, witnessing extensive destruction and seeing maimed bodies may produce severe and persistent fear reactions.

Curiosity about the events occurring while the air raid is actually in progress may also contribute indirectly to emotional adjustment by focusing attention upon discriminable signs of danger. Selective attention to air-raid stimuli may have facilitated the learning process described in the next section.

DISCRIMINATION OF DANGER CUES

It is well known that ground troops become habituated to the intense stimuli of combat. Green recruits frequently react indiscriminately to all loud noises, but, with subsequent experience, they develop a keen sensitivity to auditory and visual cues. They learn to take automatic protective action only to specific signs of danger, such as the sound of an approaching shell, and remain indifferent to all other stimuli.

Evidently, the same process occurs among civilians who are exposed to repeated air assaults. At the beginning of the air blitz, British civilians often interpreted all the loud noises of a raid as signs of enemy action. But later on they became less disturbed by the noises when they learned to distinguish the engine sounds of enemy bombers from those of British fighter planes and bomb explosions from antiaircraft fire.[7] Among Spanish civilians also, according to Langdon-Davies, there was a high degree of initial confusion of air-raid sounds, resulting in extremely exaggerated notions about the magnitude of the enemy's air assault during the first air raids.[8]

---

[7] Glover, *loc. cit.;* Vernon, *loc. cit.*

[8] J. Langdon-Davies, *Air Raid,* George Routledge & Sons, Ltd., London, 1938.

Whenever the ability to discriminate the activities of the enemy from those of the defending forces develops during successive exposure to air raids, it probably serves to reduce anxiety in a number of ways. First, there is likely to be less frequent arousal of anxiety by the noises which are "false alarms." Thus, the ability to distinguish genuine signs of danger from other stimuli reduces the number of occasions on which fear will arise. Secondly, it facilitates the acquisition of anxiety-reducing actions that can become cued to specific danger signals, e.g., throwing oneself under a table when bombs are heard falling nearby. Thirdly, there is less likelihood of overestimating the size of the enemy's attacking force or of misjudging the amount of destruction which is being produced. Fourthly, antiaircraft fire and other defensive activities during an air attack may become inherently reassuring signs, after they can be correctly recognized. Glover points out that even when antiaircraft barrages did not succeed in bringing down planes during the London blitz, the loud noise of frequent salvos produced a profound psychological reassurance. When the London defenses were augmented, the first heavy barrage produced widespread elation except in those who were unable to discriminate between a shell burst and a bomb explosion; in such cases discomfort was increased by an obsessional concern with the interpretation of the loud sounds.[9]

Although successful differentiation of various air-raid sounds may generally have the effect of reducing anxiety, it should be recognized that reliance on the presence of reassuring cues may, under certain conditions, result in increased anxiety. Glover describes one occasion when British night fighters were used in place of heavy antiaircraft fire with a consequent depressing effect upon the populace because of the "weak" barrages.[10] By and large, however, it appears that development of the ability to discriminate the noises associated with danger from those produced by defensive operations tended to have a beneficial psychological effect among British civilians.

[9] Glover, *loc. cit.*
[10] *Ibid.*

INCREASED COMMUNICATIVENESS

Another form of behavior which may have played some role in facilitating emotional adaptation to air raids was the increase in interpersonal communications which occurred, especially during the initial phases of the air war. British observers noted that in the early days of the blitz the civilian population was in a highly talkative mood.[11] People would engage in frequent conversations about their air-raid experiences with casual acquaintances and with neighbors to whom they had never spoken before. Boasting, laughing, and joking about unfortunate incidents, as well as more serious discussions about the raids, were widely prevalent among the residents in bombed cities.

Vernon[12] describes the heightened communicativeness as a form of release of emotional tension. He regards the decline in communicativeness after successive experiences of raids as an indication of decreased tension, with a corresponding decline in the need for an outlet. The spontaneous verbalization of air-raid anxieties may have had a beneficial cathartic effect, according to psychiatric observations. People who admitted they were afraid and reacted to the bombs without suppressing their fear were reported to have been less disturbed than others.[13] Woltmann claims that the open admission of fear on the part of American soldiers in England during the robot-bomb attacks resulted in increased awareness that everyone else was going through the same emotional experience, sharing the same feelings; this may have augmented group identification and permitted less stable personalities to express their fears in a socially acceptable manner without incurring ridicule or shame.[14]

The relief from emotional tension produced by verbalizing apprehensions to others is also emphasized by Schmideberg.[15] She asserts that some people are helped merely by being told that their fears

---

[11] Glover, *loc. cit.*; Matte, *loc. cit.*; Schmideberg, *loc. cit.*; Vernon, *loc. cit.*

[12] *Loc. cit.*

[13] Schmideberg, *loc. cit.*

[14] A. G. Woltmann, "Life on a Target," *Am. J. Orthopsychiat.*, Vol. 15, 1945, pp. 172–177.

[15] *Loc. cit.*

are justified; others gain emotional support by eliciting assurances that the danger is not so great as had been thought. In general, according to Schmideberg, the heightened communicativeness during the early period of the blitz was motivated by a need for help or comfort from others.

To some extent, communicativeness about air-raid experiences may have formed a part of the general pattern of increased sociability, to be discussed in the next section of this chapter. It should be noted, however, that increased gregariousness was characteristic of the entire period of the air blitz, whereas the type of communicativeness under discussion diminished markedly after the first few air raids.[16] It is probable, therefore, that different motivations were involved. The verbalization of air-raid anxieties may have functioned largely as a form of spontaneous psychotherapy, motivated by a need for emotional support from others during the initial period of adjustment to air attacks. It may have facilitated personal adjustment in much the same way that supportive therapy provides relief to a person who is facing intense environmental stress.

One may hypothesize that therapeutic mechanisms, such as the following, come into play when air-raid anxieties are verbalized to other persons: (1) reduction of secondary anxieties about one's own fear reactions by the realization that others share the same "weakness"; (2) correction of one's own exaggerated fantasies from hearing reality-oriented statements made by others who do not share the same fantasies; (3) acquisition of new anxiety-reducing symbolic responses learned from conversation with others who express reassuring ideas; or (4) identification with (or positive transference toward) stronger members of the community who are permissive listeners and who display a calm, courageous demeanor.

AVOIDANCE OF SOCIAL ISOLATION

It is a popularly accepted psychological principle that most people in our culture are able to face a dangerous situation better if they

---

[16] Glover, *loc. cit.*; Schmideberg, *loc. cit.*; Vernon, *loc. cit.*

are with others than if they are alone. That this principle holds true for air raids is indicated by many reports on the reactions of British civilians.[17] Although the local governments of numerous communities in England encouraged the use of individual family shelters, these were frequently neglected in favor of communal ones, sometimes forcing a complete change in official policy.[18] A summary report on a conference of psychologists, who discussed the problem of shelters, alludes to some evidence that people who went to collective underground shelters felt more secure than those in private surface shelters: they obtained more sleep, gained weight, and lost anxiety symptoms which had developed at home.[19]

Although the primary motive for going to communal shelters may have been the increased sense of security provided by an air-raid shelter in which large numbers of persons were present, additional social motives also came into play. Numerous observers report that the enjoyment of the "night life" found in large shelters was a major factor in preferring them to the more solitary home life.[20]

> There were shelters of every type: for the young and for the elderly, the respectable and the gay, the poor and the upper classes. In some respects, they were a little like clubs or like cafes on the continent, with their better opportunities for contact.[21]

Public shelters were not equally attractive to all sectors of the British population. In general, it was people in the "lower" classes who went to the large communal shelters in London.[22] Englishmen of higher socio-economic class, who characteristically cherish their privacy, often made arrangements to spend their nights in private homes outside the city. Nevertheless, a sizeable proportion of the

---

[17] R. D. Gillespie, *Psychological Effects of War on Citizen and Soldier,* W. W. Norton & Company, New York, 1942; Glover, *loc. cit.;* Schmideberg, *loc. cit.;* R. H. Thouless, "Psychological Effects of Air Raids," *Nature,* Vol. 148, 1941, pp. 183–185; Vernon, *loc. cit.;* Woltmann, *loc. cit.*

[18] E. D. Idle, *War over West Ham,* Faber & Faber, Ltd., London, 1943; Thouless, *loc. cit.*

[19] Thouless, *loc. cit.*

[20] Gillespie, *op. cit.;* Glover, *loc. cit.;* Schmideberg, *loc. cit.*

[21] Schmideberg, *loc. cit.*

[22] Idle, *op. cit.;* Schmideberg, *loc. cit.;* Vernon, *loc. cit.*

population in the threatened urban areas displayed a strong preference for participating in communal shelter life.

At a time when normal social activities in the city were greatly reduced, the opportunity for making new contacts under conditions where many of the usual conventions and social barriers were removed probably contributed to the attractiveness of shelter life. It is likely that the social features of shelter life were not only inherently gratifying, but they provided many people with an excellent form of distraction during the dangerous periods of air attack, thereby lessening their feelings of anxiety. Thus, both the physical presence of other people in the communal shelters and the opportunity to engage in normal social activity may have contributed to an increased sense of security.

There is some evidence which suggests that similar social factors may have been operative among the German population as well as among the English. The USSBS report on German morale calls attention to the fact that as the housing shortage became more and more acute in heavily bombed areas, the population was subjected to the discomforts of excessive crowding in shelters and in private residences; yet the interviews of German civilians reveal that there was relatively little dissatisfaction or resentment on this score.[23]

Although being in a communal shelter may serve to reduce fear reactions during air attacks, there may be some unfavorable effects as well. Schmideberg[24] points out that many people were more affected by a mild raid when in anxious company than by a more severe one when alone or among cheerful companions. But she claims that as a rule those who were most frightened "drew strength from the fearlessness of others."

Langdon-Davies[25] warns that a large crowd is likely to succumb to panic if it has nothing to do but wait. He urges that if there must be a crowd under difficult circumstances, it should be a working crowd, not a waiting crowd. As was pointed out in Chapter 6,

---

[23] USSBS Report, *The Effects of Strategic Bombing on German Morale,* Vol. 1, U.S. Government Printing Office, Washington, D.C., 1947.

[24] *Loc. cit.*

[25] *Op. cit.*

group activity may contribute to the reduction of fear; nevertheless, there is little empirical basis for Langdon-Davies' emphasis
on the danger of panic among a "waiting crowd." Although at the
beginning of the war some British A.R.P. authorities feared that
herding people together during air raids would be courting the social
danger of panic, the literature on air-raid reactions is singularly
lacking in reference to mass panic in communal shelters. On the
basis of reports he collected from a group of psychologists, Vernon
draws the following conclusion:

> Actually, suggestion almost always seems to have operated favor-
> ably. The influence of a few confident and unconcerned individ-
> uals in a group, or the cheerfulness of a warden or shelter marshal,
> calms those who are inclined to be nervous.[26]

Nevertheless, there may be unfavorable consequences of a different sort arising from the policy of permitting large numbers of
people to be a "waiting crowd" rather than a "working crowd."
Gillespie[27] claims that unless shelter life is well organized, there
may be mass apathy arising from boredom. Thouless[28] cites examples of widespread apathetic attitudes and lack of spontaneous
activity among shelterers until a suitable leader was selected. He
specifies that a necessary condition for gaining the psychological
benefits to be derived from shelter life was the "transfer of authority
attitudes from within the family to the officials of shelter groups."
It is probable that feelings of security are most effectively maintained
if the group has a leader who is able to organize collective activities
skillfully and who possesses the personal characteristics which make
it easy for people to accept him as a protective authority figure.

The fear-reducing value of being in the company of others and
of having a shelter leader who is admired and respected may arise,
in part, from a more basic psychological need. When faced with the
possibility of personal annihilation, most people experience a persistent need for emotional reassurance from others. The avoidance
of social isolation forms part of an over-all pattern of increased

---

[26] Vernon, *loc. cit.*
[27] *Op. cit.*
[28] *Loc. cit.*

group cohesiveness in times of wartime dangers, the manifestations of which include not only increased social participation within the community, but also augmented identification with the nation as a whole and readiness to devote oneself to a common cause under the authoritative guidance of idealized national leaders. Subjectively, the sense of "belonging" to protective primary and secondary groups enhances the feeling that one is valued by others, that one is worthy of affection, and that help will be available in case of need.

Schmideberg,[29] in commenting on the fact that many people could not bear the idea of being alone in an air raid, asserts that although their attitude was often rationalized as a fear that there might be nobody to rescue them, the underlying motive was an "infantile fear of being left alone." The hypothesis implied by this statement might be formulated as follows: During childhood, the presence of others is frequently associated with safety and satisfaction, whereas being left alone is often a punishment for being "bad" or entails actual deprivation and thus becomes a sign for loss of parental love. In times of high potential danger, there may be a reactivation of child-hood fears of being abandoned and, consequently, an increased need for reassurance that others will be available, particularly those upon whom one is emotionally dependent.

Certain of the observations reported by Glover,[30] based on the clinical findings of a group of psychoanalysts, offer some tentative support for this hypothesis. Among the factors found to be condu-cive to anxiety during the blitz were previous evacuation or break-up of the family, lack of friends, and social isolation. Psychoanalytic observations of transference reactions are highly consistent with the "fear of abandonment" hypothesis:

> . . . it would appear that the most notable reaction, or rather absence of reaction, of analytical patients was due for the greatest part to the effective *continuance of the transference situation*. The fact that the analyst remained to carry on his practice seemed in many cases to be decisive. . . . Change of analyst owing to war conditions provoked much more reaction than usual. Even if the change was unavoidable there was a marked resentment against

[29] *Loc. cit.*
[30] *Loc. cit.*

the "desertion." Indeed the situation was almost exactly comparable to that noted by Anna Freud and Dorothy Burlingham, viz.,
that *disruption of the family bond* was the most traumatic factor
for children living under air-raid conditions.[31]

That adults reacted strongly to separation from members of their
own families is clearly indicated by some of the material presented
in the USSBS report on German morale. Interviews of both
evacuees and members of their families left behind showed that
although they were generally satisfied with the new billets, there
was a profound lack of satisfaction with the evacuation program;
this was due principally to homesickness and the difficulties of ad-
justing to family separation. According to official German reports,
unauthorized family reunions occurred on a large scale. When the
Nazi Party attempted to prevent the illegal return of evacuees, "the
countermeasures . . . provoked a storm of resistance, the effects of
which spread right to the front lines."[32]

The need for being reassured that one has not been deserted by
important persons in the community is implied by the fact that shop
assistants, parkkeepers, and others who were compelled to remain
in London displayed immense pleasure whenever they saw well-
known persons—such as their wealthy customers or their neighborhood doctors—who had remained in the city despite having the
economic means and the opportunity to leave. Schmideberg[33] describes such reactions, together with augmented fears, which occur
when persons of prestige (or persons upon whom one is emotionally
dependent) leave the danger area.

From clinical observations of her psychoanalytic patients, Schmideberg discerned the following psychological mechanism: In order to
avoid feeling resentful or contemptuous toward such persons for
their abandonment, excuses are made for them, stressing the dangers
of remaining in the area; having thus magnified the dangers, one's
fear increases.

Other mechanisms might also be involved. For example, in some
cases abandonment on the part of parent-surrogates might be uncon-

[31] *Ibid.*
[32] USSBS, *The Effects of Strategic Bombing on German Morale,* Vol. 1.
[33] *Loc. cit.*

sciously interpreted as a form of punishment, stimulating guilt feelings and anxiety about further punishment. Reactivation of childhood attitudes might also tend to invest persons of prestige with an aura of protectiveness ("nothing bad will happen to me so long as they are around") and consequently there may be a marked decrease in feelings of invulnerability when they leave.

Whether or not the "fear of abandonment" hypothesis proves to be correct, the various observations which have been cited definitely imply that those who remain in a community subjected to air attacks tend to feel more anxious when members of their families, friends, and people with prestige in the community are evacuated. The high valuation placed upon the reassuring presence of significant persons in the community is another manifestation of the strong need for affiliation with others which is so frequently aroused in times of danger.

FATALISTIC ATTITUDES

The behavior patterns that have been discussed so far generally did not grossly conflict with correct appraisals of physical and social reality, even though the underlying motivations may have been rooted, to some extent, in the unconscious residues of childhood emotional conditioning. In fact, adjustment to the threat of wartime disasters often seems to have been facilitated in ways that were conducive to sound mental health—elimination of unrealistic beliefs, correction of exaggerated fantasies, enhancement of interpersonal rapport, and social participation in community activities. We turn now to some of the adjustment mechanisms which were much less rational in character, but which, nevertheless, may have played an important role in alleviating feelings of anxiety.

On the basis of reports from eight psychologists located in different parts of England, Vernon[34] states that fatalism was fairly widespread among the bombed populace and sometimes prevented ordinary precautions from being taken. Typical of the fatalistic attitudes

---

[34] Loc. cit.

expressed by the British was the following: "If your name is on a bomb it will get you, otherwise not, so why worry?"

In Germany, many people in the bombed cities were in a condition of "absolute fatalism," according to an official intelligence report which describes the effects of the heavy bombing attacks in the summer of 1944.[35] The dominant feeling, we are told, was that "one cannot change what's going on, therefore there is no point in worrying about it." Another official German report states that among the bombed populace of Frankfort there was a sizeable group who were neither optimistic nor pessimistic, but rather "take absolutely no position and in a sort of fatalism await what will happen."[36]

Similar attitudes apparently occurred among the bombed urban population of Japan. According to the USSBS report on Japanese morale, the following statement by a Tokyo correspondent was typical of the feelings of resignation expressed by a majority of the respondents who said that their fears decreased with continued air raids:

> There was no reason to become more frightened. Each raid was as bad as the next and there was nothing I could do. Everything would be destroyed anyway. Fate would decide who was next.[37]

The increased religious interest noted among the British during the air blitz was probably related to the development of fatalistic attitudes.[38] Reliance on a benevolent parental image in the form of a deity may have been, in itself, a profound source of reassurance. Chance, logic, and statistical odds afford little opportunity for mitigation, whereas one can hope to influence a supernatural deity by means of ritual and prayer.

Among those who were lacking in sincere religious faith, there may have been a similar tendency to fall back upon a personified image of "fate" which, as in childhood, could be magically influenced in a variety of ways. Latent attitudes of this kind may have helped to alleviate feelings of helplessness, as is implied by the apparent attempts at propitiation to be described in the next section.

[35] USSBS, *The Effects of Strategic Bombing on German Morale,* Vol. 1.
[36] *Ibid.*
[37] USSBS, *The Effects of Strategic Bombing on Japanese Morale.*
[38] S. Laird and W. Graebner, *Conversation in London,* William Morrow & Company, Inc., New York, 1942; Schmideberg, *loc. cit.*

TABOOS, RITUALS, AND SUPERSTITIONS

Among people exposed to the threat of bombing, compulsive-like avoidances, rituals, and superstitious practices were fairly common. This type of self-imposed behavior often appeared to be an instrumental attempt to prevent suffering and retaliation.

In Japan, superstitious nostrums were extremely popular.[39] For example, Western clothes were often worn because it was widely believed that they would ensure the person against air raids. Rubbing an onion on one's head or placing a pickled onion on top of a bowl of rice and beans were common Japanese recipes for protection from bombs.

Magical thinking of this kind was by no means limited to the Orient. Although somewhat more subtle in character, there were similar superstitious practices and rituals in Western European countries. Among the British, for example, gas masks or other pieces of personal equipment were often worn as talismans, with the expectation that they would prevent the occurrence of air raids.[40] Even ordinary precautions like going to a shelter or trekking sometimes acquired a magical, obsessive flavor.

> For certain persons, going to the shelters was like going to Church. They went as good children, doing what they had been told, and hoping that as a reward for their obedience they would be protected.[41]

> . . . from beginning to end of the blitz, the realistic (safety) factor in choosing shelters or in refusing to take cover was heavily overlaid by irrational reactions or rationalizations. Ordinarily sane and sensible people of every class could be heard expounding "systems" based on superstitions, feelings of omnipotence, and every possible illogicality. These systems were sometimes modified in the light of raid experiences, but this modification seldom amounted to more than changing one form of superstition for another.[42]

---

[39] USSBS, *The Effects of Strategic Bombing on Japanese Morale.*
[40] Matte, *loc. cit.;* J. Strachey, *Digging for Mrs. Miller,* Random House, New York, 1941.
[41] Schmideberg, *loc. cit.*
[42] Glover, *loc. cit.*

Personal precautionary measures were sometimes practiced with little regard for their actual effectiveness: when planes were expected, some people moved about very quietly in the way one does when attempting to avoid attracting attention to oneself.[43] In London, numerous individuals appeared to adhere obsessively to certain self-imposed formulae: "If I do this [or refrain from doing that] there will be a raid." A wide variety of verbal taboos was also observed. In target cities, some people would not permit certain ideas to be expressed, such as "there has not been a warning tonight," on the grounds that it would tempt Providence.[44] In unbombed towns, there was a similar taboo against making any comments about the air blitz elsewhere for fear that talking about what happened to other cities might bring it to them too.[45]

Many of the rituals and taboos appear to be defenses not only against anticipatory anxiety, but also against feelings of guilt. From her psychoanalytic practice, Schmideberg noted an increased tendency to deny pleasures to oneself as an attempt to propitiate fate: the raids would come as punishment if one engaged in "bad" behavior or if one indulged in highly pleasurable activities.[46] In this connection, Schmideberg calls attention to the fact that asceticism was fairly frequent among Londoners, whereas the opposite attitude of "eat, drink and be merry" was extremely rare. This point is borne out by the reports of numerous psychologists which are summarized by Vernon.[47] According to Matte, there was a momentary lifting of social conventions only at the beginning of the war—girls were seen on the streets wearing slacks; attendance increased at music halls and night clubs; popular forms of entertainment became somewhat more risqué. But this temporary loosening of social restrictions quickly gave way to the opposite reaction.[48]

It is well known that crisis situations sometimes stimulate hedonistic self-indulgences, either as a form of psychological narcosis or as

---

[43] Vernon, *loc. cit.*

[44] *Ibid.*

[45] Schmideberg, *loc. cit.*

[46] *Ibid.*

[47] *Loc. cit.*

[48] Matte, *loc. cit.*

an attempt to take advantage of the opportunity for securing pleasures that are normally forbidden. But when the crisis involves impending danger, there are powerful conscience reactions which may inhibit the loosening of moral standards. In Germany, one of the effects of bombing was an increase in feelings of guilt.[49] According to various informants, many religious people regarded the air attacks as a divine retribution for Germany's sins; others felt that Germany was being punished for having initiated the bombing of civilians. Such attitudes may have been fairly widespread during the period when German cities were subjected to bombing, since the Nazi authorities found it necessary to adopt specific propaganda and control measures designed to counteract the notion of collective guilt. Many of the rituals and avoidances which occurred among the British seem to be attempts to deal with the threat of external danger as if it were a threat of punishment for wrongdoing.

People who are facing the prospect of illness, unemployment, or any extreme form of deprivation will often attempt to ward off the danger by making sure that they do not deserve to be punished. Evidently, this was one of the dominant types of reaction among the bombed population of Britain. Stringent self-control and efforts to live up to purified moral standards seem to have submerged incipient hedonistic strivings. Perhaps the latter tendencies are likely to break through only under special conditions, such as those found in European displaced persons' camps after the defeat of Germany, where an uprooted population without reliable or respected leadership was facing an uncertain social and economic future after having already undergone intense suffering and hardship. At any rate, the increased asceticism noted in England, together with the observations of high behavioral conformity in Germany and Japan (described in the preceding chapter), implies that hedonistic abandonment of social restraints rarely occurred among people faced with the threat of air attacks. Certainly there are no indications that common moral standards were swept away in any mass outbreaks of greed, lust, or violence. On the contrary, what little evidence we have consistently

---

[49] USSBS, *The Effects of Strategic Bombing on German Morale*, Vol. 1.

points to fairly rigid conformity to social norms and increased efforts to adhere to conventional morality.

In wartime England there were other manifestations of adherence to socially conventional behavior in addition to the mildly obsessional taboos against "bad" behavior. Many people in London and other target cities preoccupied themselves with mundane matters of everyday (peacetime) life, such as going shopping or having a permanent wave. In general, there was a widespread attempt to maintain the pretense of "business as usual," a scrupulous insistence upon engaging in normal prewar activities.[50]

This clinging to peacetime normality often seems to have resembled the compulsive-like rituals and avoidances described earlier. In some instances, the refusal to deviate from the prewar way of life was so extreme as to augment the social problems arising from wartime exigencies. For example, in one provincial town, home-owners initially were completely indifferent toward people who were bombed out, refusing to take them into their homes; after several raids, however, homeless persons were no longer denied hospitality.[51]

In recounting such incidents, Schmideberg again emphasizes the mechanism of denial: The initial selfishness was essentially a refusal to acknowledge the danger; only after the belief that "nothing has changed" could no longer be maintained did they willingly begin to make sacrifices. In general, according to Schmideberg, the reassuring effect of "business-as-usual" behavior is due to the denial that one is likely to be affected by the new threat of danger, which is implied by acting as if nothing has changed.

Such behavior is probably motivated primarily by the reduction of anticipatory anxiety which comes from avoiding the signs of impending danger, but it may also represent the same sort of attempt at mitigation that underlies the more obvious avoidances discussed above. Perhaps there is a more or less unconscious expectation that refusal to take account of the threat will help to stave it off.

---

[50] Matte, *loc. cit.;* Schmideberg, *loc. cit.;* R. M. Titmuss, *Problems of Social Policy,* His Majesty's Stationery Office, London, 1950.

[51] Schmideberg, *loc. cit.*

In the next section, which deals primarily with the psychodynamics of emotional adaptation, additional hypotheses on adjustment mechanisms will be presented, some of which apply to superstitions, avoidances, and rituals and to other types of adjustive behavior patterns which have been discussed in the preceding sections.

FEELINGS OF INVULNERABILITY

In Chapter 6, we have seen that much of the available evidence tends to support MacCurdy's theory: It is primarily the experience of being a near-miss that produces emotional disturbance, and, in the absence of such an experience, fear reactions tend to diminish during a series of air attacks.[52] As yet there is little empirical evidence that helps to explain the dynamics of near-miss and remote-miss reactions.

It is probable that when a near-miss experience involves exposure to primary fear-eliciting stimuli, such as sharp pain, sudden loss of physical support, or excessively loud noises, conditioned fear reactions are acquired in the same way that such reactions are produced in experimental studies of emotional conditioning. In other words, certain of the intense and terrifying stimuli occurring during a near-miss experience may act as powerful reinforcements for building up a conditioned fear response to previously neutral air-raid cues. When the latter stimuli occur during safe (remote-miss) experiences, on the other hand, emotional relief would tend to become the prepotent reaction and fear would be extinguished.

In addition to the simple (nonverbal) conditioned response mechanism, complex symbolic processes may also be involved. Thoughts, expectations, and fantasies play an important role in determining the amount of anxiety experienced, even without any exposure to real danger. When intense fear reactions are acquired, they are not at all limited to situations containing specific cues which were temporally contiguous with the terrifying stimuli, but are manifested in a variety

---

[52] MacCurdy, *op. cit.*

of situations which do not necessarily resemble the original danger episode.

The writings of clinical psychoanalysts contain some suggestive material on mediating processes. Although based to some extent on interviews with a small number of persons who were studied intensively, their hypotheses are somewhat speculative in character. Nevertheless, they call attention to certain basic features of emotional adaptation which may help to explain some of the main phenomena of personal adjustment to wartime dangers.

According to numerous independent clinical observers, persons who face the prospect of recurrent air raids tend to develop spontaneously a variety of psychological defenses, all of which have the effect of reducing anticipatory anxieties. In preceding sections, reliance on talismans, magical rituals to ward off the danger, and other common adjustment mechanisms have been described. In addition to these, a variety of less overt personal defenses against anxiety is likely to develop. Complete denial of the impending danger, implicit trust in the protectiveness of the authorities, reversion to an infantile belief in personal omnipotence—these and other unconscious or partially conscious defense mechanisms have been described as typical modes of adjustment during a period of impending air attack.[53] Irrespective of the particular modes of defense a person employs, however, the net effect may be an illusion of personal invulnerability. According to Rado,[54] this is a "general human tendency" in situations of potential danger.

This hypothesis is consistent with the views of MacCurdy, who emphasizes the reinforcement of the feeling of invulnerability which occurs among the remote-miss group. He cites the following illustrative testimony as an extreme instance of the typical belief in personal invulnerability which counteracts fearful anticipations of personal destruction:

---

[53] Glover, loc. cit.; MacCurdy, op. cit.; J. Rickman, "Panic and Air-raid Precautions," Lancet, Vol. 1, 1938, pp. 1291–1295; Schmideberg, loc. cit.

[54] S. Rado, "Pathodynamics and Treatment of Traumatic War Neurosis (Traumataphobia)," Psychosomat. Med., Vol. 43, 1942, pp. 362–368.

"When the first siren sounded I took my children to our dugout in the garden and I was quite certain we were all going to be killed. Then the all-clear went without anything having happened. Ever since we came out of the dugout I have felt sure nothing would ever hurt us."[55]

The remote-miss survivor, after emerging unscathed from an air raid, may be able to reduce his anxieties by saying to himself, "God protects me" or "So long as I go to the shelter in the basement I am completely safe," or by reassuring himself with a variety of similar self-promulgated promises of security against subsequent danger. Some of these reassurances may be realistic and others may be purely magical. But so long as no real danger is encountered, this entire set of symbolic responses may be highly effective in evoking expectations of personal safety despite danger, which is essentially what is referred to by the term "feelings of invulnerability."

The unique emotional consequences of near-miss experiences immediately become apparent if one assumes that large numbers of civilians manage to control their fears of death, of injury, and of personal loss from air attacks primarily by developing, to varying degrees of inner conviction, a feeling of personal invulnerability. If this assumption is correct, it would be expected that one of the most critical sources of prolonged anxiety reactions and of reduced capacity for controlling emotional responses in subsequent air raids would be those narrow-escape experiences during which people feel that they are no longer protected from the impact of danger. It is only among the remote-miss group that Kris's hypothesis would be expected to hold true: "Real danger is, on the average, faced better than vague apprehensions; the fantastic or imaginary elements of anxiety are deflated by the impact of the concrete situation."[56] Among the near-miss group, on the other hand, latent anticipatory fears would be strongly reinforced because the experience of being unprotected from danger would tend to break down feelings of invulnerability which had previously been effective.

---

[55] MacCurdy, *op. cit.*

[56] E. Kris, "Morale in Germany," *Am. J. Sociology,* Vol. 47, 1941, pp. 452–461.

This is essentially the hypothesis that Schmideberg presents in her comprehensive report on psychoanalytic observations of individual reactions to air raids:

> A person's conviction that nothing can happen to him is sometimes painfully shattered if something actually *does* happen to him. In that case the shock of being hurt or losing his property will be intensified by the shock of realizing his vulnerability.[57]

Probably it is not so much the awareness of facing immediate danger as the feeling of helplessness which is the critical psychological factor. Having once had the experience of being powerless to avert the direct physical impact of an explosion, the survivor may no longer be able to convince himself that he will be safe in subsequent raids because he is unable to dispel from his fantasies, and from his image of future raids, the memory of that harrowing experience in which he was helpless.

> . . . there are two quite separable factors involved in the making of a danger into a "narrow escape." The first is that the immediate, unreflective action taken in the emergency is effective or ineffective. In the former case the emergency ends and the incident is closed without any emotional reaction and, probably, leaves no memory behind it except perhaps for a few minutes. In the latter case the ineffective action lingers in the memory and there are thoughts about what would have happened if the final scramble had been unsuccessful. So, for the production of fear there must be not merely danger but ineffective action to meet it. . . .[58]

Clinical case studies of combat personnel who developed diffuse anxiety symptoms also call attention to the loss of feelings of invulnerability once a person has experienced the reality of being powerless in the face of actual danger. Quantitative data relevant to the relationship between combat neurosis and feelings of invulnerability were obtained from a study of fliers.[59] A questionnaire was administered to 284 aircrew officers, all of whom had developed acute

---

[57] Schmideberg, *loc. cit.*

[58] MacCurdy, *op. cit.*

[59] R. R. Grinker, *et al.*, "A Study of Psychological Predisposition to the Development of Operational Fatigue," *Am. J. Orthopsychiat.*, Vol. 16, 1946, pp. 191–214.

neurotic symptoms during or immediately after their tour of combat duty. Their responses were compared with those of a control group of 260 aircrew officers who had undergone similar combat experiences but without developing symptoms. To a direct question about feelings of invulnerability ("Did you feel that while others might be hurt or killed it couldn't happen to you?"), positive responses were given by only a small percentage of the patient group, as compared with the control group. The statistically significant difference between the two groups, as well as subgroup comparisons, indicates that neurotic breakdown under conditions of danger is associated with the absence or loss of feelings of invulnerability.

Further research along these lines, with more refined methods, is needed in order to explain why some people are able to undergo harrowing danger experiences without any pronounced effect, whereas others develop neurotic symptoms. The *kind* of invulnerability defense that a person builds up during the period preceding exposure to danger may have important consequences. For example, one of the unfavorable effects of relying on magical beliefs, according to Rickman, is that when danger is actually experienced, "the magical remedy against danger may be suddenly doubted."[60] Perhaps those people who develop an illusion of invulnerability based on total denial of impending danger ("nothing at all unpleasant will happen to me") are more likely to be traumatized than those who develop a more limited sense of invulnerability, keyed to the reality of the threat ("I might be bombed out, but I will survive"). Qualitative differences of this kind might be due to personality predispositions or to situational factors, such as official communications which predict that there will be or will not be any real danger.

Although some psychological defenses may prove to be "healthier" in the long run than others, there may nevertheless be a general tendency for all of them to be impaired, to some degree, as a result of any experience which makes the person sharply aware of his personal vulnerability. If this type of awareness is assumed to be a critical psychological factor in breaking down a person's emotional resistance, it would be expected that certain other types of disaster

---

[60] Rickman, *loc. cit.*

experiences, in addition to direct personal involvement, would have the general effect of producing severe and persistent fear reactions. Loss of loved ones and loss of other objects with which the person feels identified, even when the destruction has occurred while he was far off, may have the effect of destroying his feelings of invulnerability. The discovery that the air attack has killed or injured a close relative or friend or that it has destroyed his home may produce a degree of disturbance which goes far beyond the usual emotional response to such loss. By making him consciously realize, for the first time, that he might be overwhelmed by a similar fate, such experiences may reduce the person's capacity for defending himself against air-raid anxiety. Witnessing unexpected, extensive destruction and seeing maimed bodies after the raid is over may have a similar effect upon many persons.

> An Air Raid Warden told me that for a time he did not mind the raids, but that when he had seen the dead bodies of the victims and witnessed some gruesome incidents he visualized the reality of the situation and became thoroughly alarmed. The majority of the population only saw damaged buildings and bomb-craters, heard of people being killed or injured but did not actually see the casualties. Thus many lived through the blitz without fully appreciating the realities of the situation.[61]

Thus, a strong reinforcement of fear reactions would tend to occur not only among those who experience a narrow escape, but also among those who lose members of their families, whose homes or property has been destroyed, or who happen to observe, after the raid is over, the carnage it produced.

The importance of these additional factors in eliciting profound emotional disturbances is also implied by psychoanalytic hypotheses on guilt reactions, which may be reformulated as follows. Perception of damage and injury to others may evoke a feeling of profound relief: "I'm glad it happened to him and not to me." This initial response may be followed by feelings of guilt and fear of punishment for having permitted oneself to indulge in such a narcissistic thought. If the person toward whom the invidious contrast is di-

---

[61] Schmideberg, loc. cit.

rected has been a friend or a member of the family, and particularly if there had been strongly ambivalent feelings toward him, the survivor's guilt reaction may be reinforced by regressive thought processes, e.g., "because I was glad it happened, I am responsible for it." The heightened guilt may increase the survivor's fear of punishment, giving rise to the apprehensive feeling that "next time it will be my turn." Hence, in some cases, the spontaneous reaction to the perception of damage to others may produce guilt feelings which, in turn, may form the basis for heightened air-raid anxiety. In others who experience this type of reaction, the predominant feeling may be that "I deserve to be punished." This subjective response may be responsible, in part, for the excessive docility, apathy, and other depressive symptoms observed among air-raid victims.[62]

None of the hypotheses which have been discussed precludes the possibility that some persons who are burdened with strong guilt feelings might react to the punishment of a near-miss experience with a decrease in emotional tension. From the available observations, however, it appears that the guilt-relief reaction occurred relatively infrequently among air-raid victims. Although Vernon[63] and Harrisson[64] report that there were some people who seemed to think that after one narrow escape they had "had their share" and would be safe in the future, there is no indication in the literature that optimistic reactions, relief, or elation occurred among any sizeable proportion of near-miss survivors.

SUMMARY

1. Various behavior patterns have been described which developed spontaneously during periods of air attack, particularly among the

---

[62] Glover, *loc. cit.*; T. Harrisson, "Obscure Nervous Effects of Air Raids," *Brit. Med. J.*, Vol. 1, 1941, pp. 573–574 and 832; A. M. Meerloo, *Aftermath of Peace*, International Universities Press, New York, 1946; Schmideberg, *loc. cit.*; USSBS Report, *The Effect of Bombing on Health and Medical Care in Germany*, U.S. Government Printing Office, Washington, D.C., 1945; USSBS Report, *The Effects of Bombing on Health and Medical Services in Japan*, U.S. Government Printing Office, Washington, D.C., 1947; Vernon, *loc. cit.*

[63] *Loc. cit.*

[64] *Loc. cit.*

British: curiosity about bomb damage, discrimination of danger cues during air attacks, increased communicativeness, avoidance of social isolation, fatalistic attitudes, taboos, rituals, and superstitions. These spontaneous reactions probably facilitate emotional adjustment to the threat of danger. For example, sightseeing in damaged areas following a raid may enable some people to "work through" a gradual emotional acceptance of the possibility of their own death, resulting in increased capacity to withstand the traumatic effects of a sudden confrontation with the realities of air-raid dangers; curiosity about the damage produced by a raid might also have a corrective effect upon exaggerated anticipations and fantasies about the destructiveness of air attacks, producing emotional relief and more realistic expectations.

2. During periods of high potential danger from air attacks, the presence of other persons appears to be a major source of emotional security. There are some indications that people in communal shelters felt somewhat less anxious during air raids than those who were in private shelters. In any case, many people displayed a strong preference for the former. One of the beneficial features of communal shelters may be the opportunity they offer for engaging in enjoyable and distracting forms of social activity. Those who remain in a community subjected to air raids tend to feel more anxious when members of their families, friends, and persons with prestige in the community are evacuated. The general avoidance of social isolation reflects a heightened need for the reassuring company of others, perhaps because of a reactivation of childhood fears of being abandoned.

3. Fatalistic attitudes, superstitions, and various nonrational practices which develop during periods of air attack probably represent attempts to ward off anxiety by denying the possibility of impending danger. Certain of the compulsive-like rituals and taboos may also be defenses against feelings of guilt—an effort to mitigate the threat of punishment by rigorous avoidance of wrongdoing.

4. Many of the personal defenses that minimize or deny the threat of real danger appear to be effective in reducing anxiety primarily because they serve to build up an illusion of personal invulnerability.

This hypothesis provides a plausible basis for explaining the dynamics of remote-miss and near-miss reactions. The critical disaster experiences which give rise to acute and persistent anxiety reactions are probably those which evoke a feeling of being powerless to avert actual danger. Narrow escapes from danger, loss of persons or objects with whom one feels identified, and witnessing maimed bodies may have the effect of shattering the entire set of psychological defenses (anxiety-reducing symbolic responses) involved in maintaining the expectation of personal invulnerability.

PART III
PSYCHOLOGICAL ASPECTS
OF
CIVILIAN DEFENSE

CHAPTER 9
GENERAL ASSUMPTIONS

It is generally recognized that if at some future time large-scale
A-bomb attacks are launched against the United States, the psychological impact upon the American people might prove to be as shattering as the physical devastation. Moreover, long before any wartime disaster occurs, there may be a high degree of *psychological*
vulnerability to the A-bomb threat. As the attention of the American
public becomes focused more and more upon international tensions
and the possibility of another war, the realization that our cities may
be destroyed and that millions of American civilians may be killed
or injured can in itself become a powerful stimulus capable of arousing intense emotional reactions. Any effort on the part of the Government to reduce our vulnerability to A-bomb attacks will require
careful planning in terms of the human factors involved.

For the purposes of research planning, it is necessary to take
account of the probable "shape of things to come" in order to fore-
cast the *specific* psychological problems which are likely to arise.
Only by drawing as realistic a picture as possible—sketching in the
social, political, and physical realities of anticipated future situations—will it be possible to set up research plans geared to the
future needs of civilian defense operations. As a preliminary step in
this direction, a number of reports have been prepared by the author
during the past three years in an attempt to describe some of the

major areas in which research in the human sciences is likely to be most needed. The essential points contained in those reports form the substance of the present chapter and those which follow. In Part III, various features of a full-scale civil defense program are delineated in order to bring into focus the emotional reactions which may be anticipated. The discussion of each topic is limited mainly to those problems on which adequate research might reasonably be expected to contribute to the reduction of *psychological* vulnerability to the A-bomb threat.

The forecasts and comments concerning civil defense activities are limited solely to *anti-A-bomb* preparations. Obviously, in practice, it is necessary to have a coordinated defense program which covers all major types of anticipated attack. *The material in Part III, however, is not intended as a guide for actual civilian defense policies, but rather as an initial survey of research needs in the human sciences.* Although confined to problems engendered by the threat of A-bomb attacks, the material to be presented contains many hypotheses and research proposals which might apply equally to any type of large-scale explosion and perhaps to other types of wartime disasters as well. Nevertheless, the limitations on the scope of the discussion should be borne in mind from the outset; additional material will be needed to point up the research needs arising from the special problems posed by the H-bomb, radiation poisons, biological warfare, and other threats to our national security.

In order to anticipate mass reactions, it is necessary to make a number of assumptions about the characteristics of future situations in which the American people will find themselves. Three general assumptions on which Part III is based are as follows:

1. That a potential enemy of the United States will possess a large stockpile of A-bombs and effective carriers for delivering them against targets within the United States so that, in the event of war, our cities and industries will be threatened;

2. That there will be a "cold-war" period of at least two or three years during which this country will have an opportunity to carry out defensive measures in order to minimize our vulnerability to A-bomb attacks;

3. That the A-bomb threat will not be eliminated by the development of any special counter-A-bomb weapon or by an effective international agreement for the control of atomic energy.

These assumptions are not intended as forecasts, but rather as plausible contingencies to be taken into account in planning research oriented toward future defense needs. The problems to be discussed are to be regarded as *potential* ones which will probably arise *if* the three general conditions just specified actually do occur.

Throughout the four chapters of Part III, an effort has been made to specify additional assumptions whenever they are not obviously implied by the context. Many of the assumptions to be introduced deal with official requests and demands which will be made upon the American public as necessary steps for reducing damage from A-bomb explosions. Although there is a large amount of literature on the nature of atomic warfare, very little unclassified information is available on specific protective measures which our Government is planning to institute. Since the discussion is based solely on unclassified information, it has been necessary to make a number of inferences from official and quasi-official statements.

Often, in order to indicate the kinds of hypotheses which may warrant investigation, a number of speculative suggestions about possible solutions to psychological problems are discussed—solutions which appear to have some degree of plausibility in the light of present knowledge. It should be borne in mind that some of these suggestions involve controversial issues on which little agreement will be found among social scientists until further research has been done. In general, the speculative material to be presented is intended primarily to provide a concrete picture of the difficulties which *might* have to be taken into account as a result of the A-bomb threat. Revisions of the forecasts will undoubtedly be necessary as more information becomes available on the probable nature of future atomic warfare and on the defensive measures which might be required.

CHAPTER 10

PROBLEMS OF DISASTER CONTROL

MALADAPTIVE AND DISRUPTIVE BEHAVIOR

In the event of an atomic disaster, even those survivors who are not psychiatric casualties will be in an extremely aroused emotional state. The mere perception of the vast devastation and the large number of dead and dying people will produce a terrifying effect upon almost everyone in the disaster area. Those who escape any direct experience of the explosion in and around the target city will be intensely disturbed not only by the appalling sights about them, but by the gnawing suspense of not knowing the fate of their families and close friends. Many people will also be extremely apprehensive about the possibility that they may have been exposed to lethal amounts of radiation. For many hours and perhaps days, people in and around the disaster area might fear that their lives are endangered by lingering radiation products or by other invisible toxic agents.

All of these sources of emotional stress have the effect of temporarily reducing the capacity for rational forethought and of greatly increasing the likelihood of excited, impulsive, maladaptive behavior. Under the disorganizing influence of acute anxiety, many uninjured survivors might fail to participate in essential rescue and relief activities. There may be a widespread tendency to neglect the precautions necessary for avoiding exposure to contaminated food, water, and household supplies. In attempting to escape from the raging fires, large crowds might congregate in areas which offer far less protection than other places of safety which are just as accessible. In Hiroshima, it will be recalled, hundreds of people sought refuge near a river and as the fire pressed closer the crowd began to push forward, forcing helpless injured people who were on the bank into the water. How can maladaptive responses of this kind be prevented?

There are two main ways that emotional control can be fostered: *preparatory education* preceding the outbreak of atomic attacks and *on-the-spot communication* from an authoritative source immediately following an atomic explosion. These two methods, if skillfully employed, could markedly reduce the incidence of disorganized behavior.

Civil defense authorities have repeatedly called attention to the need for a mass educational program designed to minimize casualties by preparing people to act intelligently in an atomic disaster. Such a program can serve essential psychological functions as well. In Chapter 12, which is devoted exclusively to problems of educational preparation, it will be seen that there are essential psychological needs that can be met if a concerted effort is made to reach all sectors of the population in every potential target area. The primary purpose would be to teach the most elementary knowledge necessary for appropriate behavior in an atomic disaster, with emphasis upon *what the dangers are* and a corresponding set of *do's and don'ts.* Insofar as people comprehend a danger situation and know some of the ways and means of coping with it, they are less likely to be overwhelmed by the feeling that they are trapped, abandoned, and unable to do anything to save themselves.[1]

Even if the vast majority of people acquire the necessary information in advance, they may fail to use it at the very time when it is most needed. Prior training is often forgotten, at least temporarily, when people are actually confronted by danger. Prompt authoritative communications may prove to be essential in order to reduce emotional excitement so that people can make use of the preparation they have been given.

Perhaps the most effective device would be a calm, familiar, authoritative voice giving reassurance and directions as to what should be done. Such a device might be readily available if there were an intact public-address system in every major target area. It might be possible to install an underground communication system which will withstand the damage from an A-bomb explosion. Radio-

---

[1] See the discussion of the feeling of helplessness given in Chap. 8.

broadcasting units mounted on trucks might prove to be far less effective because they would not reach the disaster area early enough to prevent confusion. Mobile broadcasting units mounted on airplanes, on the other hand, might be a highly effective adjunct to the local broadcasting system and might even be a satisfactory substitute for it.

In any case, each potential disaster area probably would benefit considerably from having a public-address system which is ready to be put into operation immediately after an explosion. It could be a tremendous asset from the standpoint of disaster control in a variety of ways. Some of the most critical instructions cannot be given in advance because they depend on too many unknown variables. For example, only the message center is likely to have access to the intelligence reports and technical details necessary for sound judgment as to when the survivors should evacuate the disaster area: if the atomic bomb has burst high in the air, survivors should wait only a few minutes and then get out of the area as quickly as possible so as to escape from the rapidly spreading fires; if the maneuvers of the attacking force raise the possibility that a second bomb may be dropped on the same city, people who survive the first explosion should dash for the best possible shelter close at hand and remain there as long as the threat persists; if the explosion is near the ground or in shallow water, survivors should remain indoors for many hours because of the lingering radiation hazards.[2]

An intact public-address system would make it possible to give the survivors in each neighborhood prompt instructions (based on coordinated information from air and ground observers) about appropriate actions to take. They could be told when to remain in their homes, when to evacuate, and where to go. They could be reminded of the precautions they had already been trained to take. In neighborhoods where there is little danger present, they could be urged to aid in rescue work and in other forms of disaster relief. But above all, a familiar voice emanating from "headquarters" might

---

[2] J. O. Hirschfelder, "The Effects of Atomic Weapons," *Bull. Atomic Scientists,* Vol. 6, August–September, 1950, p. 236.

be extremely effective in reducing confusion and emotional excitement, particularly if reassuring announcements are given about the arrival of rescue and relief teams.

There is probably little danger that a metropolitan public-address system of the kind suggested could be exploited by the enemy for purposes of psychological warfare. Appropriate code methods for putting the system into operation could easily limit its operation to designated civil defense officials who would be scattered among various communities in the defense region.

If engineering research solves the problem of devising a public broadcasting system that will withstand an A-bomb explosion, and if such a system becomes an integral part of our civil defense program, it will be worth while to investigate various means for maximizing its effectiveness. For example, it would probably be useful to give the metropolitan population some prior experience with it. The loudness, tonal quality, and location of the sound source should be sufficiently familiar so that it will be readily recognized in an emergency situation. If there are practice air-raid alerts, it might be effective to employ the public broadcasting system to announce the all-clear signal, so that the radio voice will be expected following an air attack and will be associated with the emotional relief that accompanies termination of the threat.

Returning to the general problem of preventing maladaptive and disruptive behavior, there are a few obvious implications of the extensive findings described in the preceding chapters which should be made explicit. On the basis of the available evidence on the conditions under which severe fear reactions occur, it is possible to specify the types of disaster events created by an atomic explosion that are likely to evoke acute symptoms. The most extreme forms of emotional disturbance are to be expected among survivors who undergo direct personal involvement, such as (1) being knocked down, violently shaken, buried beneath debris; (2) being injured by fire or by blast effects; (3) narrowly escaping from burning buildings; or (4) witnessing the death of a member of the immediate family.

If the population of a target city is unprotected, the vast majority would undergo traumatizing experiences of personal involvement in an A-bomb attack. It should be recognized, therefore, that the adequacy of civil defense preparations designed to increase the physical safety of the population have a direct bearing on the emotional impact of an atomic disaster. If a target city cannot be warned and evacuated before an attack is launched, if the residents cannot reach adequate shelters, and if well-trained civil defense teams are not available to carry out the essential operations of disaster control, the devastating consequences cannot be counted solely in terms of the inordinate toll of dead and injured people. The less adequate the physical protection of the population, the higher the incidence of emotional shock and disorganized behavior. In an atomic war, such reactions on a mass scale might become a crucial deterrent to national recovery.[3]

To a very large extent, the *morale* of the survivors of an A-bomb attack will be determined by the effectiveness of civil defense measures. During the air blitz against England it became increasingly apparent that the availability of welfare and relief facilities can play a decisive role in minimizing feelings of bitterness, suspicion, free-floating hostility, and other adverse morale effects.

> The rest centres, the feeding schemes, the casualty services, the compensation grants, and the whole apparatus of the post-raid services both official and voluntary occupied this role of absorbing shock. They took the edge off the calamaties of damage and destruction; they could not prevent, but they helped to reduce, a great deal of distress. Like the civil defence services, these schemes encourage people to feel that they were not forgotten. They render much less likely (in William James' phrase) an "unguaranteed existence," with all its anxieties, its corruptions and its psychological maladies.[4]

---

[3] The reassurance value and morale-building effects of various military defense measures are greatly in need of detailed study. It should be clear to the reader that the present study has not gone into military plans for active and passive defense of potential targets.

[4] R. M. Titmuss, *Problems of Social Policy,* His Majesty's Stationery Office, London, 1950.

If aid and relief measures are not well planned, or if they cannot be put into operation because of multiple A-bomb attacks, an extremely critical situation is to be expected. Following the emergency evacuation of a bombed city, homeless survivors would be widely scattered over a large region; thousands of half-starved people would be wandering about for a long period, seeking their lost families or friends; there would be frantic competition for the scarce quantities of food, water, and medical supplies available. Many groups of survivors who received no help from people in outlying communities might become extremely hostile and attempt to obtain shelter or supplies by force and violence.

Obviously, if this type of social disorganization occurs following an atomic disaster, a prolonged period of demoralization is to be expected. On the other hand, if the essential needs of the survivors are well provided for and if there is sound community leadership, there is every reason to expect that within a short period of time the vast majority will willingly participate in reconstruction work and make a fairly adequate adjustment to the deprivational situation.

For purposes of efficient organization of a community following a major disaster, it will be useful to know which types of persons can be relied on and which types are most likely to be uncooperative and demoralized. Field studies of peacetime disasters in the United States might provide a rich source of empirical material for predicting *who* will be an asset or a liability during the reconstruction phase. (Specific research proposals for investigating predispositional and situational factors have been presented in a separate report.)

If the survivors cannot be permitted to return to the target city for a prolonged period because of the presence of lingering radioactivity, there are likely to be serious problems of social reorganization which may have an unfavorable effect upon behavioral morale. Deprived of the opportunity to return to their own community and to engage in its reconstruction, they are likely to become depressed, apathetic, and deeply pessimistic about their future. To meet this contingency, special plans are required to provide for either prompt relocation of the community on a new site or the rapid absorption of survivors into other existing communities.

PSYCHIATRIC CASUALTIES

Although many survivors suffering from acute anxiety and other symptoms of emotional shock will probably recover spontaneously after the danger has subsided, there will probably be a sizeable minority whose incapacitating symptoms will persist for many weeks.[5] Those who fail to recover promptly will not be capable of productive work and will have a demoralizing effect upon others in the community. There is little likelihood that skilled psychiatric aid will be available for the majority of psychiatric casualties, but it may be possible to speed up recovery by adopting sound policies of rehabilitation. This is a special problem on which applied psychiatric research may be needed. For example, it might prove to be effective to arrange for temporary rest camps in which a therapeutic atmosphere will be maintained, so that those who are too disturbed to return to productive activity will have an opportunity to recuperate.

At present there are insufficient numbers of trained psychiatrists, psychotherapists, and psychiatric social workers to meet the current needs of the American population. In fact, this is one of the most critical shortages of skilled personnel we face. As the Armed Forces are expanded, more and more psychiatrists will be drained from the civilian supply, making the shortage all the more acute. It is generally recognized that full-scale civil defense preparation will require a considerable increase in the number of trained personnel capable of handling survivors with acute emotional disturbances. One of the obvious steps which has been proposed is to offer special inducements to attract more women into psychiatry and into the allied fields of clinical psychology and psychiatric social work, e.g., by offering free training to all qualified candidates.

Even with a greatly expanded professional training program, it will be necessary to rely on nonprofessional civil defense workers if emotional shock cases are to be given the barest minimum of adequate handling. Rescue and relief teams will come into contact with emotional shock cases, displaced persons, children who have lost their families, and bereaved parents. These civil defense work-

[5] See Chap. 5.

ers should be given at least sufficient instruction so as to avoid aggravating psychological disturbances. Cheerful chatter and ill-advised efforts to "buck up" depressed persons generally do more harm than good; crude attempts at reassurance often evoke intense feelings of humiliation and sometimes have a shattering effect upon persons who are desperately struggling to maintain their self-control.

One of the essential needs of civil defense is the development of effective psychiatric first-aid techniques to be applied on a mass scale. A considerable amount of research will be necessary, however, in order to work out psychiatrically sound procedures designed to speed up emotional recovery. As "psychiatric first aid" implies, the procedures should be designed for the emergency handling or care of acutely disturbed adults and children, under conditions where skilled psychiatric aid will not be available (immediately). The techniques should be simple enough—and safe enough—so that they can be taught to *nonprofessional* defense workers who will be in a position to apply them promptly to large numbers of disaster victims. In addition, special methods of brief individual treatment (to be administered by professional personnel) will be required for those psychiatric casualties who continue to be incapacitated.

Clinical psychiatrists have suggested and tried out many different techniques for minimizing the effects of psychological trauma, some of which may prove to be extremely valuable. But, so far, practically no systematic research has been carried out to assess the effectiveness of alternative techniques. An integrated research program should be organized in order to explore the most promising techniques in a thoroughly objective way.

Experiments in this field are rather expensive but seem to be quite feasible. Practically all psychiatric observers agree that emotional shock and other traumatic reactions evoked by bombing do not differ in any essential respect from traumatic reactions observed in peacetime. Consequently, it seems reasonably safe to assume that psychiatric first-aid techniques for application in wartime disasters can be assessed by studying their effectiveness in peacetime danger situations. Controlled experiments on the effects of various treatments, such as stimulating immediate recall and verbal rehearsal of the traumatic events, could be carried out with survivors of apartment house fires, train wrecks, automobile accidents, etc. Group therapy techniques could be tested with large numbers of persons following any major peacetime disaster. The development of sound criteria for evaluating the effectiveness of a given form of psychiatric first aid requires some special methodological research, but even the rough indices ordinarily used (remission of obvious behavioral symptoms and clinical ratings of emotional status based on psychiatric interviews) could be systematically applied so as to reveal any markedly beneficial effects.

With respect to the prevention of psychiatric casualties, some special form of psychological preparation might be discovered which would reduce the over-all incidence of severe emotional disturbances among the survivors of a disaster.[6] It seems unlikely, however, that any such preparatory device will prove to be so effective as to eliminate the need for psychiatric first aid.

"WILL THERE BE WIDESPREAD PANIC?"

Prior to World War II, government circles in Britain believed that if their cities were subjected to heavy air raids, the urban population would become so overwhelmed by fear that the dominant reaction would be panic and mass hysteria. In Part II, we have seen that this belief, based on the predictions of various specialists, proved to be a myth. Already there are some indications that a similar kind of myth is beginning to develop with respect to future A-bomb attacks—the belief that the news of the first A-bomb attacks in this country will produce panic among the residents of unbombed metropolitan centers and industrial areas.

There is, of course, a serious danger that people who expect their city to be hit at any moment might behave in an excited and socially disruptive fashion. But, for purposes of civil defense planning, it is

---

[6] See the discussion on "emotional innoculation" techniques in the following chapter.

not very useful to assume that "panic" will necessarily be the most probable response.

"Panic" is often used by both popular writers and social scientists as a colorful term to designate any collective dread that is judged to be inappropriate to the occasion. For example, the reactions following the *Invasion from Mars* radio program, which are commonly referred to as panic, consisted mainly of the following: Many people, having tuned in during the middle of the program, heard newscasts and announcements to the effect that some sort of invasion had occurred and that evacuation was necessary; they immediately felt anxious, notified others in their vicinity, phoned members of their families, and in some cases went so far as to carry out the instructions to evacuate.[7] Evidently there were relatively few in the radio audience whose behavior could be characterized as manifestly irrational or antisocial. For most participants, the panic consisted primarily in their reacting to a *false* emergency warning in a manner which, by and large, would have been appropriate for a *genuine* emergency warning, without first checking on its authenticity.

Although "panic" is an extremely ambiguous term, the image it usually brings to mind is that of a wildly excited crowd behaving in an impulsive, completely disorganized fashion, each person abandoning all social values in a desperate effort to save himself. From the available literature on extreme fear reactions, it appears that this sort of behavior rarely occurs unless (1) there is an obvious physical danger which is immediately present (e.g., a raging fire only a few feet away) and (2) there are no apparent routes of escape. Hence, panic, in the limited sense of the term, is likely to be evoked by an A-bomb attack primarily in the area where the disaster actually occurs, e.g., among those who are trapped by the general conflagration within the city. In places which are not affected by the explosion, including the cities which are potential targets for the next attack, there is far less danger of a serious outbreak of overt panic. That is to say, there is a strong likelihood that with appropriate psychological preparation such reactions can be prevented.

[7] H. Cantril, *The Invasion from Mars*, Princeton University Press, Princeton, N.J., 1940.

At a time when crucial policies of civil defense are being planned, panic-prevention should be recognized as only one of many psychological problems to be taken into account. In fact, some of the more subtle forms of fear-motivated behavior are likely to be much more prevalent and will often require preventive measures that are quite different from those designed for purposes of panic control. In England, the government's exclusive concern with the latter apparently resulted in a failure to look for—and to prevent—various nonspectacular forms of unauthorized flight. Having anticipated that a large exodus from London and other cities would take the form of an excited, chaotic stampede after the first big raids, the government failed to discover until the end of the war that over two million persons had "silently" evacuated themselves during the blitz: "So great was the flight to the western half of England that, in the reception areas of Devonshire, private evacuees outnumbered official evacuees by roughly seven hundred per cent. . . . It is astonishing that such a large number of people could, within a short period of time, leave the vulnerable areas without the government being aware of the fact."[8]

For purposes of analyzing and predicting social behavior, it is preferable to avoid using a term which connotes the sort of behavior that occurred in the Cocoanut Grove fire when referring to other, less extreme, types of action motivated by fear. In order to avoid too narrow a conception of the problems of fear control, it is necessary to reformulate the ambiguous question with which this discussion began. Instead of asking, "Will there be widespread panic?" the inquiry should be centered upon (1) what forms of fear reaction are likely to occur under various conditions of an A-bomb threat? and (2) by what means can the more extreme forms of personal disorganization and inappropriate behavior be prevented in threatened areas?

One of the major conditions under which extreme fear reactions are likely to occur is a very sudden, unexpected confrontation of the threat. In a sense, almost all the points to be discussed in the

---

[8] Titmuss, *op. cit.*

remainder of this book are directly or indirectly tied up with the problem of providing adequate psychological preparation for the American population so as to prevent inappropriate and disruptive behavior. To the extent that the public is informed about ways and means of coping with the dangers and trained to participate in civil defense operations, disruptive fear reactions will be minimized. The educational program for the general public, as well as military defenses and other features of an adequate defense program, to be discussed later, should have the effect of building up realistic expectations and of counteracting feelings of helplessness if the danger becomes imminent.

It cannot be assumed, however, that successful civil defense preparation will eliminate subjective feelings of fear. No matter how well they are prepared, the residents of all potential target areas will become extremely apprehensive as soon as they learn that the first A-bomb attack has occurred in this country. The preparation they have been given, however, should serve to *channelize* their overt reactions: if people do not feel completely unprotected, and if emergency measures have been well planned and organized in advance, they will most likely conform to the recommendations, precautions, and regulations issued by civil defense authorities.

EMERGENCY EVACUATION

Undoubtedly, the best way to avoid being killed by an A-bomb is to be as far away as possible when it explodes; and certainly the best way to avoid being afraid of an impending attack is to know that the place where one is living is far removed from the nearest possible target. These simple truisms imply that dispersing our industry and our population might be the most effective of all A-bomb defenses. But this implication evidently will have only very limited application in the total scheme of national defense planning.

A number of scientists have repeatedly urged that the entire urban population of the United States be widely dispersed so as to reduce the effectiveness of A-bomb attacks. For example, Edward Teller

claims that the enormous effort involved in large-scale dispersal
would be rewarded by a high degree of safety: "Then a few thousand Hiroshima bombs could kill only one per cent of our population."[9] Many other scientists agree that in all likelihood we shall be
attacked by large numbers of A-bombs if there is another war, but
not all of them share the optimistic expectation of achieving such a
high degree of safety by means of mass dispersal. Some predict that
a dispersed population would be just as vulnerable to bacteriological
warfare as people in cities, if not more so; this might also hold true
for radiation poisons and other unconventional weapons.

From the many official statements which have been made about
the staggering economic expense, the length of time it would take,
and the tremendous social and political consequences it would entail,
it is difficult to imagine that a policy of mass dispersal actually will
be adopted. In the summer of 1950, the Director of the United
States Civil Defense Office estimated that the financial cost would
be in the neighborhood of 300 billion dollars and that the political
cost would be a "garrison state" which might put an end to democ-
racy as we know it.[10] Accordingly, it is to be anticipated that in the
event of an outbreak of atomic warfare, a very high percentage of
our population will be concentrated in prime target areas.

Obviously, most people will have a strong urge to get away from
any metropolitan center or industrial area that is threatened. This
will be an asset or a liability from the Government's point of view,
depending on whether or not its defense plan calls for prompt
emergency evacuation. A number of social scientists have strongly
recommended that if mass dispersal is not carried out in advance,
the Government should make plans to minimize casualties by evacuating the population of metropolitan areas rapidly—as soon as the
first atomic bomb attack is launched against the United States. If
this policy is adopted by the Government, and if people have been
trained properly for orderly migration to dispersed assembly centers,

[9] E. Teller, "How Dangerous Are Atomic Weapons?" *Bull. Atomic Scientists*,
Vol. 3, February, 1947, p. 35.

[10] P. J. Larsen, "The Government's Role in Civil Defense," *Bull. Atomic Scientists*,
Vol. 6, August–September, 1950, p. 233.

there is every reason to expect a fairly high degree of conformity to emergency evacuation orders.

Evacuation on a mass scale will be a considerable undertaking requiring detailed plans not only for a controlled exodus from threatened target areas, but also for the social organization of the evacuation centers where large numbers of people may have to remain for a prolonged period. Certain types of experienced personnel will be needed to provide effective leadership in organizing constructive economic and social activities in evacuated communities. In England, for example, it was discovered too late that there was a critical shortage of experienced social workers to meet the needs of emergency centers for homeless people; those who were available were generally much more capable of taking the initiative, cutting through red tape, and handling large numbers of distressed people than were most of the local officials.[11]

The strong drive to get out of the threatened area—to be somewhere else before anything happens—can be counted on to motivate people to respond to official evacuation orders, provided there has been adequate preparation in advance. It will be necessary to make a deliberate effort to build up strong attitudes and expectations that will minimize the possibility of spontaneous, disorganized flight or of disruptive competition to be the first to reach the most advantageous safety zones. Effective preparation might require:

1. Informing the residents of each city about the local evacuation plan, and perhaps also assigning most adult members of the community to a "battle station" in specified localities where it is one's "duty" to be present;

2. Emphasizing the benefits (for oneself, one's family, and the entire community) to be derived from strict conformity to the local evacuation plan, along with emphasis on the adverse social consequences of "irresponsible" nonconformity;

3. Notifying the public of special sanctions to be applied against nonconformists in the event of an emergency evacuation.

---

[11] Titmuss, *op. cit.*

If the Government's defense plan requires the population of an obvious target area to remain there, considerable public resistance is to be expected immediately following the first A-bomb attack. The degree to which there is unauthorized evacuation from cities and reduced productive efficiency among essential industrial workers will depend on a variety of circumstances. Obviously, one of the most important factors will be the amount of public confidence in the radar warning system, the fighter plane defenses, the antiaircraft defenses, and the other protective facilities that are at hand.

Many scientists and well-informed journalists have taken great pains to explain to the reading public what A-bombs can do to the residents of an American city. In terms that most people can readily understand, the chances of survival often have been characterized more or less in the following way:

> . . . There is a very great difference between taking chances with ordinary bombs and with an A-bomb. You can always hope that a blockbuster will fall two blocks away. Furthermore, not all the blockbusters are dropped at the same instant, and you can seek shelter. With the case of the A-bomb the attack is virtually instantaneous, and, even if it explodes a mile away, your chances of survival are not good.[12]

Even without supposing that exaggerated fears of the A-bomb will flourish, it is reasonable to assume that the expectations of the majority of people will not be markedly more optimistic than are the well-publicized forecasts of the "experts." If so, people will soon come to realize, as Lapp says, "that it will be healthier to sleep in a haystack ten miles from the city limits rather than in a feather bed in the heart of the city." Assuming that this becomes the dominant feeling, it may still be relatively easy to discourage people from acting upon it, so long as there are no signs of an imminent attack. But if an initial A-bomb disaster occurs—and especially if it comes without warning before war has been declared—the spontaneous tendency of most people in unbombed cities probably will be to leave immediately, whether that action is authorized or not.

---

[12] R. E. Lapp, "The Strategy of Civil Defense," *Bull. Atomic Scientists,* Vol. 6, August–September, 1950, p. 241.

Probably the most critical factor in preventing unauthorized migration—short of a convincing official announcement to the effect that no further attacks are possible—will be the availability of protective shelters. If the shelters are regarded as inadequate or useless, there may be a very sizeable proportion of the urban population who will pack up and leave, unless prevented from doing so by coercive force, in which case there is likely to be considerable resentment and protest as well as a marked deterioration in job performances. Hence, from the standpoint of preventing widespread confusion and avoiding nonconformity to official demands immediately following an initial A-bomb attack, the key problems are (1) to develop a feasible plan for organized emergency evacuation of those who will not be needed and (2) to supply adequate shelters and an efficient warning system for those who will be required to remain.

THE SHELTER PROBLEM

In all probability there will be a definite priority system for the construction of shelters, underground installations, and other protective facilities. With a large proportion of the manpower and raw material resources of the country allocated to building offensive weapons and well-protected retaliatory installations, the construction of shelters in urban areas will undoubtedly be limited to the barest essentials. Underground shelters may be constructed for key military, administrative, and industrial personnel; for critical supplies; for irreplaceable libraries of blueprints, maps, and industrial and military data. Some facilities, such as underground dormitories, may also be provided for essential industries. But it is highly unlikely that there will be sufficient manpower and material to provide adequate shelters for the majority of the civilian population, even in the most vulnerable urban centers. Although there has been a good deal of publicity about current plans for financing the construction of large public shelters, especially in the downtown sections of large cities, it seems doubtful that these will accommodate more than a small fraction of the residents in any metropolitan area.

Noting the ever-increasing signs of hectic preparation, seeing and sometimes participating in the construction of shelters for others, urban residents are likely to become increasingly alarmed by the fact that no attempt is being made to provide them with protection from direct exposure to an A-bomb attack. If the potential danger of such an attack becomes more and more apparent, the demand for public shelters may become a major political issue. On the occasion of an imminent threat of attack, this issue might fulminate into a national crisis.

These anticipated problems might be greatly diminished by a single technological advance. If engineers and scientists are able to solve the technological problem of providing the American people with relatively simple and inexpensive means for constructing adequate physical protection against A-bomb explosions, many of the social and psychological problems to be discussed in the remainder of this book might be eliminated.

Assuming that the only substances available are concrete, earth, and bricks, the critical factor preventing construction of adequate public shelters will most likely be the manpower shortage. If this should prove to be the case, there is a partial solution to the problem to be considered which may prove to be both feasible and psychologically sound: the policy of encouraging people to build their own shelters. If people are told how to build private or neighborhood shelters, and if they feel apprehensive about the danger of an A-bomb attack, it is probable that a fairly large proportion of the urban population would contribute their spare time to providing this measure of security for themselves and their families.

From the published information about effective A-bomb shelters, it would appear that there is nothing unusually complicated about the construction of home shelters of a type which would give a fair degree of protection in an A-bomb attack. According to some experts, it would be difficult to build a shelter that would give close to 100 per cent protection, because it would have to be blastproof and airtight, with an oxygen supply that would last for many hours or even days without becoming contaminated by radioactive particles from the outside. But in an atomic disaster, tens of thousands of lives might be saved even by shelters which are only partially effective. Specifications for such shelters should meet scientifically established requirements in order to prevent dangerous as well as wasteful effort.

Front-line combat troops are encouraged to dig foxholes even though they offer no protection against a direct hit. If the urban population are exposed to the threat of an A-bomb attack, they will probably feel that they are in a comparable danger situation; they might be quite willing to provide themselves at least with something equivalent to a foxhole, if nothing better can be obtained. For example, by lining the walls of the basement of a private dwelling or apartment house with concrete, bricks, or sandbags, and by providing for emergency exits to be used in case the building catches fire or collapses, a fairly adequate shelter might be accessible. If entered before the detonation occurs, the shelter could provide excellent protection against the intense heat of the explosion and prevent injuries from shattered glass and flying debris. Depending on the distance from the explosion, there would be some degree of protection against direct-blast effects and gamma rays.[13]

The problem of what *kinds* of shelters people could build for themselves has been tackled by practical engineering technicians. A set of specifications—ranging from complicated structures that are highly protective to simple ones which provide a slight amount of protection—could be made available to the public. Full details could be given about how to carry out each step, where to get the materials, and so on. For those who live in towns near mountains or hills, additional recommendations might be included on the possible uses of caves and other special features of the terrain. Details could also be given on the probable amount of time there will be between a warning signal and the A-bomb explosion, along with some advice on how close the shelters should be to one's own home. In some neighborhoods, for example, the residents might wish to build collective shelters if they could expect to have sufficient time to get to them.

---

[13] Los Alamos Scientific Laboratory, *The Effects of Atomic Weapons,* U.S. Government Printing Office, Washington, D.C., 1950.

If specifications for various kinds of private and communal shelters are to be publicized, the information could be incorporated into the public educational program. The Government might be able to give additional encouragement by providing certain types of materials free or at a nominal cost. Each community could set up, perhaps as part of the local civil defense organization, a board of local construction experts who would be able to give advice to those in need of it and to inspect homemade shelters for the purpose of suggesting simple ways of improving them.

One of the major drawbacks of a homemade-shelter program is that it may arouse acute social resentments among those classes of the population which are not in a position to acquire or build expensive private shelters. To prevent disruptive social antagonisms from arising, it would probably be necessary to resort to careful rationing of the most suitable materials and to provide some form of government subsidies to equalize the opportunity for constructing shelters among all economic classes.

If the problem of class differences in safety can be solved, the homemade-shelter program might be extremely successful at a time when there are strong feelings of insecurity about impending A-bomb attacks. Participation in this form of self-protective activity would contribute to the feeling that "I am really able to do something about it." Moreover, if personal responsibility for providing one's own shelter is accepted, there is less tendency to place full reliance for one's protection on the authoritative figures of the Government. Consequently, there would be less likelihood of reacting to apparent "neglect" on the part of the Government with anxiety and resentment. After the homemade shelters are constructed, they may become an important source of reassurance. Awareness of their real protective value as well as nonrational factors (e.g., "I made it myself.") may invest them with considerable symbolic value as an anxiety-reducing feature of the environment.

Thus, even though surprise attacks may preclude their usefulness for some people, the shelters will probably be psychologically advantageous. So long as people do not expect all A-bomb attacks to come without warning, homemade shelters may be expected to serve this function. And, if our population is ever exposed to A-bomb attacks which are *not* surprise attacks, the feelings of security provided by the shelters will prove to be highly realistic.

CHAPTER 11

TRAINING AND EMOTIONAL INOCULATION

At present it is generally recognized that the devastating effects of an A-bomb attack can be greatly mitigated if the civilian population in and around the target city has been organized and trained to cope with the disaster. Investigators of the Hiroshima and Nagasaki bombings have emphasized that insufficient personnel to give medical aid was a critical factor in augmenting casualties. Because of the high death toll among the local physicians and nurses, untrained volunteers had to be pressed into caring for the injured. The amount of fire damage to buildings in peripheral areas also might have been reduced if trained emergency squads had been available.

Government authorities have repeatedly announced that civil defense plans call for local organizations of civilians to carry out various disaster-control operations. The Hopley Report[1] estimated that in a future war some fifteen million people may be needed for civil defense operations. The over-all plan on United States civil defense by the National Security Resources Board[2] specified four progressive stages of training for local civil defense workers: (1) basic training; (2) team training in technical and service duties; (3) collective training under realistic field conditions; (4) participation in a series of combined operations covering progressively larger geographical areas.

It may be assumed, therefore, that one of the major forms of national defense preparation will be the organization and training of civil defense units in which a sizeable proportion of the American population will be expected to participate. It may be assumed further

---

[1] U.S. Office of Civil Defense Planning (Russell J. Hopley, Director), *Civil Defense for National Security*, U.S. Government Printing Office, Washington, D.C., 1948.

[2] National Security Resources Board, *United States Civil Defense*, U.S. Government Printing Office, Washington, D.C., September, 1950.

that these local units, particularly in urban areas, will be set up with two general purposes in mind: (1) to carry out necessary disaster-control measures immediately after a bombing attack occurs, during the critical period before any outside help can arrive, and (2) to be prepared to cope with the entire disaster on a local scale in the event that a multiple A-bomb attack occurs which might require that specialized, mobile units be diverted elsewhere. Accordingly, there will be a large number of disaster-control functions to be apportioned among local civil defense teams. Intensive training will be required for a variety of specialized tasks: aircraft detection, fire fighting, rescuing survivors, administering first aid, assisting in the medical care of patients in emergency hospitals, detecting radiological contamination, setting up decontamination centers for people exposed to radiation, aiding the police in traffic control, collecting and hygienically disposing of corpses, eliminating public-health hazards, repairing power lines and essential utility systems, constructing camps for evacuees, etc.

PROBLEMS OF RECRUITMENT AND ASSESSMENT

If the defense program requires that a large proportion of the able-bodied civilian population participate in special emergency units, a number of problems in connection with recruitment may arise. Obviously, the number and quality of available volunteers, the existing state of public opinion, and long-range political considerations will play a determining role in shaping recruitment policies. But there are also some general psychological problems to be taken into account.

Successful recruitment is not simply a matter of getting people to join defense units and to attend meetings. In most units there will be a considerable amount of essential information to be learned and there will be a variety of new techniques to be mastered. If the training is to be successful, it is necessary to rely on strong personal motivations. The learning process will be a difficult and painful one for many people unused to devoting their free time after working hours to anything other than relaxation and amusement. Much of the technical material to be mastered will be inherently uninteresting to the average civilian and often the specific content will be anxiety arousing. Only if the participants feel strongly committed to their civil defense assignments are they likely to be conscientious in acquiring the skills necessary for efficient action. Moreover, a strong sense of duty toward their personal role in the organization may prove to be an important determinant of successful performance if they are ever required to carry out an assigned task in the face of harrowing disaster conditions.

During the initial stage of organizing civil defense units, a policy of voluntary recruitment is probably necessary in order to build up a strong nucleus of a highly motivated and devoted cadre. When the defense program calls for expansion of the entire organization, the problem of enlisting sufficient numbers of volunteers may become an acute one. Even if there is a favorable response from influential community leaders, there may be large sectors of the public and many essential-skill groups who will find that they have insufficient time to spare for active participation.

It is at this stage that social scientists may be able to make an important contribution as advisors on policy decisions. Well in advance of this stage, social research should be alerted to the need for information relevant for eliciting mass participation in a civil defense organization.

Many of the basic difficulties in recruiting personnel for civil defense units, particularly those tied up with the arousal of anxiety, are closely linked with other problems of public resistance (discussed in later chapters). In the present context, attention is merely called to a few of the practical problems of recruitment toward which opinion research and social surveys might be oriented:

1. What special incentives, such as job-relevant training, opportunity for new social contacts, and monetary compensations, would be most effective for attracting and holding large numbers of recruits from each social stratum?

2. To what extent could the cooperation of schools, colleges, and professional organizations be obtained so as to incor-

porate essential civilian defense training into existing training programs?

3. What sorts of cooperation might be elicited from large-scale employers so that workers could receive some of the defense training as a regular part of their jobs?

4. What type of organizational affiliation is most attractive to recruits? (For example, would there be more middle-class volunteers for fire-fighting units if such units were not an adjunct to the local fire department?)

5. If nonvoluntary recruitment becomes necessary, what kinds of "draft" procedures are least likely to elicit resentment among those affected?

6. What types of information and publicity themes are most effective in eliciting willingness to volunteer for active participation in civil defense?

Assuming that the practical difficulties of attracting sufficiently large numbers of recruits can be overcome, various problems of selection and assessment are to be anticipated.

Some of the tasks to be carried out by civil defense teams, e.g., medical first aid, radiological detection, and certain types of rescue work, will require personnel who are capable of becoming highly skilled technicians. Other tasks, such as stretcher-bearing and building firebreaks, could be learned by people who have relatively little skill potential. Although there is great variation in the aptitudes and skills required, the ultimate goal of the training in every one of the many different emergency tasks is the same: efficient performance of disaster-control operations under the intensely stressful conditions of a large-scale disaster. Hence, there are two major factors to be taken into account in selecting and assigning civilian personnel to civil defense units: (1) their learning ability or skill potentialities and (2) their ability to withstand the disruptive impact of intense stress.

With respect to both of these factors, mass screening and assessment devices are already available which could be utilized: group intelligence tests, mechanical aptitude tests, job background questionnaires, personality inventories, etc. It should be recognized, however, that such devices are still relatively crude and are useful mainly for very rough purposes, such as the elimination of those who are grossly unfit. Moreover, the routine application of mass-testing procedures might arouse some resentment, particularly among recruits for skilled operations who are likely to be status conscious. It would be highly undesirable to institute any selection procedures which might have the effect of creating unfavorable attitudes toward the organization or of adding another obstacle to the already numerous sources of psychological resistance which interfere with recruitment. Thus, it may prove to be necessary to apply techniques which can be part of an informal "placement" interview rather than to subject large groups of recruits to routine-testing situations. For the most efficient assignment of key personnel, however, special techniques are needed which could be readily applied without producing resentment.

One of the most important research needs is that of developing more refined techniques for selecting civil defense leaders. It is generally recognized that decisive and skillful leadership is a fundamental requirement for efficient teamwork in a confused and uncertain danger situation. Whenever the unit leader is lacking in the essential personal attributes, there is a grave risk that at the critical moment his entire unit will become completely disorganized and fail to carry out its mission.

> The graver the emergency, i.e., the less consciousness is able to grapple with the problem, the greater is the tendency to fall back on earlier and primitive tendencies; in other words, the more does the man become the child. So in grave danger the average individual will look about for someone who is prepared to play a parental role. The immediately commanding officer has all eyes turned on him inevitably; his actions are the ones that will be imitated. If he is made of the right stuff the emergency will, just as automatically, induce in him a tendency to guide and guard those under his command. Morale will then be good. On the other hand, if he is not a true leader, the emergency will make him too one who looks for direction. His indecision will then

indicate to the group that nothing effective can be done, and confusion will be worse confounded.[3]

A related problem is that of selecting the rank and file for those special units which will be required to carry out crucial assignments. There are many vital defense operations for which it is essential to have persons who are capable of maintaining a high level of emotional control. For example, the entire strategy of controlling an incipient conflagration immediately after an atomic explosion may depend on the efficiency of scouting teams who have the job of detecting local fire threats, locating and testing available water supplies, mapping possible routes through which equipment can be moved, etc. Members of such units must be capable of performing adequately despite the intense stresses of facing danger, of witnessing widespread death and destruction, and of having lost relatives and friends in the disaster. Psychological research, if directed toward these problems, may be expected to make an important contribution in developing valid and efficient selection methods.

In the report prepared by the Assessment Staff of the Office of Strategic Services,[4] there is a description of a very elaborate series of tests which their candidates were required to undergo, including a number of unusually strenuous tests of stress tolerance. The claim is made that this arduous assessment program had no deleterious effects upon the morale of their recruits but rather produced relatively favorable attitudes toward the organization. Whether recruits for positions of leadership and for other essential activities in the civil defense organization will respond to assessment tests in the same way is an open question. Hence, it is important not only to determine the validity of various testing procedures, but also to study the consequences of introducing each of the validated procedures into the testing program. In other words, assessment research should have the goal of providing a set of simple testing devices which can be relied on to meet two essential requirements:

---

[3] J. T. MacCurdy, *The Structure of Morale,* The Macmillan Company, New York, 1943.

[4] OSS Assessment Staff, *Assessment of Men: Selection of Personnel for the Office of Strategic Services,* Rinehart & Company, Inc., New York, 1948.

(1) their validity greatly exceeds that of ordinary personnel interviews, and (2) their utilization does not produce unfavorable effects upon the attitudes or morale of the recruits. Since the over-all success of the civil defense organization will be determined in no small measure by the adequacy with which its personnel are assigned to critical jobs, practical research on these two aspects of assessment procedure can make an important contribution to the national defense effort.

There is another aspect of assessment which should not be overlooked: the opportunity to evaluate personnel on the job, after they have already had their basic training. For instance, fire-fighting units might be given a chance to "show their stuff" by participating in actual fire fighting when local conflagrations occur during the training period; various medical units might be given comparable experience in dealing with casualties in the emergency rooms of local hospitals. Such participation may prove to be extremely valuable for eliminating workers who are emotionally unfit for their assignment and for reassigning leaders, especially if objective-rating procedures are developed specifically for such purposes. In addition, as will be pointed out shortly, active participation in local emergencies may prove to be extremely effective in maintaining group morale.

ATTITUDES TOWARD THE DEFENSE REGION

During World War II, the rank and file in civil defense units in the United States, England, Germany, and Japan were organized on a purely local basis. Units of fire fighters, for example, regarded themselves as defenders of their own home town. Although the members of such units might willingly aid a neighboring community in an emergency, it is to be expected that there would be strong resistance against a demand to devote their energies to preparing primarily to give aid to some "outside" community at a time when their own community is seriously threatened.

In preparing for atomic warfare, primary feelings of loyalty can no longer be limited to the home town community. In Hiroshima and Nagasaki, according to an official estimate, about 70 to 80 per cent of the equipment and personnel prepared for civil defense activities were wiped out.[5] Civil defense authorities have emphasized the implications of the fact that in an A-bomb attack the entire local defense force may be destroyed. One of the main conclusions which has been drawn is that civil defense organizations should be based on a larger area than the city and that plans should be worked out to foster mutual aid between neighboring towns. A report by the U.S. Atomic Energy Commission states:

> From the experience at Hiroshima and Nagasaki it is clear that if an attack comes to an unwarned population, the most that can be expected of them will be that the uninjured will rescue those who are trapped or injured before they are reached by fire. Because of the confusion and destruction which will follow a bomb burst, general relief must come from the outside. Washington, if attacked, would look for help—that is, for workers, supplies, and equipment—from its outlying undamaged ring and its suburban areas and from cities as distant as Baltimore, Philadelphia, and Richmond. Relief must be organized with this in view. Supplies, supplementary fire-fighting equipment, and new hospitals must be kept outside vulnerable areas.[6]

The geographical regions that require coordination on a functional basis for effective civil defense operations might in some parts of the country coincide with arbitrary state boundaries and in other parts not. In either case, however, the necessity for organizing civil defense on a regional rather than on a municipal basis poses a number of new problems. If the early stages of organization and training were carried out solely as a local community enterprise, sooner or later the recruits would have to be told or would "figure out" for themselves that this setup was unrealistic. They would realize that their preparation actually is not so much to defend their own home town as to aid other communities. If this realization were to come as a surprise, after the trainees had already built up

---

[5] Los Alamos Scientific Laboratory, *The Effects of Atomic Weapons,* U.S. Government Printing Office, Washington, D.C., 1950.

[6] Atomic Energy Commission, "The City of Washington and an Atomic Attack," *Bull. Atomic Scientists,* Vol. 6, January, 1950, p. 29.

a misconception of their mission, there would undoubtedly be considerable resentment toward the civil defense authorities, together with disaffection and loss of motivation to continue the training. In order to avoid unfavorable morale effects among trainees, it will be necessary to develop realistic expectations from the very beginning.

It may prove to be relatively easy to explain the reasons for preparing to carry out civil defense activities in neighboring cities rather than in one's own and to convince trainees that this orientation is an essential one. But it may be extremely difficult to attract large numbers of local residents into an arduous training program when the goal is not that of protecting the local community. If the threat of atomic disasters is perceived by the general public to be a real one, many people will undoubtedly be strongly motivated to protect their own neighborhood; they might be quite willing to devote their time and energy to local preparation activities. It is quite another thing, however, to become active in a unit which is preparing to avert disaster in some other community many miles away. Even among those who feel it is their duty to join such an organization, there is likely to be a perfunctory attitude toward the training coupled with chronic, anxious concern: "What is being done for my own neighborhood?"

This problem might be solved by building a strong conviction that participation in a regional civil defense program is equivalent to defending one's own local community. From a psychological point of view there are two major requirements for developing this kind of attitude among civil defense workers. First, there must be continual reassurance that one's own primary group is, in fact, being given the full benefit of defensive preparation; secondly, there should be a feeling of identification with the entire region for which defense activities are oriented. In other words, willing and devoted participation is not likely to be widespread unless the participants feel that they are part of an organization which is preparing to protect their own families, friends, and neighbors, and that their participation will directly aid the community to which they "belong."

To some extent, this problem may be met by adopting appropriate communication policies designed to focus attention on regional symbols and to induce favorable attitudes toward them. For example, emphasis might be placed on the theme that the entire regional defense organization and all of its resources will be brought into action, if necessary, to cope with any local emergency that might arise anywhere within the region; peacetime analogies such as insurance policies might be used to convey the notion that "If you ever need help you will get much more out of it than you put into it." But publicity and information alone may not be effective unless reinforced by organizational practices.

Ways and means of fostering personal identification with the entire population of the defense region require careful investigation. The possibility of setting up paired communities which are mutually responsible for each other in the event of a wartime disaster is already being considered by experts on civil defense operations. Some of the additional devices to be evaluated in terms of their effectiveness in breaking down psychological distance within the defense region are:

1. Adopting an organizational structure so that the major units are based on function rather than on geographic locale. For example, instead of neighborhood units there might be fire-fighting units or medical aid units composed of members who come from widely scattered neighborhoods. Similarly, instead of having municipal divisions with a city official as the director, there might be functional divisions headed by a regional director for fire-fighting units, another for medical aid units, etc.

2. Setting up regional basic-training schools for the rank and file with appropriate transportation facilities so that persons from different towns have part of their training together.

3. Encouraging group competitions (membership drives, sports, public demonstrations of civil defense skills such as fire-fighting, etc.) in which members from different parts of the region find themselves on the same team.

4. Holding frequent joint meetings and social get-togethers for members from different local communities (perhaps organized via a network of local civil defense social clubs which welcome and provide lodging for out-of-town members).

5. Organizing regional defense training problems so that people in each municipality, in turn, have the opportunity of seeing a vast array of regional units going into action in their own local area.

6. Using regional defense units to aid in controlling local peacetime disasters which occur anywhere within the defense region.

7. Including in the training curriculum tours of the various communities within the region, focusing on their relevant resources, such as location of hospitals and natural firebreaks.

GROUP IDENTIFICATION

Recent studies of combat personnel have emphasized the importance of group identification as a major motivational factor underlying efficient performance in the face of danger. When the physical survival of each individual in the group is at stake, the tendency to abandon one's duty or to seek an escape from the situation is often held in check by reliance on the "protectiveness" of the group and by a strong motivation to avoid "letting the others down."

Although the psychological processes involved in group identification are not as yet well understood, it is possible to foresee serious problems which may arise in civil defense operations if this factor is not taken into account. If the members of stable defense units receive their training together, and carry out arduous tasks together, and if in the later stages of training they face actual danger situations together (e.g., by participating in fighting local fires), a strong "group spirit" may be expected to develop spontaneously, together with strong bonds of mutual loyalty and dependence among the members of the unit. When called into action, their ability to carry out an assignment in the face of danger will be far superior, other things being equal, to a group composed of equally well-trained men who are strangers to each other. From this point of view, it would seem that group identification should be fostered within civil defense units.

It cannot be overlooked, however, that this policy may prove to be psychologically detrimental if a large number of organized groups suffer high casualties in an A-bomb attack. The survivors of a decimated unit, having lost their leader and many of their teammates, may become demoralized by the loss. A study of cohesion in the German army revealed that group solidarity of an intense sort does not always have favorable behavioral consequences.[7] Prolonged isolation from the nucleus of the primary group often resulted in increased fear of being killed and sometimes had a generally disintegrative effect.

An alternative policy that has been suggested is to train individuals in such a way that they identify with a large and continually shifting group, being psychologically prepared to function as potential replacements, to join up with any random group of survivors who have had similar specialized training. Such a policy would be extremely difficult to carry through successfully if it should prove to be necessary to resort to it. There is little prior experience to draw upon for devising effective techniques to achieve this type of preparation. It would undoubtedly require intensive research to check on the effectiveness of alternative procedures—periodically shifting each member of a training unit into a new unit; instituting formal disciplinary rules for obeying orders given by any unit leader; discouraging unit social activities which contribute to mutual friendship among the members of the group.

To a large extent, the psychological problem under discussion hinges upon the expected nature of A-bomb disasters. If it is most

---

[7] E. A. Shils and M. Janowitz, "Cohesion and Disintegration in the Wehrmacht in World War II," *Public Opinion Quart.*, Vol. 12, Summer, 1948, p. 280.

probable that within a given defense region only one local community will be destroyed, leaving the majority of civil defense units intact, then stable units in which group spirit is fostered would appear to be the preferable policy. (It should be noted that the attempt to minimize the number of units suffering a partial loss of personnel from an A-bomb explosion may require setting up stable units on a neighborhood basis, even though dispersion of membership might be preferable from the point of view of building up regional identification, as was discussed in the preceding section.)

On the other hand, in an area where multiple A-bomb attacks might occur, with high losses throughout the entire region, it would be necessary to make some attempt to train civil defense workers in such a way that those who survive will be prepared to carry out their functions without being demoralized by the loss of specific leaders or teammates.

Some defense regions may face the focalized type of attack (e.g., those containing many small towns with only one large industrial target), and some the diffuse type (e.g., those with heavy industry scattered throughout the entire region). Hence, it may be necessary to determine the appropriate policy separately for each region.

ASSIGNMENT OF EMERGENCY DUTIES

In the preceding discussion, the point has been stressed that wherever intact units are likely to survive an A-bomb explosion, the members should be trained to function as a stable unit so as to encourage the development of group identification. The members of such units probably will be assigned the duty of assembling and reporting for specific assignments immediately upon being notified that an A-bombing has occurred in their region. But what about those defense workers who survive the explosion within the disaster area itself? There may be thousands of them on the periphery of the target area who are uninjured, even though exposed to the dangers of fire, blast, and lingering radioactivity in their immediate vicinity. They will be the civil defense workers who can most promptly go into action during the critical, initial phase of the disaster. Should they be expected to assemble promptly with their defense unit for a detailed, coordinated assignment? More specifically, should civilian defense workers be instructed and trained in advance that irrespective of the conditions in their immediate locale, their duty, if they are not injured, is to assemble immediately with their civil defense organization?

Having an assigned task to perform may be beneficial in preventing distraught, irrational behavior among those who are in a destroyed area. But rigorous instruction to assemble immediately for duty often will be incompatible with other powerful motives which are aroused immediately following an explosion. Conscientious defense workers who feel it is their duty to report immediately to an assembly area may experience intense conflict if they are inside the disaster area: it may be highly dangerous to leave their particular locale (because of the presence of radioactive dust clouds); their immediate neighborhood might be threatened by fire hazards requiring prompt action to avert danger; a member of the family or a close friend may require immediate aid. In the Halifax disaster, according to Prince,[8] the only people who engaged in rescue work immediately after the explosion were visitors in the city and local residents with no social or family ties. The others generally ran first to their own homes to check on the safety of their families.

Conflicting loyalties may augment behavioral disturbances and greatly reduce the effectiveness of performances during the initial period when prompt and efficient action is most needed. For example, a man who reports for fire-fighting duty at a time when one of his children is missing or injured may be highly disturbed, not only because he is anxious about his child, but also because he feels guilty about having abandoned his family at such a critical moment.[9]

It is necessary to take account of the potentially adverse consequences of rigorous assignment to civil defense duties and to work

---

[8] S. H. Prince, *Catastrophe and Social Change,* Columbia University Studies in Political Science, etc., Columbia University Press, New York, 1920.

[9] See the discussion in Part I, Chap. 3, of guilt reactions among A-bomb survivors.

out a solution which will minimize emotional disturbances. One possibility to be investigated is the following: Defense workers might be instructed that if their immediate vicinity is undamaged, their duty is to report promptly to the designated assembly area; if, however, they find themselves in a neighborhood which has undergone some destruction, their primary duty is to protect themselves, their families, and their neighbors before reporting for duty with their organization. Such a policy might have the added advantage of minimizing the deleterious emotional effects of loss of personnel among civilian defense units within the disaster area. The members of each unit would know that their group is intended to function as a team only if they are in a locale which is not directly endangered; otherwise, they are expected to function on their own as individual civil defense workers. Under these conditions they would be less likely to discover the extent to which their own unit suffered initial casualties from the disaster and they might be psychologically prepared, to some extent, to function alone.

Although the policy under discussion might prove to have a number of beneficial effects, it is an open question as to whether or not the advantages outweigh the obvious disadvantages of providing the opportunity for avoiding prompt emergency mobilization. Investigations of the reactions of disaster-control personnel during peacetime disasters might provide some empirical basis for evaluating policies of this type.

EMOTIONAL RESPONSES OF RELIEF WORKERS

One of the major goals of civil defense operations will be to give immediate aid to thousands of survivors within the A-bombed area. It will be necessary for specialized teams to enter the disaster area as soon as it is reasonably safe to do so. Rescue units will be urgently needed to help people escape from burning buildings, to dig out survivors buried under debris, to carry the injured and unconscious to safety; medical units will have the task of giving prompt first aid for severe burns, lacerations, and fractures; other units will be required to act quickly in order to minimize fire hazards and to facilitate the evacuation of survivors. The number of lives lost may be drastically increased if civil defense teams fail to carry out their assignments efficiently. Consequently, it is important to consider the emotional reactions which may seriously interfere with the performance of essential rescue and relief operations.

The tremendous devastation in the disaster area will be a disturbing factor. Even more upsetting will be the sight of people who have been killed and injured. Especially among medical aid personnel, the problem of preventing emotional shock reactions is an acute one because of the extreme disfigurement and mutilation of human bodies produced by an atomic explosion. John Hersey[10] gives a graphic account of the unnerving experiences that beset survivors who set about the task of aiding the injured in Hiroshima:

> [Father Kleinsorge, a German priest] . . . heard a voice ask from the underbrush, "Have you anything to drink?" . . . When he had penetrated the bushes, he saw there were about twenty men, and they were all in exactly the same nightmarish state; their faces were wholly burned, their eyesockets were hollow, the fluid from their melted eyes had run down their cheeks. . . . Their mouths were mere swollen, pus-covered wounds, which they could not bear to stretch enough to admit the spout of the teapot.

> Mr. Tanimoto [a Japanese clergyman] found about twenty men and women on the sandspit. . . . He reached down and took a woman by the hands, but her skin slipped off in huge, glove-like pieces. He was so sickened by this that he had to sit down for a moment. Then he got out into the water and, though a small man, lifted several of the men and women, who were naked, into his boat. Their backs and breasts were clammy, and he remembered uneasily what the great burns he had seen during the day had been like: yellow at first, then red and swollen, with the skin sloughed off, and finally, in the evening, suppurated and smelly. . . . On the other side, at a higher spot, he lifted the slimy living bodies out and carried them up the slope away from the tide. He had to keep consciously repeating to himself, "These are human beings."

> . . . bewildered by the numbers [inside the hospital], staggered by so much raw flesh, Dr. Sasaki lost all sense of profession and stopped working as a skillful surgeon and a sympathetic man; he

---

[10] John Hersey, *Hiroshima*, Alfred A. Knopf, Inc., New York, 1946.

became an automaton, mechanically wiping, daubing, winding, wiping, daubing, winding.

Near the entrance to the park, an Army doctor was working but the only medicine he had was iodine, which he painted over cuts, bruises, slimy burns, everything—and by now everything that he painted had pus on it.[11]

To avoid distraught and inept performances among medical-aid personnel, it may be necessary to give them an opportunity to build up some degree of emotional adaptation to the job of handling large numbers of casualties. One method would be to introduce them gradually to the experience of working with patients in medical clinics and hospitals, ending up, if possible, in the emergency room of a large metropolitan hospital.

Even those civil defense workers whose jobs do not require such close physical contact with casualties may become so agitated by the appalling sights about them that they are unable to perform adequately. Some form of preparation—some special kind of *emotional inoculation*—is necessary for the average civilian who is being trained to carry out an assignment in a disaster area. Certain of the devices which have been used on a limited scale in the psychological preparation of soldiers for combat may prove to be effective for this purpose, but considerable research will be needed in order to be sure that they do not do more harm than good.

Perhaps the most successful general approach would be to give civil defense trainees detailed descriptions of the perceptual experiences to be expected in wartime disasters so that they will be stimulated to develop appropriate anxiety-reducing responses. On general theoretical grounds, it seems probable that personal psychological defenses are most likely to be effective in the actual danger situation if the individual previously has acquired correct anticipations of the disturbing sights and sounds that will be encountered: when the danger materializes, those who have mentally rehearsed the situation in advance are least likely to be surprised, shocked, and overwhelmed by feelings of helplessness. Purely verbal descriptions,

---

[11] *Ibid.*

however, may fail to elicit imaginative rehearsals of coping with the danger; more graphic presentations, on the other hand, might have a somewhat traumatizing effect, resulting in emotional sensitization rather than adaptation.

One inoculation device which has been suggested is that of exposing trainees to increasing doses of realistic sound films (preferably in color) showing actual disaster scenes. Other possible devices that might enable trainees to become emotionally adapted to the sight of the dead and injured are tours of the local morgue, courses in human anatomy, and disaster exhibits using a World's Fair type of presentation, e.g., blown-up photographs of damage, full-scale models of destroyed communities, and lifelike plaster dummies to demonstrate each type of casualty.

Before introducing anything of this kind into the training program, however, careful research is needed to test its over-all effectiveness and to determine the optimal conditions for its use: At what stage in training should it be used? How gradual should the doses be? Should extreme mutilations and other shocking sights be included at all?

In evaluating the effects of exposure to emotional stimuli it is necessary to answer two important questions: (1) How much good does it do when the trainees are ultimately exposed to an actual disaster situation? and (2) How much harm does it do during the training period? The second question is relatively easy to investigate. Experimental presentations of the stimuli could be administered within a training organization and the subsequent changes in experimental and control groups could be investigated by means of psychiatric interviews, attitude scales, and behavioral indices (overt attempts to quit the training program or to transfer to a different type of training). But the first problem, the evaluation of the ultimate value of the device, is extremely difficult to investigate. As yet, no validated tests have been developed which could be used to predict subsequent reactions to danger. This methodological deficiency has long been recognized as a major obstacle to the development of sound techniques of fear control; e.g., it precluded the possibility of making any precise evaluation of the effectiveness of the United

States Army's battle-inoculation course during World War II.[12] The possibility of observing trainees in peacetime disaster situations, as well as other, less costly ways of investigating emotional inoculation, remain to be explored. Such research, if successful, might lead to the development of emotional-training techniques which are effective both for civil defense workers and for those industrial workers who are likely to be exposed to wartime disasters.

Another source of stress which will affect many civil defense workers arises from the fact that they will be dealing with disaster victims who are extremely anxious or depressed. Quite aside from the severe emotional-shock cases who will require special psychiatric treatment, there may be large numbers of survivors who are extremely apprehensive about the realistic possibility that they may be doomed to die from radiation sickness within a week or two. There will also be large numbers of persons, both among the sick and the well, who have been unable to locate members of their families. Knowing that there are huge numbers of unidentified dead and injured, they will be in a severely agitated state. In addition to apprehensiveness about radiation sickness and anxious concern about missing loved ones, there will be other kinds of emotional disturbance as well: bereavement, anxiety about disfigurement, and jitteriness about the danger of another A-bomb attack.

There is a twofold problem here. First, the disaster victims will require calm, reassuring, patient handling during the days and weeks following the attack. Secondly, the relief personnel who come in close contact with disaster victims must be able to withstand the emotional strain and demoralizing influence of working with persons who are in an extremely anxious or depressed state of mind.

Such problems require careful consideration in planning the organization of medical and social services. For example, in setting up a system of sorting medical casualties so as to give priority to those who have the best chance of recovering, it may be desirable

---

12 I. L. Janis, "Problems Related to the Control of Fear in Combat," Chap. 4 in S. Stouffer, et al., The American Soldier: Combat and Its Aftermath, Vol. 2, Princeton University Press, Princeton, N.J., 1949.

to arrange for segregating those radiation victims who are expected to die, so that they will not have a demoralizing effect on a large number of medical-aid personnel and on other patients. For the patients who will be worried about epilation, ugly scar tissue, and other disfigurements, a special series of pamphlets and posters might be prepared in advance, containing reassuring information about treatment and the chances of recovery. These printed materials could be included in emergency supply kits for distribution at the appropriate time in disaster-aid centers.

The training of civil defense personnel might also take account of the problem. In the preceding chapter, the suggestion was made that all those who are likely to be in extensive contact with emotionally upset survivors be given some instruction and practice in elementary psychiatric principles and techniques. To the extent that defense workers are able to give appropriate supportive help to disaster victims, the unfavorable effects of widespread emotional upset will be reduced *within their own ranks* as well as among the people they are trying to help.

COUNTERACTING FEELINGS OF INSECURITY AND PESSIMISM

If civil defense workers are to be psychologically prepared to cope with the dangers of atomic bombing, they must be given realistic information about the destructive impact of the A-bomb. This aspect of their training, however, may have a demoralizing effect. As people become more and more aware of the realities of atomic disasters, they will, of course, become increasingly anxious. Concurrently, they may develop a profound sense of futility which would seriously interfere with their participation in defensive preparations. Moreover, if at some future time it becomes generally known that Russia possesses a large stockpile of A-bombs, or has developed H-bombs, bacteriological agents, or other weapons of mass destruction which could be applied against this country, many people may become so impressed by the magnitude of the threat that they will feel highly pessimistic about their own chances of survival.

Within the ranks of the civil defense organization and among the entire urban population, there will be some individuals who will begin to ask a variety of disquieting questions: "After an A-bomb explosion will any of us be left to carry out these instructions?" "Isn't all this training and preparation going to be a drop in the bucket compared with the enormous devastation of an atomic attack?" "Suppose that some newer weapon like a cloud of radiation poison is used—won't our defense activities be useless?"

If a sense of futility becomes widespread among civil defense workers, there is little chance for carrying out successful training. There probably would be openly expressed resistance against "wasting any more time" on "useless" preparations; even those who remain active in the organization would have little motivation to invest time and energy in the enterprise. Similarly, if this attitude permeates the mass audience for whom the public educational program is intended, there would be relatively few people willing to apply themselves to the task of learning the basic material.

Feelings of insecurity and pessimism cannot be prevented by suppressing information about the probable nature of A-bomb attacks. A sizeable number of people who are being trained in disaster-control activities will be sufficiently interested to seek out the information for themselves and they will undoubtedly pass it on to others. The official and unofficial predictions already published would provide ample material upon which the more imaginative members of civil defense organizations could elaborate. If civil defense officials attempt to suppress such material, urban communities would undoubtedly be faced with an even more demoralizing influence. Highly exaggerated rumors would spread rapidly and their impact would be augmented by the sharp awareness that "the authorities are afraid to let us know the truth."

During the air blitz against England, according to Glover, there was always a minority of fearful people who would pass on any frightening idea they heard in the hope of having it contradicted. In the early phases of the blitz, when people suspected that the government and the news services were suppressing the truth, anxious rumor-mongering flourished. From what is generally known about the spread of fear rumors, the best antidote is confidence "that you have been told the worst, and that you always will be told the worst."[13] Once the authoritative channels of communication are taken to be unreliable, people begin to feel isolated from their government and can no longer be reassured by official denials.

There is no clear-cut set of psychological principles that can be applied to prevent the development of feelings of insecurity and pessimism, especially when such reactions do, in fact, have some basis in reality. At present one can only speculate about ways of counteracting the debilitating effects of realistic anticipations of danger.

Official communications directed to the rank and file of the civil defense organization and to the public at large might adopt some general information policies designed to take account of the need for counteracting feelings of futility. For example, in presenting any information about wartime dangers emphasis might be placed on the theme that adequate preparation definitely increases the odds in favor of survival. However, the effectiveness of communication policies of this kind requires empirical investigation. It might turn out, for instance, that emphasis on "increasing the odds in favor of survival" sometimes has a boomerang effect; perhaps many Americans are so used to being assured that appropriate action totally eliminates the danger (e.g., "Cancer can be *cured* . . . if detected early.") that anything short of such assurance may be interpreted as implying a relatively hopeless outlook.

Pessimism arising from the expectation that the regional defense organization will not be capable of coping with a major atomic disaster might be reduced by focusing attention upon the potential aid available from other defense regions and, above all, from a mobile, full-time defense organization. Highly efficient elite outfits, composed of well-trained technicians who are prepared to supplement the rescue and relief operations of local civilian units, might be organized, perhaps as part of the United States Armed Forces. If such an organization were created, the residents of each commu-

---

[13] E. Glover, *The Psychology of Fear and Courage*, Penguin Books, Inc., New York, 1940.

nity would probably feel far more secure about the prospects of successful disaster control. Civil defense workers and the entire urban population might be less worried about the bungling, inefficiency, inadequate training, and over-all weakness of their local civil defense organization if they knew that there was a powerful "big brother" organization capable of doing a really effective job and ready to back them up in case of an emergency. Occasional opportunities to witness demonstrations by the experts in the elite organization might serve to reinforce this attitude.

To some extent, focusing attention upon military defenses—radar-detection network, fighter planes, and antiaircraft weapons—in the zone of interior may foster feelings of security. But very little is known about the reassurance value of active defense measures within the United States. It would certainly be unsafe to assume that when people see or hear about protective military installations in the immediate vicinity of their home town, they will necessarily feel less worried about being bombed. Perhaps by investigating the attitudes of people in areas where nearby installations are currently being constructed, some useful information will be obtained concerning the differential reassuring functions of various defensive measures.

Within the civilian defense organization, it should be possible to sponsor discussion-group sessions in which community leaders and civil defense personnel are encouraged to express their attitudes concerning anticipated wartime disasters.[14] If the discussion-group leaders are well prepared, they might be able to refute grossly exaggerated expectations and call attention to the reassuring features of this country's defensive preparations. At the same time, discussion groups might serve as a channel of communication to civil defense authorities, enabling them to adjust their communication policies to the current state of public opinion.

It is difficult to estimate whether or not suggestions of the sort which have just been made will be sufficiently effective to prevent the spread of demoralizing expectations and attitudes. This is a

---

[14] D. C. Cameron, "Psychiatric Implications of Civil Defense," *Am. J. Psychiat.*, Vol. 106, 1950, p. 587.

problem which pertains not only to members of the civil defense organization, but to the entire population in all vulnerable regions of the country. In the last chapter, this topic will be discussed again and a number of research proposals will be suggested.

CHAPTER 12
EDUCATION FOR SURVIVAL

In an Army Medical Bulletin devoted to the problems of atomic warfare, it is estimated that of the 50,000 or more deaths which would ordinarily result from a single attack on a modern city about 10,000 could be avoided if every person in the city were adequately informed beforehand as to what he could do for himself in case of an A-bomb disaster.[1] The Hopley Report on civil defense recommends a public educational program as a major undertaking of vital importance to national security, referring not only to the tremendous number of lives that may be saved, but also to the psychological dangers that may be averted:

> As war of the future will directly affect our total civilian as well as our military resources, the entire civilian population must be made aware of the problems and hazards, as well as the limitations, of an enemy attack which might employ unconventional as well as conventional weapons. . . .
>
> Individual citizens and families must be prepared to exercise maximum self-protection before expecting help from others. They must be so informed and instructed that they will be able to act with assurance and self-confidence. Such knowledge and ability to take the proper action in an emergency will dispel fear, prevent panic and confusion, minimize loss, and maintain morale.[2]

The more recent civil defense plan, prepared by the National Security Resources Board, reaffirms the need for teaching the general public what to do in an emergency.[3] This plan recommends that

---

[1] U.S. Army Medical Department, "What Every Medical Officer Should Know about the Atomic Bomb," *Bull. U.S. Army Med. Dept.*, Vol. 8, July, 1948, p. 493.

[2] U.S. Office of Civil Defense Planning (Russell J. Hopley, Director), *Civil Defense for National Security*, U.S. Government Printing Office, Washington, D.C., 1948.

[3] National Security Resources Board, *United States Civil Defense*, U.S. Government Printing Office, Washington, D.C., September, 1950.

the Federal Civil Defense agency should have responsibility for releasing basic information and that state and local defense officials should develop an intensive educational program for their own areas.

It can be assumed, therefore, that as part of the general preparedness program there will be some form of educational program on atomic warfare devised to reach the American public. Thus, while one sector of the general population will be receiving intensive special training for the type of civilian defense functions discussed in the preceding chapter, the remainder of the population will also be receiving instruction designed to prepare them to cope with A-bomb emergencies.

OBJECTIVES OF A PUBLIC EDUCATIONAL PROGRAM

That there will be enormous problems involved in attempting to carry out a successful program of mass education becomes apparent as soon as one considers the quantity and the content of the elementary material to be learned. The following is a brief outline of typical items of information which would be essential for the average civilian to know if he is to maximize his chances for survival following an atomic explosion:

1. Appropriate actions during an A-bomb alert: the best place to go if one is at home, at work, out in the open; the best position of the body for protection against blast effects; etc.
2. Appropriate emergency responses to the bright flash of an A-bomb explosion in case of a surprise attack: what the flash will look like; how to avoid injury from the secondary heat wave and the concussion wave; what to do immediately after the concussion wave has passed.
3. Ways of averting fire hazards: how to escape from burning buildings; what to do if one's clothes catch fire; where the safest places of refuge are if one is caught inside the fire area; how the potential fire hazard can be reduced if one

is at the periphery of the explosion; under what conditions one should evacuate to escape from a developing conflagration.

4. Essential precautions against radiological hazards: how to tell whether or not one should remain indoors; how to find an uncontaminated area; which kinds of food are safe to eat and which are unsafe; decontamination rules concerning removal of exposed clothing, scrubbing of exposed parts of the body, etc.

5. Probable location of emergency facilities: nearest medical-aid station if at home or at work; where food, clothing, shelter, and supplies can be obtained after escaping from the disaster area.

The above items pertain only to *individual* survival. If the average person is to be adequately prepared to give the most elementary kind of aid to members of his family and to others, there are many more topics to be included—such as, how to extract a person from beneath debris without injuring him unnecessarily; how to carry injured persons; how to give emergency first aid for burns, cuts, broken bones.

Certain kinds of technical information might also be included. For instance, in order to reduce confusion about the large number of "do's" and "don'ts" concerning radiological hazards—and to prevent the undesirable extremes of irrational indifference and excessive fear—it will probably be helpful to give some basic information about the nature of the radioactivity emitted by an A-bomb explosion. Perhaps by presenting the material pictorially and graphically, so as to reify the radioactive particles, people will come to regard them as a familiar and real part of the physical world. Conceivably, this material might be supplemented by training in certain types of technical "know-how."

It may turn out to be feasible to mass-produce various kinds of radiological safety equipment at a relatively low cost: detection meters, film badges to register total amount of personal exposure, gas masks or respirators, canvas suits and boots, etc. If so, this equipment could be issued to the residents of metropolitan areas, but it would have little value unless detailed instructions were given on its care and its appropriate use.

Other material which should be incorporated into the public educational program has already been discussed in Chapter 10, the most important of which concerns the construction of homemade shelters and the local emergency plan for predisaster evacuation. It may also be desirable to include information about other precautionary measures, such as the following:

1. *Fire Precautions.* Factories, workshops, business establishments, and homes should be carefully checked from the standpoint of eliminating readily inflammable material in order to reduce fire hazards following an A-bomb explosion.[4] Public cooperation on these fire precautions will undoubtedly be requested by civil defense authorities. Use of special paints (which are fire resistant or non-heat-reflectant, or both) on the wall surfaces of dwellings in metropolitan areas might also be recommended.

2. *Prevention of Flying-Glass Casualties.* In both Hiroshima and Nagasaki there were thousands of persons, particularly at the periphery of the city, who were injured by flying-glass particles from nearby windows shattered by the blast.[5] Industrial establishments might be requested to secure their workers against this hazard by making use of shatterproof glass or by changing the physical layout of workshops. Similarly, if there is danger of a surprise attack, the public at large might be requested to place their furniture away from windows.

3. *Protective Clothing.* It will probably be of value, from the standpoint of minimizing casualties, to encourage people in urban and industrial areas to adopt a new style of clothing which will offer a fair degree of protection against flash burns. Numerous authorities have emphasized the following characteristics in clothing as being desirable: light colors, loose fit, thick cloth (double layers),

---

[4] Los Alamos Scientific Laboratory, *The Effects of Atomic Weapons,* U.S. Government Printing Office, Washington, D.C., 1950.

[5] *Ibid.*

and fire-resistant material. With sufficient cooperation from style designers, clothing manufacturers, and retail advertisers, a new fashion of clothing incorporating these features might be successfully introduced to the American public. In addition, as a means of protection against radiation hazards, it may be considered desirable to have industrial workers, civil defense personnel, and perhaps the entire urban population in certain target areas provided with special canvas clothes and boots to be worn immediately following an A-bomb disaster.[6] If such clothing, meeting scientifically valid specifications, cannot be manufactured in sufficient quantity, recommendations might be issued to housewives urging them to make the appropriate apparel for their own families and to keep it in easily accessible places so that it can be readily donned in the event an emergency arises.

4. *Immunization and Other Medical Procedures.* Medical authorities might find it advisable to have the entire population in vulnerable areas immunized against tetanus as a precautionary measure to reduce infections from burns and cuts. Other anticipated public-health problems following an atomic explosion may require special forms of immunization, and perhaps some other procedures: blood-typing for subsequent transfusions, leucocyte counts for subsequent detection of radioactive exposure, etc. If these services are offered free of charge, a large proportion of the population would probably appear voluntarily at the designated medical centers. But special efforts might be required to elicit the cooperation of those who would otherwise fail to come for the requisite medical procedures.

In addition to teaching adaptive skills and purely factual information about emergency measures, an effective public educational program might be capable of inculcating general attitudes which will facilitate appropriate action in the event of wartime disasters. For example, an effort might be made to call attention to the undesirable consequences of ignoring strangers who need help in order to search for one's own family. Communication themes such as the following, if reinforced by civil defense policies and practices, might

---

[6] *Ibid.*

help to build up the appropriate predisposition: After an A-bomb explosion, separated or missing members of your family will have the best chance of being helped promptly, at the time that they most need help, if everyone follows the same rule—i.e., always give whatever aid you can to people who are nearby before trying to find your own relatives.

Other communications might be designed to develop attitudes and expectations that will help to counteract psychological warfare techniques which the enemy might use in an attempt to produce panic and confusion among our urban population. Atomic weapons offer rich opportunities for the enemy to exploit fear of unseen, insidious dangers. Enemy broadcasts, for instance, might give a list of target cities in which radiation poisons or delayed-action A-bombs are alleged to have been planted by their underground agents. The American public could be warned that such propaganda tricks might be attempted; assurances could be given that in case of any genuine threat, military and defense authorities will act promptly to protect the population. If the public develops a high degree of confidence in the efficiency of our national security apparatus, such forewarnings might greatly reduce the effect of enemy "scare" announcements.

PROBLEMS OF MOTIVATION

Certain types of motivational problems that might interfere with the success of a public educational program are suggested by the results of a pilot study which was carried out in the Los Angeles area during the summer of 1950. Twenty-nine men and women of diverse occupational and educational backgrounds were given intensive interviews for the purpose of obtaining some initial indications of the range and quality of reactions that might be investigated in large-scale studies of current attitudes. The interviews were focused upon expectations concerning atomic bombing, beliefs about the magnitude of the danger, anticipated personal reactions to an imminent A-bomb attack, and related topics. The standard set of questions included several that dealt directly with civil defense preparations:

1. What do you think could be done in the United States at the present time to prepare for the possibility of A-bomb attacks?
2. There are some plans to set up a large civil defense organization so that in case of war there will be people ready to fight fires, give first aid, and so on. What do you think of this idea?
3. Suppose that the Government announced, sometime soon, that millions of people were needed in a civil defense organization in order to prepare for the possibility of bombing attacks against our cities. What would your attitude be if the Government called for volunteers?
4. Do you think that you would volunteer to spend some of your spare time getting civil defense training?

Most of the respondents expressed lukewarm approval of civil defense preparations. The favorable sentiment seemed to be of a rather superficial character, reflecting primarily the conventional appraisal of rescue and relief activities as a humanitarian and patriotic enterprise. In most of the interviews, one finds manifest approval accompanied by the attitude that there is no real need for us to do very much about the A-bomb threat at the present time. Two of the outstanding beliefs that apparently bolstered this complacent view were the following:

1. The threat of bombing attacks against this country is extremely remote.
2. If we are ever faced with real danger, the Government will see to it that the population of the United States is well protected; the individual citizen does not need to engage in any preparatory activity.

Almost all of the respondents explicitly denied that they felt any anxiety about the possible danger of A-bomb attacks. In general, they tended to minimize the threat. There was considerable variation in the specific arguments given, but all the respondents gave some reason or other for believing that the A-bomb threat was too remote to worry about. Some of the optimistic expectations were expressed in terms of fairly concrete arguments. In a few cases, emphasis was placed upon the remoteness of war. For example, a middle-class housewife said:

> "I haven't been thinking at all about the possibility of war or anything like that because I think it is such a long ways off— about fifteen years or so from now. I believe that Russia has so much to do in order to prepare for war that they won't start anything and I don't think the United States is planning to."[7]

Others admitted the possibility of war within a few years but felt that the Russians would be deterred from attacking us with A-bombs: they have few A-bombs and no way of delivering them against American cities; they would not dare to start using A-bombs because they realize that we can retaliate.

A number of the respondents offered no definite arguments at all for their optimistic expectations. Adducing rather vague religious or patriotic grounds, they declared their faith that it simply could not happen. This is illustrated by the following statements from the interviews of three working-class people:

> "I don't think there will be any atom bombs dropped because it would be too awful a thing to happen. . . . I'm not worried about it because I have faith in God and I think everyone's life is in God's hands."

> "Russia might be able to bomb the U.S. but I don't worry about that at all. The United States has always won every war it fought and has always managed to keep its home territories protected and that is what will happen in any war that we ever get into."

> "In the last war we thought that they were going to come over here to bomb us and nothing really happened. . . . I think it will be the same thing this time. . . . I feel that it can't happen here, as they say."

Even those few respondents who admitted having felt some slight degree of concern about the A-bomb showed no evidence of regarding it either as a major threat or as a factor to be taken into account in their personal image of the future. Typically, when discussing

---

[7] These and subsequent statements are taken from the records of the interviews carried out in the pilot study mentioned on page 233 under "Problems of Motivation."

the possibility of A-bomb attacks against this country, these respondents spoke in terms of using *one* A-bomb and thereby minimizing the threat:

> "I don't really feel concerned about the possibility of atom bombs being used here. Of course, it's always possible that *one of them could be smuggled in* but I don't think that's very likely. I think we're quite a long way from any danger on that score."

> "If there is another war I imagine the Russians might try to bomb some of our cities. . . . I believe they would drop atom bombs on our cities if they could. I hope that they couldn't do it but I realize that *they might be able to slip one of them in with a ship.*"

There were some respondents who were definitely opposed to civil defense preparations, apparently as a consequence of their optimistic expectations about the prospects of a future atomic war. These people viewed current civil defense preparations as a waste of time and money or as a premature policy that should not be acted upon until there is a real threat. The following three examples are typical of the negative attitudes that were grounded in the expectation that real danger is an exceedingly remote possibility:

> "In the last war we built shelters, we turned the schools into shelters and set up first aid stations and we never had any occasion to use them. I think that it will be the same thing this time. We will prepare all those things again, but we really won't have any use for them again." [Fifty-five-year-old practical nurse]

> "I don't think that very much needs to be done for the present, because I believe that it will be such a long time before war is at all imminent. So I don't think that civil defense plans are necessary at present. I think the public should know something about it and the material that's coming out now in the newspapers is taking care of that all right." [Thirty-year-old housewife]

> "I suppose that shelters and things like that might be needed but that costs a lot of money, and all that cost comes out of our own pockets. We have to pay for it ourselves. That is, the American people have to pay for it and so I'd be very skeptical about any plan like that. I think I would be undecided if the government came out with an announcement saying that it was all necessary. We as a people often don't look at both sides. We frequently jump into things without bothering to figure out

whether it's really the right thing to do. I would be very cautious about spending any money on civil defense." [Twenty-one-year-old college student]

So long as highly optimistic beliefs persist, a certain amount of public indifference toward civil defense is to be expected. Nevertheless, this type of resistance might prove to be relatively superficial in the sense that a change in attitude might easily be evoked. Although practically all the respondents asserted that they felt unconcerned about the A-bomb threat, there were definite indications that this surface reaction cannot be relied on to give a complete or accurate description of their current state of feeling. In fact, the most salient feature of the entire set of interviews is the mixed, inconsistent attitude expressed toward the threat of A-bomb attacks. The manifest denial of concern was characteristically coupled with signs of uncertainty and indirect expressions of covert feelings of insecurity. For example, a number of respondents who claimed that they were not at all concerned about the possibility that their own city might be bombed, nevertheless revealed that they had given some thought to their own proximity to bombing targets or had even considered the possibility of moving away from the metropolitan area. This type of inconsistency is illustrated by the comments of a twenty-year-old housewife. She repeatedly claimed to be completely unworried because she felt that A-bombs will not be used at all in any future war, since both sides would fear mutual destruction. But after recalling that she had heard about some people who were planning to move away from Los Angeles because of the possibility of A-bomb attacks, she was asked how she felt about that:

"Maybe it's not such a bad idea after all. I've thought about that a lot. I don't really care about Los Angeles anyhow. I'd just as soon live someplace else. I think it might be a good idea to go to Nevada—it ought to be much safer there."

Some of the interview material suggests that communications which call attention to the magnitude of the danger would be effective in evoking heightened awareness of the need for civil defense. A number of the respondents showed a marked shift, from outright disapproval to qualified approval, merely in response to a few statements by the interviewer that had been intended to test the stability of the individual's opinion. For example, an insurance salesman promptly abandoned his economic arguments against expanding our defense efforts when "expert opinion" regarding the danger of A-bomb attacks was cited to him. At the beginning of the interview, he confidently announced that if we do not stop overtaxing ourselves, we shall be giving in to Russia's "phoney" threats that are designed to "bleed us white." But at the end of the session he revised his opinion after being told about the "real danger" posed by the A-bomb:

> "Well, I think we shall have to consider using subterranean cellars. And we'll have to set up all kinds of look-out planes and spotters who can notify us in time. We would have to take all kinds of air-raid precautions—we should prepare for that now. Our local governments should set up some kind of arrangements to take care of the situation. . . . This time there could be some real danger and I think that civil defense might be much more important than it was in the last war."

Similar changes occurred in a number of cases when the interviewer introduced ideas that ran counter to the optimistic expectations expressed by the respondent. But not all the changes evoked by statements about the magnitude of the danger were in the direction of increased interest in civil defense. A few respondents reacted by expressing extremely hostile attitudes directed against the potential enemy or against groups within the United States. This reaction is illustrated by the following case material. A forty-year-old aircraft worker repeatedly asserted during the interview that he felt unconcerned about the possibility of A-bomb attacks and he adduced numerous optimistic arguments: Probably there won't be another war and anyhow it would be to the advantage of both sides to postpone war for many years; if there is a war, Russia might try to use *an* A-bomb against us, but they probably wouldn't succeed and, besides, all the advantages would be on our side; it's all a very remote possibility and there is no need to do anything about it at present; etc. At the end of the interview he was told that some experts believe that Russia now has a sizeable stockpile of A-bombs and has been building long-range planes that could reach American cities. His response was:

> "Yes, I guess that's true. Their planes could get through. It would be a terrible thing. I hate to think of what would happen."

After being told a few more details (that some experts estimate that Russia will have over one hundred A-bombs by next year; that Russian submarines can launch A-bombs against coastal cities; etc.), this man displayed overt signs of emotional tension and asserted:

> "I'm really afraid about that. Probably the only thing we can do is to hit them first, hit them real hard. . . . We might be able to knock them out first."

In this case, it is to be noted that although initially there was consistent denial of concern and elaborate minimization of the threat on seemingly reasonable grounds, the threshold for anxiety arousal was actually extremely low. Merely exposing this person to a brief communication (by a total stranger) was sufficient to evoke an entirely different reaction. Perhaps the most important feature of this example is the readiness with which the original optimistic unconcern was abandoned and replaced—at least temporarily—by an aggressive political attitude (demand for preventive war).

In other interviews, a similar transformation occurred when the A-bomb threat was sharply posed, sometimes resulting in the expression of hostile political attitudes directed toward domestic targets. A forty-five-year-old mechanic, who had given typical minimizing arguments, switched to an exaggerated conception of the threat when his attention was called to Russia's capabilities: "They might try to wipe this nation off the face of the earth." He then proceeded to make extremely derogatory statements about the present administration in Washington, such as the following:

> "I suppose some of those Communist scientists in the government know what the score is. But the government doesn't seem to see fit to let the American people in on any information."

A thirty-five-year-old waitress expressed a similar hostile attitude after being told about the A-bomb threat:

"We should stay out of the war. It was a mistake for us to go into Korea. We should give up the idea of trying to make money on other countries. People like MacArthur shouldn't be permitted to run this country. We should sit back and give up our interests in other countries; in that way we can stay out of war. Also, we have too many foreigners in this country. We have been too lenient with people coming here and should crack down on that. The Communists in this country are very dangerous and they should be sent back to Russia or should be carefully watched so that they can't cause any trouble. We have too many foreigners here now and we should do something about that."

The case illustrations just presented are typical examples of the mixed, unstable attitudes toward the A-bomb threat encountered in many of the interviews. When comfortable beliefs about the future were temporarily shaken by the interviewer's counterarguments, the initial unconcern was often abandoned. Without any apparent forethought or considered judgment, some of the respondents seemingly were ready to support gross changes in American political policies, such as preventive war, extreme isolationism, and drastic curbs against foreigners and Communists. It is obvious that if such predispositional tendencies exist among a sizeable proportion of the American public, serious social and political consequences may ensue from an ill-devised campaign which attempts to elicit popular support for civil defense solely by arousing strong anxiety about the A-bomb threat.

Although only a few respondents expressed open objections to civil defense, practically all of them manifested a *very low degree of interest*. The dominant answer given to questions about civil defense plans was to the effect that "I don't know much about it, but I suppose that it might be a good idea." Most of the respondents admitted that they had paid little attention to discussions of civil defense and had not given much thought to the topic before. A few mentioned having noticed relevant material in the newspapers and on the radio—explanations of what to do if an A-bomb drops and announcements of current defense plans. But the details of the material were almost completely forgotten. Even the better-educated respondents, whose comments about the current international situation showed that they had kept themselves informed about world affairs, knew very little about the nature of atomic disasters or about the possible measures for reducing our vulnerability. Probably as a result of their general lack of interest, the respondents had acquired very little specific information, despite the fact that a good deal of material on civil defense had appeared in their local newspapers, in popular magazines, and on the radio during the preceding months.

In most cases, this lack of information was clearly apparent when they spoke about the power of atomic weapons. Evidently, because of grossly exaggerated notions about the destructiveness of an A-bomb, the favorable sentiment toward civil defense was frequently qualified by strong doubts as to how much good any sort or preparation would do. In some cases, these doubts were clearly based on the tacit assumption that an atomic disaster is so devastating that preparatory measures would be utterly futile. Typical comments were the following:

> "I think that the atom bomb would destroy all shelters. So there isn't much that anyone could do about escaping from an atom bomb."

> "I don't think there is any way of preparing for the danger. . . . The bombs are such that it doesn't help out at all to have that sort of thing [civil defense teams] available. It just wouldn't do any good in any case."

> "Nothing can be done about the danger of an atom bomb. Once a bomb falls everybody is killed who is anywheres around there and no one can be saved. I believe that there is no protection against it."

As these statements imply, some of the respondents assumed that an A-bomb attack would be a totally inescapable, uncontrollable form of mass annihilation. Perhaps this stereotyped image underlies much of the personal indifference toward civil defense. Obviously, a person will not derive any reassurance from the fact that defense preparations are under way if he conceives of an atomic attack as a kind of "end-of-the-world" catastrophe. To the extent that current opinions concerning civil defense arise from misconceptions about the destructive impact of the A-bomb, it should be possible to bring about favorable changes merely by publicizing the facts about Hiroshima and Nagasaki.

Even the most sophisticated persons among those who were interviewed evidenced a markedly oversimplified conception of the antipersonnel effects of an atomic explosion: everyone within range is killed and everyone else is presumably far enough away to be unharmed. There was considerable surprise on the part of those respondents who were told a few simple facts about the survivors at Hiroshima and Nagasaki—that there were thousands of injured people requiring prompt medical treatment; that many violent deaths occurred hours after the explosion as a result of secondary fires; that there were tens of thousands who suffered from lack of food and shelter, etc. In some cases, this type of information elicited an immediate change in opinion toward civil defense. For example, a teacher who originally was very doubtful about the efficacy of civilian defense, made the following statement after being told about the various types of A-bomb casualties:

> "Oh, well, in that case I would be completely in favor of a civil defense organization. I would feel that we ought to get going on it right away if it really could make that much difference. I really haven't read much about atom bomb casualties and I didn't realize that so many could be saved. . . . My conception of it was that there isn't very much that could be done to alter a person's chances of surviving, once an atom bomb is dropped. But if what you say is true, then I think that the government should be doing something about it right away to prepare for any such emergency."

Obviously, one cannot generalize about American public opinion from a very small number of interviews. But the pilot study does serve to call attention to certain types of attitudes and expectations that warrant careful investigation in subsequent cross-section studies of the United States population. From the intensive interviews, one may surmise that there are important motivating functions to be taken into account in planning a program of public education.

Information about Russia's capabilities might evoke a sharper awareness of the need for civil defense among people who remain complacently over-optimistic. Material that is designed to create a realistic conception of atomic warfare might help to correct exaggerated beliefs among those who feel that preparation is futile. But, in order to have the effect of increasing personal willingness to participate in preparatory activities, such information will require careful assessment and planning to counteract potentially unfavorable effects.

Popular magazine articles, newspaper features, radio and television programs, movies, free pamphlets, and other mass media ordinarily employed in a national publicity campaign may be quite effective in launching the educational program. Initially, these media can be counted upon to arouse interest, to increase motivation to learn, and to foster favorable attitudes toward civil defense among a broad sector of the American population. But how many people will devote the amount of time necessary to master the basic information and skills that are essential for self-preservation and for effective emergency action?

It will be noted that a number of items included in the sample "curriculum" outlined at the beginning of this chapter will probably require more than purely verbal instruction; for example, item 2—on how to respond adaptively to the flash of an A-bomb explosion—requires overt practice as well. In order to reduce their reaction time to the point where the effects of the secondary heat wave and the concussion wave (which occur up to several seconds after the flash of the explosion) could be avoided, most people would have to rehearse the reaction of hurling themselves down to a prone position ("hitting the dirt") and of ducking away from windows in response to an unexpected light signal. There is reason to believe that if these reactions are *not* practiced by the population of a city, thousands of people who could save themselves will be killed or severely injured in a surprise A-bomb attack.[8] Other items may also require a certain amount of overt practice, such as learning how to select the correct direction for escaping from the disaster area by inferring the locus of the explosion from the shadow burns cast by objects in its path.

---

[8] Los Alamos Scientific Laboratory, *op. cit.*

The necessity for overt practice is only one of many reasons for expecting that adequate training of the general population, if it is seriously attempted, will necessitate an intensive educational program that goes far beyond the usual publicity campaign. The anxiety aroused by the subject matter will interfere with the motivation to learn and will often keep the size of self-selected audiences to a minimum. Even if the content of the educational program is limited to the most essential material, there is still so much to be learned—and it must be *learned well* to be effective—that special training courses may be necessary.

Members of the civil defense organization could certainly be given thorough preparation as part of their regular training, and many of them might pass on the most relevant information to others in the community. Special neighborhood evening classes could be set up, perhaps conducted by members of the local defense organization, which might be attended by those nonmembers in the community who would be willing to come. If the basic material is incorporated into the public-school and high-school curricula, the majority of school children and large numbers of adolescents might become well trained; many of them could be counted on to introduce some of the information to older members of their families. Even with such devices to supplement the national publicity program, however, there will probably be a very sizeable proportion of the urban population who will fail to learn the material and consequently will not know what to do to save themselves and their families in an A-bomb disaster.

Investigations of audience exposure and response to national publicity campaigns might help to identify problem groups, e.g., those who lack ability to comprehend fully the usual content of newspapers or those who are not reached by the usual mass media. Special techniques, such as those employed with low I.Q. groups in the army, might be developed for instructing people who have learning difficulties.

With the cooperation of educators experienced in the techniques of mass education, the material to be learned could undoubtedly be presented in such a way that the vast majority of the population would be *capable* of learning it, provided it were conscientiously studied and rehearsed (in the way so many people apply themselves to handbooks of traffic rules when they are required to pass an information test in order to secure a driver's license).

Specialists in educational methods, when called upon to aid in setting up the program, will undoubtedly find that their major problem is to develop effective incentives for that very large fraction of the public for whom the learning of this new information is a highly disagreeable chore. Should publicity about the educational program present strongly negative characterizations of nonparticipants, i.e., accuse them of being unpatriotic, of neglecting the welfare of their families, or of being too "stupid" to comprehend the need for individual preparation? Should the point be stressed that "you will feel less worried as soon as you begin learning the appropriate know-how"? To what extent, if at all, should an appeal be made by playing up the terrifying consequences which might be in store for those who are unprepared? Questions of this sort may require special investigations of the over-all effectiveness of alternative ways of building up motivations among those who initially lack interest or who seek to avoid the unpleasant material. In evaluating certain of the alternatives, it will be necessary to pay careful attention to the problem of minimizing the unfavorable effects of arousing anxiety.

ANXIETY-REDUCING INFORMATION

When people are presented with material dealing with possible dangers and are told about the ways and means of saving themselves, they are likely to ignore such information or to resent it unless they believe there is some chance that they *actually will* be exposed to the threats being discussed. For the present, it will be assumed that the educational program will not be initiated on a large scale unless public opinion in this country warrants the attempt; i.e., it will not be introduced until such time that there is widespread belief that A-bomb attacks against this country represent a probable danger for which preparation is essential to survival.

Under such conditions, information about atomic warfare will most likely be received with a high degree of serious interest. But when the details about the dangers are presented, and when the complicated and extreme lengths to which one has to go to avert the dangers are spelled out, there is likely to be a marked increase in anxiety. As people develop a greater awareness of the concrete realities of the threat, they may become increasingly insecure and pessimistic about their chances of survival. Such reactions would not only impede the learning of the material, but would also have unfavorable morale effects in general.

Marked individual differences in reactions to anxiety-arousing information are to be expected. In a potentially threatening situation, some people feel less disturbed when they are given an authoritative statement of what the dangers really are, whereas others are made more fearful by such information. Psychological investigations might provide some useful indications of communication techniques which are most effective in minimizing anxiety among different social strata with unique predispositions (e.g., presenting realistic details about the danger to be anticipated might be found to have relatively favorable motivating effects among male adolescents and among urban working-class families, even though it might have demoralizing effects among other subpopulations).

To counteract the disruptive effects of presenting anxiety-evoking material to the public at large, it will be necessary to give careful consideration to anxiety-reducing devices. One obvious technique which might be used is that of giving reassuring items of information whenever a potential danger is being discussed. For example, in presenting the warning that drinking water in the disaster area might be contaminated and that internal absorption of radioactive water might be fatal, such reassurances as the following would help to emphasize the ways in which this danger will be avoided: "just remember not to drink any water if you are ever in a disaster area and you will avoid this hazard"; or "there will be a small emergency supply of pure water on hand so that you and your family will not have to go thirsty"; or "teams of well-equipped civil defense workers have been trained to test and purify large amounts of water very quickly." In general, it might be most effective to avoid featuring the danger to be anticipated except where the material will serve the purpose of explaining (and motivating adherence to) rules about what to do and what not to do in facing specific sources of danger.

Another aspect of sound psychological strategy is to provide realistic and reassuring information *in advance,* before misconceptions, personal fantasies, and exaggerated rumors have a chance to develop. This requires skill in anticipating the sources of anxiety which are likely to be touched off by any given item of information.

The following illustration may serve to highlight some of the psychological considerations involved in making judgments about *which* facts should be given to the public. Suppose that an audience has already learned, in connection with radiological safety rules, that radiation sickness is an unpleasant and sometimes fatal disease. What information, if any, should be given about the minor symptom of epilation? The fact that some people in the audience already know that in Hiroshima many people lost their hair would require that some realistic details be given; otherwise, there is the likelihood that the strange symptom of losing one's hair will become generally known via exaggerated rumors. What specifically should the audience be told about epilation? To answer this question, it is necessary to consider two other questions: (1) What fears will a simple description of the epilation symptom arouse? and (2) How can these fears be allayed? Sometimes the answers to these questions may require a certain amount of research on typical subjective responses of the audience to the given topic. With respect to the particular example under discussion, one might predict that two main fears are likely to be aroused by the information that small doses of radioactivity produce epilation. Some people will probably be worried that this strange symptom, coming several days or weeks after the explosion, implies that one will suffer from other, far worse effects (e.g., "If all of one's hair falls out, will other parts of the body also be affected in a similar way?"). Another likely source of worry is that the disfigurement may be permanent (e.g., "If I get a mild case of radiation sickness, will I remain completely bald-headed for the rest of my life?"). It becomes obvious, once these specific anxieties are taken into account, that any discussion of epilation should place a strong emphasis upon the fact that this symptom is *not* a sign that any other kind of bodily impairment will necessarily occur and that in most cases of moderate or mild radiation sickness the hair grows back again in normal fashion within a few months.

There are many other topics requiring careful presentation, with emphasis being placed upon facts that serve to allay anxieties which might otherwise be aroused. It should be noted that this presentation problem will sometimes require the inclusion of information which would not ordinarily be considered essential from the standpoint of teaching people what they should do in a disaster situation. Nevertheless, the skillful employment of anxiety-reducing information is likely to be an essential factor in determining the over-all success of the public educational program.

In the light of the above discussion, it is clear that emotional factors should be taken into account at an early stage in the preparation of the material for the public educational program. Before that stage is reached, research should be encouraged on the general problem of minimizing the anxiety aroused by mass communications dealing with potential dangers.

CHAPTER 13
APPREHENSIVENESS AMONG THE URBAN POPULATION

Closely linked with the special problems of anxiety-arousal, discussed in the preceding chapter, is a much more general one affecting the entire civil defense enterprise. In purely psychological terms, ignoring the specifics of the international situation, the problem might be formulated as follows: How can people in vulnerable areas build up a tolerance for insecurity, i.e., the ability to maintain emotional control and to act intelligently despite being confronted with the threat of impending danger? From what little is known about reactions to objective anxiety situations, one would expect that socially disruptive and irrational reactions are most likely to occur if intense awareness of the A-bomb threat is elicited unexpectedly without adequate psychological preparation; i.e., if the perception of a rather vague and remote threat is suddenly transformed (by actual events or by official communications) into a perception of a clear and almost present danger.

Suppose that complacent expectations were rudely shaken by a drastic event or warning—an official announcement that Russia has a large stockpile of A-bombs ready for immediate use and that we may be attacked at any moment. Feelings of anxiety would be so highly aroused among the urban population that large numbers might take drastic action, whether it is rational or not. This is especially probable if no obvious defensive measures were visible that could be relied on for protection. In a crisis of this kind, there may be (1) spontaneous migration from cities and from industrial areas; (2) widespread attitudes of pessimism ("Nothing that can be done will do us any good.") or of fatalism ("It is all a matter of luck, so it doesn't matter whether you try to do anything about it or not."); (3) resentment and lack of trust

249

in government authorities. Under these extreme conditions, it would be extremely difficult to obtain public support for a long-range civil defense program. The type of training and preparation required probably would not meet popular demands for dramatic protective action; the sense of futility (discussed in Chapter 11) might spread throughout the entire nation, handicapping the entire civil defense program ("All of this business is just a drop in the bucket—what good will it do?"). Then, if the "war scare" crisis subsides and is followed by a period in which the danger again appears to be remote, people may become wary about "being taken in by false alarms"; appeals for participation in civil defense activities which attempt to arouse a realistic degree of concern about potential wartime dangers would then become relatively ineffective.

In order to avoid extreme reactions of anticipatory anxiety, it is probably essential to bring about a stepwise increase in awareness of the reality and proximity of the bomb threat, before the danger appears to be actually at hand. In each person's private image of his own future, the threat must come gradually into focus at a time when the menace is not perceived as being overwhelmingly great.

A stepwise increase in awareness of impending danger, with a corresponding increase in feelings of insecurity, has two advantages from the standpoint of personal adjustment. First, it stimulates each individual to rehearse the future danger situation in his own imagination and this, in turn, often leads to the spontaneous development of a variety of personal techniques for handling one's own anxiety.[1] This process of internal preparation probably leaves the person in a less vulnerable psychological position when he is confronted with subsequent anxiety-arousing events. Secondly, a slight dose of insecurity often serves as a powerful motivation for participating in group activities which are designed to ward off the danger; such participation with others can become an important source of reassurance, and, with subsequent increases in insecurity, the person is likely to turn more and more of his energies into this form of activity.

---

[1] See Chap. 8.

One of the important implications of the tentative, schematic analysis just presented is that the most favorable time for introducing a full-scale civil defense program and for demanding all-out public participation would be during a period when war does *not* appear to be imminent but during which public attention is focused more and more upon the threat looming up on the distant horizon. Thus, one would expect the full program to be most successfully introduced at the time of a comparatively limited, cushioned crisis (e.g., when it becomes generally known that "Russia will have sufficient weapons and equipment for launching an attack against our cities in about one or two years from now") rather than in a full-blown crisis (e.g., "Russia is now capable of launching an attack at any moment").

Similar considerations apply to the effects of anxiety-arousing appeals in obtaining public cooperation in various action programs. Consider, for example, the potential problems of industrial relocation during a prolonged "cold-war" period. Large-scale dispersal of United States urban centers is not a very likely prospect,[2] but it seems quite probable that a small segment of the population will be directly affected by a limited decentralization program. According to some reports, relocation of industry has already begun in a very small way and may be increasingly encouraged by the Government. Numerous commentators have called attention to the vulnerability of centralized administrative agencies of the Government and it is to be expected that these, also, will be subject to a certain amount of dispersal. So long as relocation is kept down to a very small scale, little public resistance is likely to occur; but if large industrial plants are removed from areas in which they employ a substantial percentage of the resident population, considerable objection and protest will probably arise, particularly among the people whose jobs are at stake. To some extent, resistance might be overcome by offering attractive inducements to encourage and help workers to move with the industrial organization that had been employing them. If this method fails, however, the problem may become an acute one.

---

[2] See Chap. 10.

One of the obvious ways of attempting to convince dissident industrial workers that they should accept relocation is to arouse their anxiety. Strong emphasis upon the dangers of A-bomb attacks and upon the avoidance of this threat by taking advantage of the opportunity to move to a less vulnerable section of the country may appear to be a successful way to overcome resistance to relocation. But it may also be effective among broad sections of the population for whom no such plans are intended. Instead of the problem of resistance to the limited relocation program, the Government may be faced with public clamor for far more extensive dispersal plans; at the same time there may be a considerable amount of spontaneous, unplanned migration away from vulnerable areas.

Other kinds of boomerang effects may arise in connection with various security measures, such as antisabotage precautions. Government officials have already issued public warnings concerning espionage, sabotage, and underground activity; they have urged that everyone be alert to report suspicious circumstances to proper authorities. At some future time, when atomic warfare is felt to be much less remote than at present, people may become extremely apprehensive about the possibility that A-bombs can be launched by submarines, planted in innocent-looking merchant craft, or even smuggled into the country piece by piece and reassembled secretly inside any factory, office building, or apartment house. At such a time, the public might become all too cooperative, especially if anxiety is strongly aroused by playing up dramatic incidents which demonstrate that underground agents are actively at work trying to plant A-bombs in American cities. The national security apparatus might then become overloaded with a multitude of false leads, coupled with urgent requests for prompt investigations of questionable activities in every local community. Concurrently, in a national atmosphere of apprehensiveness and suspicion, critical issues might arise with respect to the political dangers of "scapegoat" reactions toward minority groups and popular demands for extreme security measures of an antidemocratic character.

The possibility of unfavorable consequences of the sort just mentioned highlights once again the need for careful studies on the effects of anxiety-arousing communications and for systematic attitude research on predispositional tendencies among the American population. Intensive research is needed, not only to gauge the impact of alternative communication policies, but also to increase our general psychological understanding of personal adjustment to impending danger. The scientific and popular literature on reactions of persons exposed to threats of death or injury contains relatively little pertinent information. Perhaps the most cogent data on adjustment to situations of danger are those sparse clinical observations made during World War II, which have been summarized in Chapters 5 through 8. By concentrating on comparable danger situations that arise in peacetime, research workers in the human sciences should be able to discover a great deal more that will point the way to effective principles of psychological strategy for counteracting the demoralizing effects of anxiety and pessimism.

After all, there are many more-or-less "doomed" individuals—for instance, among certain types of military combat units and among civilians with incurable diseases—who are able to face the prospect of death without becoming demoralized and without losing their strong motivation to take every precaution to maximize their chances of surviving, even though they realize that the odds in their favor are low. Investigations centered upon the psychological mechanisms that come into play in extreme conditions may serve to illuminate the critical determinants of personal adjustment.

Exploratory studies might be encouraged along the following lines. In order to obtain an initial estimate of the validity of current speculative hypotheses and to arrive at some new insights, intensive interviews and behavioral studies could be carried out with persons who are exposed to an extreme threat of personal danger, such as:

1. Persons who have cancer or some other serious disease, particularly those who suffer little discomfort but know that they might have only a short time to live.

2. Persons who are scheduled to undergo an extremely serious operation.

3. Men in hazardous occupations for which there is a relatively high casualty rate (e.g., test pilots).
4. People in communities threatened by epidemics or by other periodic disasters.

Interviews and other methods of case study could be applied in order to obtain insights into the mechanisms that help to explain how such persons adjust to the threat. The most plausible hypotheses could then be investigated further by making use of more precise research techniques for testing relationships among specific factors, e.g., correlational studies with a larger sample of subjects and controlled experiments.

Three types of problems on which intensive case studies might be expected to provide valuable leads are the following:

1. What are the dominant fears and psychological needs that are aroused by the threat of impending personal disaster? (For example, does the threat of danger regularly evoke increased fear of social isolation, as the material in Chapter 8 suggests?) Latent as well as manifest trends aroused by the threat of personal disaster may be revealed by observations of changes in attitudes toward significant persons in the environment, by the manifest content of anxiety feelings, and by daydreams or other fantasy productions.

2. What sorts of reassurances and nonreassurances are given by others and with what effect? (For example, in connection with an investigation of anticipatory anxiety reactions of surgical patients, some useful data on the effects of different kinds of communications were obtained by asking the patients what their physicians had told them and how they felt about the information they were given.)

3. What specific factors in the current life situation tend to augment emotional tension and what factors tend to diminish it? Tentative inferences may be made from observations of (1) the nature of the activities which the person is required to carry out in order to maximize his chances for survival; (2) relationships with family members, friends,

and authority figures; (3) opportunities for engaging in preferred activities.

From intensive case studies designed to provide information on each person's thoughts, feelings, and behavior when confronted with the threat of an impending personal disaster, it should be possible to discover key variables in the adjustment process and to derive plausible hypotheses for systematic investigation. Primary attention should be given to comparisons between those who adjust well and those who adjust poorly to the same type of threat. One of the aims of these comparisons should be to discern differences in *communication factors* which appear to make a difference in promoting one type of reaction as against another. For example, it might be found that among patients with serious diseases, those who are told to adhere to a strict set of health rules tend to be less anxious and less pessimistic than others. Findings of this kind could then be examined from the standpoint of their implications for hypotheses on communication contents which facilitate adequate personal adjustment to the prospect of danger or imminent death; some of the hypotheses may provide suggestive leads to practical manipulative devices for minimizing disturbed reactions.

If research teams for investigating peacetime disasters are organized, it would be possible to arrange for special field studies in order to test the most plausible hypotheses with entire communities under actual disaster conditions. Partially confirmed hypotheses might then be tested with a variety of persons exposed to different *kinds* of threat in order to arrive at general principles which will apply to a wide range of impending danger situations. For example, from on-the-spot studies of peacetime disasters, valuable data may be obtained on the conditions under which official communications issued during a crisis are successful or unsuccessful. By contacting the relevant authorities, field investigators could obtain fairly complete information about the *media* and the *content* of practically every official communication issued to the public before, during, and after each disaster, including such items as (1) warnings of impending danger; (2) recommendations concerning preventive and protective measures; (3) reassurances about anticipated dangers;

(4) evacuation orders and other emergency demands; (5) information releases about the progress of disaster control, the damage sustained, or the damage anticipated; (6) notices about the enforcement of emergency laws and regulations; (7) warnings and recommendations about public health and safety measures during the postdisaster period; (8) announcements about postdisaster relief and rehabilitation activities. Often, by means of systematic interviews and other observational techniques, reliable information can be obtained on the effectiveness of different types of communication with respect to:

1. Communication exposure (Was it perceived by those for whom it was intended?).
2. Comprehension (Was it correctly understood?).
3. Acceptance (Was it believed?).
4. Transmission (Was the information passed on to others?).
5. Arousal of affect (What emotional feelings did it produce?).
6. Instigation of action (Did it elicit appropriate or inappropriate action?).
7. Morale (What effect did it have on attitudes toward authorities, expectations about the future, etc.?).

Similar studies could also be made of the effects of newspaper stories, radiobroadcasts, spontaneous word-of-mouth rumors, and other pertinent communications which are disseminated without official verification. Thus, it should be possible to observe the psychological impact of various media and content characteristics so as to identify the communication factors which appear to maximally effective in preventing adverse mass reactions under conditions of objective threat. Opportunities might then be sought for checking the main findings by conducting controlled experiments in communities where peacetime disasters are anticipated. By comparing the responses of two equivalent groups, one of which is given appropriately designed communications, and the other not, the effects could be determined with a fairly high degree of precision.

The types of research proposed have at least two obvious drawbacks from the standpoint of coordinated research planning. First, such studies are very costly and time consuming. It would require painstaking work on the part of many highly skilled investigators before even the most tentative findings relevant to civil defense planning could be derived from intensive case studies; field investigations and controlled experiments are even more costly. Secondly, even if effective manipulative devices are developed for handling localized peacetime threat situations, they may not be applicable on a mass scale to a collective wartime threat.

Despite these objections, the proposals which have just been outlined represent what seems to be a promising line of attack for making basic scientific advances relevant to the practical problem of minimizing anxiety, pessimism, and disruptive behavior in times of anticipated danger. One has only to contemplate the potential magnitude of the problem to feel that in the absence of any safe bet, it is worth while to take the best possible research gambles.

Bibliography

PART I: REACTIONS AT HIROSHIMA AND NAGASAKI

BRUES, A. M., "With the Atomic Bomb Casualty Commission in Japan," *Bull. Atomic Scientists,* Vol. 3, June, 1947, pp. 143–144.

GLOVER, E., "Notes on the Psychological Effects of War Conditions on the Civilian Population," Part III, "The Blitz," *International J. Psychoanal.,* Vol. 23, 1942, pp. 17–37.

HERSEY, JOHN, *Hiroshima,* Alfred A. Knopf, New York, 1946.

Los Alamos Scientific Laboratory, *The Effects of Atomic Weapons,* prepared for and in cooperation with the U.S. Department of Defense and the U.S. Atomic Energy Commission, U.S. Government Printing Office, Washington, D.C., 1950.

NAGAI, T., *We of Nagasaki: The Story of Survivors in an Atomic Wasteland,* Duell, Sloan and Pearce, Inc., New York, 1951.

Report of British Mission to Japan, *The Effects of the Atomic Bombs at Hiroshima and Nagasaki,* His Majesty's Stationery Office, London, 1946.

SIEMES, FATHER, "Hiroshima—August 6, 1945," *Bull. Atomic Scientists,* Vol. 1, May, 1946, pp. 2–6.

SPIEGEL, H. X., "Psychiatric Observations in the Tunisian Campaign," *Am. J. Orthopsychiat.,* Vol. 14, 1943, pp. 381–385.

U.S. Army Medical Department, "What Every Medical Officer Should Know about the Atomic Bomb," *Bull. U.S. Army Med. Dept.,* Vol. 8, April, 1948, pp. 247–326.

USSBS Report, *The Effects of Atomic Bombs on Health and Medical Services in Hiroshima and Nagasaki,* U.S. Government Printing Office, Washington, D.C., 1947.

——, *The Effects of Atomic Bombs on Hiroshima and Nagasaki,* U.S. Government Printing Office, Washington, D.C., 1946.

————, *The Effects of Strategic Bombing on Japanese Morale,* U.S. Government Printing Office, Washington, D.C., 1947.

PART II: EFFECTS OF AIR WAR

BODMAN, F., "Child Psychiatry in Wartime Britain," *J. Educational Psychol.,* Vol. 35, 1944, pp. 293–301.

BRANDER, T., "Psychiatric Observations among Finnish Children during the Russo-Finnish War of 1939–1940," *Nervous Child,* Vol. 2, 1943, pp. 313–319.

BROWN, F., "Civilian Psychiatric Air-raid Casualties," *Lancet,* Vol. 1, 1941, pp. 686–691.

COX, G., "Eyewitness in Madrid," *Harper's Magazine,* Vol. 175, 1937, pp. 27–30.

CRICHTON-MILLER, H., "Somatic Factors Conditioning Air-raid Reactions," *Lancet,* Vol. 2, 1941, pp. 31–34.

DENNY-BROWN, D., "Effects of Modern Warfare on Civil Population," *J. Lab. Clin. Med.,* Vol. 28, 1943, pp. 641–645.

DESPERT, J. L., *Preliminary Report on Children's Reactions to the War, Including a Critical Survey of the Literature,* Cornell University Medical College, New York, 1942.

DUNSDON, M. I., "A Psychologist's Contribution to Air-raid Problems," *Mental Health,* Vol. 2, London, 1941, pp. 37–41.

EHRSTROM, M. Ch., "Psychogene Blutdruckssteigerung," *Acta Medica Scand.,* Vol. 72, fasc. VI, 1945, p. 546.

FRASER, R., I. M. LESLIE, and D. PHELPS, "Psychiatric Effects of Severe Personal Experiences during Bombing," *Proc. Roy. Soc. Med.,* Vol. 36, 1943, pp. 119–123.

FREUD, A., and D. BURLINGHAM, *Infants without Families,* International Universities Press, New York, 1944.

————, *Young Children in Wartime,* George Allen & Unwin, Ltd., London, 1942.

GARNER, H. H., "Psychiatric Casualties in Combat," *War Med.,* Vol. 8, 1945, pp. 343–357.

GILLESPIE, R. D., *Psychological Effects of War on Citizen and Soldier,* W. W. Norton & Company, New York, 1942.

————, "Résumé of His Addresses before the New York Academy of Medicine," *So. J. Med.,* Vol. 41, New York, 1941, pp. 2346–2349.

GLOVER, E., "Notes on the Psychological Effects of War Conditions on the Civilian Population," Part III, "The Blitz," *International J. Psychoanal.,* Vol. 23, 1942, pp. 17–37.

GRINKER, R. R., B. WILLERMAN, A. D. BRADLEY, and A. FASTOVSKY, "A Study of Psychological Predisposition to the Development of Operational Fatigue," *Am. J. Orthopsychiat.,* Vol. 16, 1946, pp. 191–214.

HADFIELD, J. A., "Treatment by Suggestion and Hypnoanalysis," Chap. 7 in E. Miller (ed.), *The Neuroses of War,* The Macmillan Company, New York, 1940.

HALDANE, J. B. S., *A.R.P.,* Victor Gollancz, Ltd., London, 1938.

HARRISSON, T., "Obscure Nervous Effects of Air Raids," *Brit. Med. J.,* Vol. 1, 1941, pp. 573–574 and 832.

HENRY, J., "Initial Reactions to the Americans in Japan," *J. Soc. Issues,* Vol. 2, 1946, pp. 19–25.

IDLE, E. D., *War over West Ham,* Faber & Faber, Ltd., London, 1943.

INGERSOLL, R., *Report on England,* Simon and Schuster, Inc., New York, 1940.

JANIS, I. L., "Objective Factors Related to Morale Attitudes in the Aerial Combat Situation," Chap. 8 in S. Stouffer, *et al., The American Soldier: Combat and Its Aftermath,* Vol. 2, Princeton University Press, Princeton, N.J., 1949.

KARDINER, A., *The Traumatic Neuroses of War,* Paul B. Hoeber, Inc., New York, 1941.

KLEIN, E., "The Influence of Teachers' and Parents' Attitudes and Behavior upon Children in Wartime," *Mental Hygiene,* Vol. 26, New York, 1942, pp. 434–445.

KOGAN-YASNY, V. M., "Some Aspects of Peptic Ulcer during Wartime," *Am. Rev. of Soviet Med.,* Vol. 2, 1945, pp. 233–237.

KRIS, E., "Danger and Morale," *Am. J. Orthopsychiat.,* Vol. 14, 1944, pp. 147–156.

————, "Morale in Germany," *Am. J. Sociology,* Vol. 47, 1941, pp. 452–461.

LACASSIE, R., "Formes cliniques de l'énurésis de l'Adulte et Perturbations de Guerre du Rythme urinaire," *Paris Médicale,* Vol. 37, 1947, pp. 168–171.

LAIRD, S., and W. GRAEBNER, *Conversation in London,* William Morrow & Company, Inc., New York, 1942.

LAMBLING, GOSSET, BERTRAND, and VIARE, "Le Génie évolutif de la Maladie ulcereuse avant et pendant la Guerre," *Paris Médicale,* Vol. 1, 1946, pp. 146–152.

LANDER, J., "The Psychiatrically Immunizing Effect of Combat Wounds," *Am. J. Orthopsychiat.,* Vol. 16, 1946, pp. 536–541.

LANGDON-DAVIES, J., *Air Raid,* George Routledge & Sons, Ltd., London, 1938.

LINDEMANN, E., "Symptomatology and Management of Acute Grief," *Am. J. Psychiat.,* Vol. 101, 1944, pp. 141–148.

MacCURDY, J. T., *The Structure of Morale,* The Macmillan Company, New York, 1943.

MACKINTOSH, J. M., *The War and Mental Health in England,* Commonwealth Fund, Division of Publication, New York, 1944.

"Mass Observation," T. H. Harrisson and C. Madge (eds.), *War Begins at Home,* Chatto & Windus, London, 1940.

MATTE, I., "Observations of the English in Wartime," *J. Nervous Ment. Disease,* Vol. 97, 1943, pp. 447–463.

MEERLOO, A. M., *Aftermath of Peace,* International Universities Press, New York, 1946.

Military Mobilization Committee of the American Psychiatric Association, *Psychiatric Aspects of Civilian Morale,* Family Welfare Assoc. of America, New York, 1942.

MIRA, E., "Psychiatric Experiences in the Spanish War," *Brit. Med. J.,* Vol. 1, 1939, pp. 1217–1220.

MORRIS, J. M., and R. M. TITMUSS, "Epidemiology of Peptic Ulcer," *Lancet,* Vol. 2, 1944, pp. 841–845.

PHILLIPS-WOLLEY, C. J. F., "An Analysis of Gastric and Duodenal Ulcers in Vancouver General Hospital," *Can. Med. Assoc. J.,* Vol. 49, 1943, pp. 113–117.

PINKERTON, F. J., "Wartime Experiences in Hawaii after the Blitz on Pearl Harbor," *J. Am. Med. Assoc.,* Vol. 126, 1944, pp. 625–630.

RADO, S., "Pathodynamics and Treatment of Traumatic War Neurosis (Traumataphobia)," *Psychosomat. Med.,* Vol. 43, 1942, pp. 362–368.

RICKMAN, J., "Panic and Air-raid Precautions," *Lancet,* Vol. 1, 1938, pp. 1291–1295.

SCHMIDEBERG, M., "Some Observations on Individual Reactions to Air Raids," *International J. Psychoanal.,* Vol. 23, 1942, pp. 146–176.

SEYDEWITZ, M., *Civil Life in Wartime Germany,* The Viking Press, Inc., New York, 1945.

SOLOMON, J. C., "Reactions of Children to Blackouts," *Am. J. Orthopsychiat.,* Vol. 12, 1942, pp. 361–362.

STENGEL, E., "Air-raid Phobia," *Brit. J. Med. Psychology,* Vol. 20, 1944, pp. 135–143.

STERN, J., *The Hidden Damage,* Harcourt, Brace and Company, Inc., New York, 1947.

STEWART, D. N., and D. M. WINSER, "Incidence of Perforated Peptic Ulcer," *Lancet,* Vol. 2, 1942, pp. 259–260.

STOCKS, P., "Vital Statistics of England and Wales in 1941," *Brit. Med. J.,* Vol. 1, 1942, pp. 789–790.

STOKES, A. B., "War Strains and Mental Health," *J. Nervous Ment. Disease,* Vol. 101, 1945, pp. 215–219.

STRACHEY, J., *Digging for Mrs. Miller,* Random House, New York, 1941.

SULLIVAN, H. S., "Psychiatric Aspects of Morale," *Am. J. Sociology,* Vol. 47, 1941, pp. 277–301.

THOULESS, R. H., "Psychological Effects of Air Raids," *Nature,* Vol. 148, 1941, pp. 183–185.

TITMUSS, R. M., *Problems of Social Policy,* His Majesty's Stationery Office, London, 1950.

UNRRA (Special Committee), *Psychological Problems of Displaced Persons,* London, 1945. (Mimeo.)

USSBS Report, *Over-all Report (European War),* U.S. Government Printing Office, Washington, D.C., 1945.

———, *The Effect of Bombing on Health and Medical Care in Germany,* U.S. Government Printing Office, Washington, D.C., 1945.

———, *The Effects of Atomic Bombs on Health and Medical Services in Hiroshima and Nagasaki,* U.S. Government Printing Office, Washington, D.C., 1947.

———, *The Effects of Atomic Bombs on Hiroshima and Nagasaki,* U.S. Government Printing Office, Washington, D.C., 1946.

———, *The Effects of Bombing on Health and Medical Services in Japan,* U.S. Government Printing Office, Washington, D.C., 1947.

———, *The Effects of Strategic Bombing on German Morale,* Vols. 1 and 2, U.S. Government Printing Office, Washington, D.C., 1947.

———, *The Effects of Strategic Bombing on Japanese Morale,* U.S. Government Printing Office, Washington, D.C., 1947.

VERNON, P. E., "Psychological Effects of Air Raids," *J. Abnorm. Soc. Psychol.,* Vol. 36, 1941, pp. 457–476.

WEATHERBY, F. E., "War Neuroses after Air Attack on Oahu, Territory of Hawaii, Dec. 7, 1941," *War Med.,* Vol. 4, 1943, pp. 270–271.

WHITACRE, F. C., and B. BARRERA, "War Amenorrhea," *J. Am. Med. Assoc.,* Vol. 124, 1944, pp. 399–403.

WILLIAMS, R. M., and M. B. SMITH, "General Characteristics of Ground Combat," Chap. 2 in S. Stouffer, *et al., The American Soldier: Combat and Its Aftermath,* Vol. 2, Princeton University Press, Princeton, N.J., 1949.

WITTKOWER, E., and J. P. SPILLANE, "A Survey of the Literature of Neuroses in War," Chap. 1 in E. Miller (ed.), *The Neuroses in War,* The Macmillan Company, New York, 1940.

WOLTMANN, A. G., "Life on a Target," *Am. J. Orthopsychiat.,* Vol. 15, 1945, pp. 172–177.

PART III: PSYCHOLOGICAL ASPECTS OF CIVILIAN DEFENSE

Atomic Energy Commission, "The City of Washington and an Atomic Attack," (Memorandum to Mr. Steelman, Chairman of the NSRB), *Bull. Atomic Scientists,* Vol. 6, January, 1950, p. 29.

BRODIE, B. (ed.), *The Absolute Weapon: Atomic Power and World Order,* Harcourt, Brace and Company, Inc., 1946.

BROMAGE, A. W., "Public Administration in the Atomic Age," *Am. Pol. Sci. Rev.,* Vol. 41, 1947, p. 947.

CAMERON, D. C., "Psychiatric Implications of Civil Defense," *Am. J. Psychiat.,* Vol. 106, 1950, p. 587.

CANTRIL, HADLEY, *The Invasion from Mars,* Princeton University Press, Princeton, N.J., 1940.

COALE, A. J., *The Problem of Reducing Vulnerability to Atomic Bombs,* Princeton University Press, Princeton, N.J., 1947.

COTTRELL, L. S., JR., and S. EBERHART, *American Opinion on World Affairs in the Atomic Age,* Princeton University Press, Princeton, N.J., 1948.

GLOVER, E., *The Psychology of Fear and Courage,* Penguin Books, Inc., New York, 1940.

HERSEY, JOHN, *Hiroshima,* Alfred A. Knopf, Inc., New York, 1946.

HIRSCHFELDER, J. O., "The Effects of Atomic Weapons," *Bull. Atomic Scientists,* Vol. 6, August–September, 1950, p. 236.

JANIS, I. L., "Problems Related to the Control of Fear in Combat," Chap. 4 in S. Stouffer, *et al., The American Soldier: Combat and Its Aftermath,* Vol. 2, Princeton University Press, Princeton, N.J., 1949.

———, "Psychological Problems of A-Bomb Defense," *Bull. Atomic Scientists,* Vol. 6, August–September, 1950, p. 256.

———, "Review of David Bradley's *No Place To Hide," The Yale Law Journal,* Vol. 58, 1949, p. 818.

KUBIE, L. S., "Manual of Emergency Treatment for Acute War Neuroses," *War Med.,* Vol. 4, 1943, p. 582.

LAPP, R. E., *Must We Hide?,* Addison-Wesley Press, Inc., Cambridge, 1949.

———, "The Strategy of Civil Defense," *Bull. Atomic Scientists,* Vol. 6, August–September, 1950, p. 241.

LARSEN, P. J., "The Government's Role in Civil Defense," *Bull. Atomic Scientists,* Vol. 6, August–September, 1950, p. 233.

Los Alamos Scientific Laboratory, *The Effects of Atomic Weapons,* prepared for and in cooperation with the U.S. Department of Defense and the U.S. Atomic Energy Commission, U.S. Government Printing Office, Washington, D.C., 1950.

MACCURDY, J. T., *The Structure of Morale,* The Macmillan Company, New York, 1943.

MARSHAK, J., E. TELLER, and L. R. KLEIN, "Dispersal of Cities and Industries," *Bull. Atomic Scientists,* Vol. 2, April, 1946, p. 13.

National Security Resources Board, *United States Civil Defense,* U.S. Government Printing Office, Washington, D.C., September, 1950.

OPPENHEIMER, E., "The Challenge of Our Time," *Bull. Atomic Scientists,* Vol. 3, December, 1947, p. 370.

OSS Assessment Staff, *Assessment of Men: Selection of Personnel for the Office of Strategic Services,* Rinehart & Company, Inc., New York, 1948.

PRINCE, S. H., *Catastrophe and Social Change,* Columbia University Studies in Political Science, etc., Columbia University Press, New York, 1920.

SHILS, E. A., *The Atomic Bomb in World Politics,* Peace Aims Pamphlet 45, National Peace Council, London, 1948.

————, and M. JANOWITZ, "Cohesion and Disintegration in the Wehrmacht in World War II," *Public Opinion Quart.,* Vol. 12, Summer, 1948, p. 280.

TELLER, E., "How Dangerous Are Atomic Weapons?" *Bull. Atomic Scientists,* Vol. 3, February, 1947, p. 35.

TITMUSS, R. M., *Problems of Social Policy,* His Majesty's Stationery Office, London, 1950.

U.S. Army Medical Department, "What Every Medical Officer Should Know about the Atomic Bomb," *Bull. U.S. Army Med. Dept.,* Vol. 8, July, 1948, p. 493.

U.S. Office of Civil Defense Planning (Russell J. Hopley, Director), *Civil Defense for National Security,* U.S. Government Printing Office, Washington, D.C., 1948.

USSBS Report, *The Effects of Atomic Bombs on Health and Medical Services in Hiroshima and Nagasaki,* U.S. Government Printing Office, Washington, D.C., 1947.

————, *The Effects of Atomic Bombs on Hiroshima and Nagasaki,* U.S. Government Printing Office, Washington, D.C., 1946.

Index

A

Abortions, among A-bombed survivors, 56

Absenteeism, in Britain, during periods of air attack, 85, 147

Adjustment mechanisms, and curiosity about bomb damage, 154–156
and discrimination of danger cues, 156–157
and expectations of personal invulnerability, 171–177
and fatalistic attitudes, 165–166
and interpersonal communicativeness, 158–159
and rituals, taboos, and superstitious practices, 167–171
summary, 177–179
(*See also* Psychodynamic hypotheses)

Adjustment to stress, and basic personality structure, 78–83

Affect (*see* Depression; Fear)

Aggressive attitudes, among A-bombed survivors, 61–62
toward the enemy, 129–133
evoked by disaster experiences, 134–135
and fear reactions, 126
toward home-front authorities, 126–129, 133, 136–138
and spacing of air attacks, 128, 136–137
summary, 150, 152
targets of, 133–138

Aggressive impulses of children, 95–96

Aid to others, among A-bombed survivors, 28–30, 32–37, 39–40, 50–51
(*See also* Rescue and relief activity)

Air attack, discrimination of danger cues during, 119, 156–157
emotional adaptation to, 100, 109–116

Air attack, physical magnitude of, 101–103
and acute anxiety symptoms, 87
and emotional adaptation, 116
and morale, 107, 140–144
and "near-miss" experiences, 104
and personal involvement, 145
spacing of, 117–118, 128, 136–137
(*See also* A-bomb attacks; Blitz [Britain])

Air-raid alerts, British attitudes toward, 109–111

A. R. P. (Britain), 106, 110, 162

Alcoholism, incidence following bombings, in Britain, 75
in Germany, 76

Allies, German resentment toward, 130, 131, 143

Amazement of A-bombed survivors, 5

Amenorrhea, 91–92

American Psychiatric Association, Military Mobilization Committee of, 105

Amnesia, among A-bombed survivors, 58

Anginal attacks, during periods of air attack, 91

Antiaircraft barrages, in Britain, criticisms of home authorities for insufficient, 119, 137–138
as psychological reassurance, 156–157

Anticipations of danger, 102–103, 109–111

Antisabotage precautions, problems connected with, 252

Anxiety, and discrimination of danger cues, 119, 156–157
states, 26–27, 46, 81, 98, 104, 106
symptoms, acute, 21, 23, 85–87, 89
of children, 93–95
among combat personnel, 114–115
incidence of, related to magnitude of air attack, 87

267

C

Battle of Britain, 128
(*See also* Blitz [Britain])
Bed-wetting, 92, 93
Behavior patterns, spontaneous, during periods of air attack, 154
Behavioral disturbances (*see* Psychiatric casualties)
Behavioral morale, and food shortages, 146
Beliefs, exaggerated, about destructiveness of A-bombs, examples of, 241–242
Bizarre verbalizations, absence of in interviews of A-bombed survivors, 241–242
Black-market activity, during periods of air attack, 148
Blackouts, in San Francisco, reaction of children to, 93
Blast and concussion effects of A-bomb explosion, 10, 13, 14–15, 16, 19, 229
Blitz (Britain), 74, 75, 80, 98, 105, 111, 112, 127, 128, 136, 137, 156, 157, 158, 159, 163, 166, 167, 168, 188, 194, 224
Blood disease, among A-bombed survivors, 48
Bomb, type of, as factor in emotional stress during air raids, 122–123
"Bomb Berlin" policy, 127
Bombing experience in relation to morale, 138–144
Boston, 134
Brander, T., 94
Bristol, 90, 94
Britain (England), 27, 69, 73, 75, 77, 84, 88, 90, 91, 103, 109, 113, 128, 129, 133, 137, 138, 147, 149, 158, 160, 165, 169, 170, 188, 192, 194, 197, 210, 224
British Mission to Japan, 30
British morale, 128–129
Brown, F., 82, 86
Brues, A. M., 47
B-29 raids in Japan, 4, 60, 138
Burlingham, Dorothy, 93, 95, 164
"Business-as-usual" attitude in Britain during bombings, 170

Calder, Ritchie, 117
Casualties, from A-bomb attacks, 5, 14, 19–20, 228
(*See also* Perception of casualties; Psychiatric air-raid casualties)
Cerebral hemorrhage, during periods of air attack, 91
Characterological disorders among children, 96
Childhood fears, reactivation of during bombing, 81
Children, aggressive impulses of, 95–96
behavioral disturbances among, 92–96
knowledge about air-raid dangers among, 95
psychiatric disorders among, summary, 97
reactions of during blackouts and alerts, 93
Civilian defense, attitudes concerning, examples of, 240–242
communications, on-the-spot, need for, 185–187
educational program, need for, 185, 195
objectives of, 229–233
problems of motivation for, 233–245
and specifications for homemade shelters, 202
measures, adequacy of, and fear reactions, 118–119, 188–189
criticism of, following British raids, 127–128, 137–138
increased in Tokyo, following Doolittle raid, 142
popular support for preparations, 142
problems of treating psychiatric casualties, 190–192
publicity campaigns, limitations of, 243–244
units, assessment of personnel for, 207–210
conflicting loyalties of members of, 217–218
emergency duties of, assignment of, 216–218
participation of in local emergencies, 210